Study Guide

Volume 2: From the Renaissance

A HISTORY OF WESTERN SOCIETY

Study Guide

Volume 2: From the Renaissance

A HISTORY OF WESTERN SOCIETY

Third Edition

James A. Schmiechen
Central Michigan University, Mt. Pleasant

John P. McKay
University of Illinois at Urbana-Champaign

HOUGHTON MIFFLIN COMPANY • BOSTON

Dallas   Geneva, Illinois   Lawrenceville, New Jersey   Palo Alto

Library of Congress Catalog Card Number: 86-81468

ISBN: 0-395-42410-0

BCDEFGHIJ-FFG-8987

CONTENTS

To the Student   vii

Chapter 12   THE CRISIS OF THE LATER MIDDLE AGES   155

Reading with Understanding Exercise 1:   A—1-8
Learning how to underline or highlight
major points   *following page* 166

Reading with Understanding Exercise 2:   B—1-3
Learning to improve your underlining skills   *following page* A—8

Chapter 13   EUROPEAN SOCIETY IN THE AGE OF THE
RENAISSANCE   167

Reading with Understanding Exercise 3:   C—1-3
Learning how to identify main points that are effects,
results, consequences   *following page* 180

Chapter 14   REFORM AND RENEWAL IN THE
CHRISTIAN CHURCH   181

Chapter 15   THE AGE OF EUROPEAN EXPANSION AND
RELIGIOUS WARS   195

Chapter 16   ABSOLUTISM AND CONSTITUTIONALISM IN
WESTERN EUROPE (ca 1589-1715)   211

Chapter 17   ABSOLUTISM IN EASTERN EUROPE TO 1740   227

Chapter 18   TOWARD A NEW WORLD-VIEW   241

Reading with Understanding Exercise 4:   D—1-3
Learning to classify information according
to sequence   *following page 254*

Chapter 19   THE EXPANSION OF EUROPE IN THE
EIGHTEENTH CENTURY   255

Chapter 20   THE LIFE OF THE PEOPLE   269

Chapter 21   THE REVOLUTION IN POLITICS, 1775-1814   281

Chapter 22   THE REVOLUTION IN ENERGY AND INDUSTRY   297

Reading with Understanding Exercise 5:   E—1-5
Learning how to identify main points that are
causes or reasons   *following page 310*

Chapter 23   IDEOLOGIES AND UPHEAVALS, 1815-1850   311

Chapter 24   LIFE IN URBAN SOCIETY   327

Chapter 25   THE AGE OF NATIONALISM, 1850-1914   341

Chapter 26   THE WEST AND THE WORLD   355

Chapter 27   THE GREAT BREAK: WAR AND REVOLUTION   371

Reading with Understanding Exercise 6:   F—1-3
Learning how to make historical comparisons   *following page 386*

Chapter 28   THE AGE OF ANXIETY   387

Chapter 29   DICTATORSHIPS AND THE SECOND WORLD WAR   401

Chapter 30   THE RECOVERY OF EUROPE AND THE AMERICAS   417

Chapter 31   LIFE IN THE POSTWAR ERA   435

Chapter 32   THE RECENT PAST, 1968 TO THE PRESENT   445

Answers to Objective Questions   *following page 456*

TO THE STUDENT

HOW TO STUDY HISTORY AND PREPARE FOR EXAMS

The study of history can be rewarding but also perplexing. Most history courses require you to read and understand large bodies of detailed information. The history student is expected to perform many tasks—memorize information, study the reasons for change, analyze the accomplishments and failures of various societies, understand new ideas, identify historical periods, pick out broad themes and generalizations in history, and so forth. These jobs often present difficulties. This guide will make your study easier and increase your efficiency. It has been developed to help you read, study, and review *A History of Western Society*, and regular and systematic use of it will improve your grade in this course. You may use the guide in a variety of ways, but for best results you might choose the following approach:

1. *Preview the entire chapter* by reading the chapter objectives and synopsis; then quickly read through the study outline, noting the reading with understanding exercises. All of this will take only a few minutes but is an important first step in reading. It is called *previewing*. By pointing out what the chapter is about and what to look for, previewing will make your reading easier and improve your reading comprehension.

2. *Now read your assignment in the textbook.* Pay attention to features that reveal the scope and major emphasis of a chapter or section, such as the chapter title, chapter and section introductions, questions, headings, conclusions, and illustrative material (e.g., maps and photographs). Note study hint 3 on page ix about underlining.

3. After reading, *review what you have read* and check your comprehension by going over the chapter outline once again—but this time make sure that you understand

all the points and subpoints. If you do not fully understand a particular point or subpoint, then you need to return to the text and reread. It is not at all uncommon to need to read the text at least twice.

4. Continue your review. *Answer the review questions* that follow the study outline. It is best to write out or outline your answer on a sheet of paper or a note card. Be sure to include the supporting facts. Reread your answers periodically. This process will help you build a storehouse of information and understanding to use at the time of the exam.

5. Now work on the definitions, identifications, and explanations in the study-review exercises provided in each chapter of the *Study Guide*. This will help you to understand and recall both concepts and specific facts. Know not just who or what, but also why the term is significant. Does it illustrate or represent some fundamental change or process? Note that if a particular term appears in the text *and* in your lecture notes, it is of special importance. Do the geography exercises found in all appropriate chapters. This is important because they will enable you to visualize the subject matter and thus remember it better. It will take a few minutes, but the payoff is considerable.

6. Last, *complete the multiple-choice and fill-in exercises* for each *Study Guide* chapter. Some of these questions look for basic facts, while others test your understanding and ability to synthesize material. *The answers are at the end of the Guide.* If you miss more than two or three, you need to restudy the text or spend more time working on the *Guide*.

ADDITIONAL STUDY HINTS*

1. *Organize your study time effectively*. Many students fail to do well in courses because they do not organize their time effectively. In college, students are expected to read the material before class, review, and do the homework on their own. Many history teachers give only two or three tests during the semester; therefore, assuming personal responsibility for learning the material is vital. Mark up a semester calendar to show scheduled test dates, when term projects are due, and blocks of time to be set aside for exam study and paper writing. Then, at the beginning of each week, check the calendar and your course outlines and notes to see what specific preparation is

---

*For a complete text and workbook written to meet the needs of students who want to do their best in college, see James F. Shepherd, *RSVP, The Houghton Mifflin Reading, Study, and Vocabulary Program*, Second Edition (1984).

necessary for the coming week, and plan your time accordingly. Look at all the reading with understanding exercises in this *Study Guide* and try to estimate how much time you will need to master study skills. Set aside a block of time each day or once every several days for reading your text or studying your lecture notes and working in the *Study Guide*. Despite what one observes on college campuses, studying is not done most effectively late at night or with background music. Find a quiet place to study alone, one where you can tune out the world and tune into the past.

2. *Take good lecture notes.* Good notes are readable, clear, and above all reviewable. Write down as much of the lecture as you can without letting your pen get too far behind the lecturer. Use abbreviations and jot down key words. Leave spaces where appropriate and then go back and add to your notes as soon after the lecture as possible. You may find it helpful to leave a wide margin on the left side for writing in subject headings, important points, and questions, as well as for adding information and cross-references to the text and other readings. One way to use your notes effectively is by *reciting*. Reciting is the act of asking a question and then repeating the answer silently or aloud until you can recall it easily. Above all, do not wait until the night before an exam to use lecture notes you have not looked at for weeks or months. Review your lecture notes often and see how they complement and help you interpret your reading.

3. *Underline.* Too often students mark almost everything they read and end up with little else than an entire book highlighted in yellow. Underlining can be extremely helpful or simply a waste of time in preparing for exams; the key is to be selective in what you underline. Here are some suggestions:

a. Underline major concepts, ideas, and conclusions. You will be expected to interpret and analyze the material you have read. In many cases the textbook authors themselves have done this, so you need to pinpoint their comments as you read. Is the author making a point of interpretation or coming to a conclusion? If so, underline the key part. Remember, learning to generalize is very important, for it is the process of making history make sense. The author does it and you must learn to identify his or her interpretation as well as conflicting interpretations; then to make your own. Here is where your study of history can pay big rewards. The historian, like a good detective, not only gathers facts but also analyzes, synthesizes, and generalizes from that basic information. This is the process of *historical interpretation*, which you must seek to master.

b. Underline basic facts. You will be expected to know basic facts (names, events, dates, places) so that you can reconstruct the larger picture and back up your analysis and interpretations. Each chapter of this guide includes several lists of important items. Look over these lists before you begin to read, and then underline these words as you read.

c. Look at the review questions in the *Study Guide*—they will point to the major themes and questions to be answered. Then, as you read, underline the material that answers these questions. Making marginal notations can often complement your underlining.

4. *Work on your vocabulary*. The course lectures and each chapter in the text will probably include words that you do not know. Some of these will be historical terms or special concepts, such as *polis*, *feudalism*, or *bourgeoisie*—words that are not often used in ordinary American speech. Others are simply new to you but important for understanding readings and discussion. If you cannot determine the meaning of the word from the context in which it appears or from its word structure, then you will need to use a dictionary. *Keep a list of words* in your lecture notebook or use the pages in the back of this guide. Improving your historical and general vocabulary is an important part of reading history as well as furthering your college career. Most graduate-school entrance exams and many job applications, for instance, have sections to test vocabulary and reading comprehension.

5. *Benefit from taking essay exams*. Here is your chance to practice your skills in historical interpretation and synthesis. Essay exams demand that you express yourself through ideas, concepts, and generalizations as well as by reciting the bare facts. The key to taking an essay exam is preparation. Follow these suggestions:

a. *Try to anticipate the questions on the exam*. As you read the text, your notes, and this guide, jot down what seem to be logical essay questions. This will become easier as the course continues, partly because you will be familiar with the type of question your instructor asks. Some questions are fairly broad, such as the chapter-objective questions at the beginning of each chapter in this guide; others have a more specific focus, such as the review questions. Take a good look at your lecture notes. Most professors organize their daily lectures around a particular theme or stage in history. You should be able to invent a question or two from each lecture. Then answer the question. Do the same with the textbook, using the *Study Guide* for direction. Remember, professors are often impressed when students include in their essay textbook material not covered in class.

b. *Aim for good content and organization*. Be prepared to answer questions that require historical interpretation and analysis of a particular event, series of events, movement, process, person's life, and so forth. You must also be prepared to provide specific information to back up and support your analysis. In some cases you will be expected to give either a chronological narrative of events or a topical narrative (for example, explaining a historical movement in terms of its social, political, and economic features). Historians often approach problems in terms of cause and effect, so spend some time thinking about events in these terms. Remember, not all causes are of equal importance, so you must be ready to make distinctions—and to back up these distinctions with evidence. This is all part of showing your skill at historical interpretation.

When organizing your essay, you will usually want to sketch out your general thesis (argument) or point of interpretation first, in an introductory sentence or two. Next move to the substance. Here you will illustrate and develop your argument by weighing the evidence and marshaling reasons and factual data. After you have completed this stage (writing the body of your essay), go on to your conclusion, which most likely will be a restatement of your original thesis. It is often helpful to outline your major points before you begin to write. Be sure you answer all parts of the question. Write clearly and directly. All of this is hard to do, but you will get better at it as the course moves along.

6. *Enhance your understanding* of important historical questions by undertaking additional reading and/or a research project as suggested in the "Understanding History Through Reading and the Arts" and "Problems for Further Investigation" sections in the *Study Guide*. Note also that each textbook chapter has an excellent bibliography. Many of the books suggested are available in paperback editions, and all of the music suggested is available in most record-lending libraries and record stores.

7. *Know why you are studying history.* Nothing is worse than having to study a subject that appears to have no practical value. And indeed, it is unlikely that by itself this history course will land you a job. What, then, is its value, and how can it enrich your life? Although many students like history simply because it is interesting, there are a number of solid, old-fashioned reasons for studying it. It is often said that we need to understand our past in order to live in the present and build the future. This is true on a number of levels. On the psychological level, identification with the past gives us a badly needed sense of continuity and order in the face of ever more rapid change. We see how change has occurred in the past and are therefore better prepared to deal with it in our own lives. On another level, it is important for us to know how differing political, economic, and social systems work and what benefits and disadvantages accrue from them. As the good craftsperson uses a lifetime of experience to make a masterpiece, so an understanding of the accumulated experiences of the past enables us to construct a better society. Further, we need to understand how the historical experiences of peoples and nations have differed, and how these differences have shaped their respective visions. Only then can we come to understand how others view the world differently from the ways in which we do. Thus, history breaks down the barriers erected by provincialism and ignorance.

The strongest argument for the study of history, though, is that it re-creates the big picture at a time when it is fashionable and seemingly prudent to be highly specialized and narrowly focused. We live in the Age of Specialization. Even our universities often appear as giant trade schools, where we are asked to learn a lot about a little. As a result, it is easy to miss what is happening to the forest because we have become obsessed with a few of the trees. While specialization has undeniable benefits, both societies and individuals also need the generalist perspective and the ability to see how the entire system works. History is the queen of the generalist disciplines. Looking at change over time, history shows us how to take all the parts of the puzzle—politics, war, science, economics, architecture, sex, demography, music, philosophy, and much more—and put them together so that we can understand the whole. It is through a study of the interrelationships of the parts over a long expanse of time that we can develop a vision of society. By promoting the generalist perspective, history plays an important part on today's college campus.

Finally, the study of history has a more personal and surprisingly practical application. It is becoming increasingly apparent to many employers and educators that neglect of the liberal arts and humanities by well-meaning students has left them unable to think and reason analytically and to write and speak effectively. Overspecialized, narrowly focused education has left these students seriously deficient in basic verbal skills, placing them at a serious disadvantage in the job market. Here is where this course can help. It is universally recognized that studying history is an excellent way to develop the ability to reason and write. And the moving pageant of centuries of human experience you are about to witness will surely spark your interest and develop your aptitude if you give it the chance.

CHAPTER 12

THE CRISIS OF THE
LATER MIDDLE AGES

CHAPTER OBJECTIVES

After reading and studying this chapter you should be able to answer the following questions:

Q-1. What were the causes and the effects of the fourteenth-century disasters?
Q-2. Was war a catalyst for change?
Q-3. What provoked the division in the church in the fourteenth century?

CHAPTER SYNOPSIS

The fourteenth century was a time of disease, war, crime, and violence. The art and literature of the period are full of the portrayal of death, just as the historical accounts are full of tales of conflict and violence. There were several major causes for this century of human suffering. Natural disasters—including changes in climate and horrible new diseases—attacked Europe. A long series of wars between France and England not only brought death and economic ruin but increased personal violence and crime as well. In addition, a serious shortage of labor, created by the bubonic plague, resulted in intense social conflict among landlords. Economic crisis during the century also resulted in a bitter struggle between urban workers and their guild masters.

Amid such violence the church lost power and prestige, partly because of the religious disillusionment that accompanied the plague. In short, the institutional church failed to fill the spiritual vacuum left by the series of disasters. A more immediate reason for the decline of the church's influence and prestige was the Babylonian captivity and the Great Schism. The call for reform, often in the form of the conciliar movement, by people such as Marsiglio of Padua and John Wyclif, was a signal of things to come in the sixteenth-century Reformation.

But the century of disaster was also a century of change, some of it for the good of ordinary people. It is in this light that the chapter examines some important changes in marriage practices, family relations, and the life of the people. The decline in population meant that those who survived had better food and higher wages. Peasants in western Europe used the labor-shortage problem to demand higher wages and freedom from serfdom. These demands often resulted in conflict with their lords. The disillusionment with the organized church also led to greater lay independence and, ultimately, ideas of social and political equality. The wars actually fostered the development of constitutionalism in England. All in all, it was a period of disaster but of disaster that brought with it important changes.

STUDY OUTLINE

I. Death and disease in the fourteenth century
    A. Disaster in the fourteenth century
        1. Climate changes and inflation caused economic decline
        2. Diseases killed many people and animals
        3. The population was undernourished, and population growth came to a halt
        4. Weak governments were unable to deal with these problems
    B. The Black Death
        1. Genoese ships brought the plague—the Black Death—to Europe in 1347
        2. This bubonic bacillus lived in fleas that infested black rats
        3. Unsanitary and overcrowded cities were ideal breeding grounds for the black rats
        4. Most people had no rational explanation for the disease, and out of ignorance and fear many blamed it on Jews
        5. The disease, which killed millions, recurred often and as late as 1700
    C. The social and psychological consequences of the Black Death
        1. The plague hit the poor harder than the rich, but all classes suffered
        2. The decline in population meant labor shortages, thus wages went up and social mobility increased
        3. The psychological consequences of the plague were enormous: depression, gross sensuality, flagellantism, and obsession with death
II. The Hundred Years' War (1337-1453)
    A. The causes of the war
        1. Edward III of England, the grandson of the French king Philip the Fair, claimed the French crown
            a. French barons used Edward's claim as a way to check their king

    2. Flemish wool merchants supported the English claim to the crown

    3. Both the French and the English saw military adventure as an excuse to avoid domestic problems

    4. The French barons passed the crown to Philip Valois and not Edward III

B. The popular response to the war

    1. Royal propaganda for war and plunder was strong on both sides

    2. The war meant opportunity for economic or social mobility for poor knights, criminals, and great nobles

C. The Indian summer of medieval chivalry during the Hundred Years' War

    1. Chivalry was a code of conduct for the knightly class

      a. Knights were supposed to be brave, loyal, courteous, and generous

      b. Chivalry and feudal society glorified war

    2. Chivalry enjoyed its final days of glory during the war

D. The course of the war to 1419

    1. The battles took place in France and the Low Countries

    2. At the battle of Crécy (1346), the English disregarded the chivalric code and used new military tactics: the longbow and cannon

E. Joan of Arc and France's victory

    1. Joan of Arc's campaigns meant a turning point and victory for France

    2. Joan was turned over to the English and burned as a heretic

F. Costs and consequences

    1. The war meant economic and population decline for France and England

    2. War financing caused a slump in the English wool trade

    3. In England, returning soldiers caused social problems

    4. The war encouraged the growth of parliamentary government, particularly in England

      a. The "Commons" acquired the right to pass on taxation and developed its own organization

      b. In France, neither king nor the Provincial assemblies wanted a national assembly

    5. The war generated feelings of nationalism in England and France

III. Vernacular literature

A. The emergence of national consciousness is seen in the rise of literature written in national languages—the vernacular

B. Three literary masterpieces manifest this new national pride

    1. Dante's *Divine Comedy*, a symbolic pilgrimage to the City of God, embodies the psychological tensions of the age and contains bitter criticism of some church authorities

    2. Chaucer, in his *Canterbury Tales*, uses a religious setting to depict the materialistic and worldly interests of a variety of English people in the fourteenth century

     3. Villon used the language of the lower classes to talk about the reality, beauty, and hardships of life here on earth

IV. The decline of the church's prestige

    A. The Babylonian Captivity (1309-1377)

       1. The pope had lived at Avignon since the reign of King Philip the Fair of France and thus was subject to French control

       2. This Babylonian Captivity damaged papal power and prestige

       3. Pope Gregory XI brought the papacy back to Rome in 1377, but then a split occurred when the newly elected Urban VI alienated the church hierarchy in his zeal to reform the church

       4. A new pope, Clement VII, was elected, and the two popes both claimed to be legitimate (the Great Schism)

    B. The Great Schism lasted until 1417

       1. England and Germany recognized Pope Urban VI

       2. France and others recognized Pope Clement VII

    C. The conciliar movement was based on the idea of reform through a council of church leaders

       1. Marsiglio of Padua claimed that authority within the church should rest with a church council and not the pope

       2. The English teacher John Wyclif attacked papal authority and called for even more radical reform of the church

       3. Wyclif's ideas were spread to Bohemia by John Hus and then to the University of Paris

       4. Finally, the council at Constance (1414-1418) ended the schism with the election of Pope Martin V

V. The life of the people in the fourteenth and fifteenth centuries

    A. Fur-collar crime

       1. In England, nobles returning from war had little to do and were in need of income; thus they resorted to crime at home

       2. Kidnaping, extortion, and terrorism by the upper classes were widespread

       3. Central governments were not able to stop abuses

       4. As a result, "outlaws" such as Robin Hood sought to protect the people

    B. Peasants' revolts

       1. Peasants revolted in France in 1358 and in England in 1381

       2. One cause was the lords' attempt to freeze wages

       3. In general, the revolts were due to rising expectations

       4. The 1381 revolt in England began as a protest against taxes

       5. As in England, workers in Italy, Germany, and Spain revolted

    C. Marriage and the family

       1. Economic factors, rather than romantic love, usually governed the decision to marry

    2. Marriage usually came at 16 to 18 years for women and later for men; divorce did not exist

    3. Many people, however, did not observe church regulations and married without a church ceremony

D. Life in the parish

    1. The land and the religion were the centers of life

    2. Mobility within guilds declined in the fourteenth century, and strikes and riots within guilds became frequent

    3. Cruel sports, such as bullbaiting, and drunkenness reflect the violence and frustrations of the age

    4. Lay people increasingly participated in church management

E. Catalysts for change

    1. The crises and wars of the fourteenth and fifteenth centuries altered traditional ways of life

    2. Rising social consciousness, changes in government, and advances in technology were some of the changes brought by the events of the times

REVIEW QUESTIONS

Q-1. What were the causes of the population decline that began in the early fourteenth century?

Q-2. What was the source of the bubonic plague and why did it spread so rapidly in Europe?

Q-3. What impact did the plague have on wages and the demand for labor? Can you guess what happened to land values?

Q-4. Describe the psychological effects of the plague. How did people explain this disaster?

Q-5. What were the immediate and other causes of the Hundred Years' War?

Q-6. Why did the people support their kings in war?

Q-7. In your opinion, did feudalism tend to encourage or prevent war? Explain.

Q-8. What were the results of the Hundred Years' War? Who were the winners and losers within both countries?

Q-9. Why did a national representative assembly emerge in England but not in France?

Q-10. Drawing on the writings of Dante, Chaucer, and Villon, describe vernacular literature in terms of its form and subject matter. What makes it "modern"?

Q-11. The Babylonian Captivity greatly weakened the power and prestige of the church. Explain.

Q-12. In 1409 there were three popes. Why? Who were they and how and why did this situation occur?

Q-13. What was the conciliar movement and who were its advocates? Was this a revolutionary idea?

Q-14. Why was Wyclif a threat to the institutional church? Even many powerful and rich lords feared the Lollards. Why?

Q-15. What was fur-collar crime and why did it become a central feature of European life in the fourteenth and fifteenth centuries?

Q-16. Did peasant conditions improve or deteriorate in the fourteenth and fifteenth centuries? Explain.

Q-17. What were the reasons for the French *Jacquerie* of 1358 and the English Peasants' Revolt of 1381?

Q-18. Describe how guilds worked, and explain why a great amount of conflict and frustration was evident among guild members in the fourteenth century.

STUDY-REVIEW EXERCISES

Define each of the following key concepts and terms.

fur-collar crime

English Statute of Labourers

conciliar movement

Pasteurella pestis

vernacular

craft guild

Identify each of the following and give its significance.

Robin Hood

Marsiglio of Padua

Battle of Crécy (1346)

Martin V

Joan of Arc

Babylonian Captivity

Margaret Paston

Lollards

House of Commons

Edward III

John Hus

John Wyclif

Jacquerie

Explain the importance of each of the following concepts in late medieval life and describe what changes it was subject to in this period.

pluralism

marriage and womanhood

feudal chivalry

individual Christian faith

leisure time

nationalism

Provide approximate dates for the following important events.

1. The first instance of the bubonic plague in Europe

2. The Babylonian Captivity

3. The Hundred Years' War

4. The Council of Constance

5. The battle of Crécy

6. The French Jacquerie revolt

7. Dante's *Divine Comedy* (1321)

Test your understanding of the chapter by answering the following questions.

1. In reaction to the calls for reform in the fourteenth century, the church *did/ did not* enter into a period of reform and rejuvenation.
2. Prior to the plague in 1348, Europe experienced a period of unusually *good/bad* harvests.

3. The Hundred Years' War was between the kings of _____

    and _____ .

4. The followers of the English theologian Wyclif were called _____ .
5. Up to the nineteenth century, *economic/romantic* factors usually determined whom and when a person married.
6. For the most part, job mobility within the late medieval guilds tended to *increase/ decrease.*

MULTIPLE-CHOICE QUESTIONS

1. The conciliar movement was
    a. an effort to give the pope the power to use councils to wipe out heresy.
    b. the effort by the French lords to establish a parliament.
    c. a new monastic order vowing poverty.
    d. an attempt to place ultimate church authority in a general council.

2. The plague was probably brought into Europe by
    a. Chinese soldiers.
    b. Spanish warriors returning from South America.
    c. English soldiers pushing into France.
    d. Genoese ships from the Crimea.

3. In general, farm laborers who survived the bubonic plague faced
   a. higher wages.
   b. food shortages.
   c. the need to migrate.
   d. excommunication from the church.

4. Generally, the major new source of criminals after the Hundred Years' War was
   a. the urban mobs.
   b. the rural peasants.
   c. the nobility.
   d. the bourgeoisie.

5. Which of the following statements about the fourteenth century is *false*?
   a. The population declined.
   b. The standard of living fell drastically.
   c. The power of the church declined.
   d. War between England and France was frequent.

6. Most people in the fourteenth century believed that the plague (Black Death) was caused by
   a. bad air.
   b. poor sanitation and housing.
   c. a bacillus living in fleas.
   d. black rats.

7. Generally, the plague disaster of the fourteenth century resulted in all but one of the following for European society.
   a. higher wages for most workers
   b. a severe decline in the number of German clergymen
   c. a decline in flagellantism
   d. an obsession with death

8. Which of the following was *not* a participant in the Hundred Years' War?
   a. Edward III of England
   b. King Philip the Fair
   c. Joan of Arc
   d. the Dauphin Charles of France

9. One reason for peasant-landlord conflict in the fourteenth century was
   a. peasants' opposition to declining wages and inflation.
   b. landlords' attempts to legislate wages.
   c. land scarcity.
   d. peasants' refusal to be drafted for war service.

10. The author of *Defensor Pacis* and proponent of the idea that authority in the Christian church rested in a general council rather than in the papacy was
    a. Cardinal Robert of Geneva.
    b. Pope Urban V.
    c. John Wyclif.
    d. Marsiglio of Padua.

11. The Hundred Years' War had all but one of the following effects on English society.
    a. It encouraged representative government.
    b. It depressed the English wool trade.
    c. It increased the amount of arable land in England.
    d. It created a severe manpower shortage.

12. The followers of the English theologian-reformer Wyclif were called
    a. Protestants.
    b. Outlaws.
    c. Lollards.

13. Which of the following was not a social consequence of the agricultural catastrophes of the fourteenth century?
    a. people married earlier
    b. unemployment
    c. increase in crime
    d. increased serfdom

14. After 1347, the Black Death generally moved
    a. from north to south.
    b. from west to east.
    c. from south to north.
    d. from east to west.

15. Initially the Hundred Years' War was fought over
    a. Aquitaine.
    b. King Edward III's claim to the French crown.
    c. the control of the Flemish wool trade.
    d. religion.

16. English military innovation(s) during the Hundred Years' War included
    a. the crossbow.
    b. the cannon and the longbow.
    c. cavalry.
    d. the pike.

17. Each of the following statements represents marriage during the Middle Ages
    except
    a. some marriages were made privately.
    b. most marriages were arranged.
    c. divorce did not exist except in rare cases.
    d. divorce was common.

18. Who of the following was not a writer of vernacular literature?
    a. Dante
    b. Villon
    c. Clement VII
    d. Chaucer

19. All but one of the following was true of Joan of Arc.
    a. She dressed like a man.
    b. The English king was her greatest supporter.
    c. She was accused of being a heretic and was burned.
    d. She was from a peasant family.

20. For the French, the turning point of the Hundred Years' War was
    a. the relief of Paris.
    b. the defeat of the English fleet in the English Channel.
    c. the relief of Orleans.
    d. the battle of Poitiers.

GEOGRAPHY

A. Using Map 12.2 in the text
   1. Locate the extent of the English possessions in France. What were the origins
      of English claims to French land?

   2. Why was it unlikely that England could have held these territories permanent-
      ly?

B. Using Map 12.3 in the text
   1. Locate the main centers of popular revolt in France and England.
   2. Why were so many of the English revolts in the highly populated and advanced areas of the country?

UNDERSTANDING HISTORY THROUGH READING AND THE ARTS

One of the results of the Black Death was a revival of Christian mysticism—a search for meaning in life through a personal relationship with God. One of the most popular books of this movement was *The Imitation of Christ** by Thomas à Kempis.

An excellent introduction to the music of this period is a recording, *Instruments of the Middle Ages and Renaissance*, with an accompanying illustrated book by David Munro (Angel recording number SB2-3810 [1976]), and for the French chansons and the English Madrigals listen to the recording titled *The King's Singers Sing of Courtly Pleasures*, which includes text and translations (Angel recording number s-37025 [1974]).

Students interested in the history of disease in general or in the plague in particular should check the chapter bibliography. Three interesting accounts of the subject are G. C. Coulton, *The Black Death* (1929); P. Zeigler, *The Black Death* (1960); and W. McNeill, *Plagues and Peoples* (1976). E. Perroy, *The Hundred Years' War** (1951), is a good start for anyone interested in that subject. Boccaccio's *Decameron* is a series of bawdy tales told by a group of Florentine men and women who fled to the countryside to escape the plague.

PROBLEMS FOR FURTHER INVESTIGATION

What was the cause of the conflict between Philip the Fair of France and the pope? Was the French king out to destroy the power of the papacy? These and other questions are debated by a number of historians in C. T. Wood, ed., *Philip the Fair and Boniface VIII** (1967).

* Available in paperback.

READING WITH UNDERSTANDING
EXERCISE 1

LEARNING HOW TO UNDERLINE OR HIGHLIGHT THE MAJOR POINTS

Underlining (or highlighting with a felt-tipped pen, as many students prefer) plays an important part in the learning process in college courses. Underlining provides you with a permanent record of what you want to learn. It helps you in your efforts to master the material and prepare for exams.

The introductory essay (pp. vii-xii) provides some good guidelines for learning how to underline effectively, and you should review it carefully before continuing.

Further Suggestions

1. In addition to underlining selectively, *consider numbering the main points* to help you remember them. Numbering helps make the main points stand out clearly, which is a major purpose of all underlining or highlighting.

2. *Read an entire section through before you underline or highlight it.* Then, as you read it a second time, you will be better able to pick out and underline key facts, main points, and sentences or paragraphs that summarize and interpret the information.

3. *Avoid false economies.* Some students do not mark their books because they are afraid that the bookstores will not buy them back. This is a foolish way to try to save money for two reasons. First, students must of necessity invest a great deal of time and money in their college education. By refusing to mark their books, they are reducing their chances of doing their best and thus endangering their whole college investment. Probably the only alternative to marking your books is making detailed written notes, which is more difficult and much more time consuming.

Second, carefully underlined books are *a permanent yet personal record of what you study and learn.* Such books become valuable reference works, helping you recall important learning experiences and forming the core of your library in future years.

Exercise

Read the following passage once as a whole. Read it a second time to underline or highlight it. Consider numbering the points. On completion, compare your underlining with the model on the next page, which is an example of reasonable and useful underlining. Finally, compare the underlined section with the chapter outline in the *Study Guide.* You will see how the outline summary is an aid in learning how to underline major points.

EGYPT, THE LAND OF THE PHARAOHS
(3100-1200 B.C.)

The Greek historian and traveler Herodotus in the fifth century
B.C. called Egypt the "gift of the Nile." No other single geographical factor had such a fundamental and profound impact on
the shaping of Egyptian life, society, and history as the Nile. Unlike the rivers of Mesopotamia it rarely brought death and destruction. The river was primarily a creative force. The Egyptians
never feared the relatively calm Nile in the way the Mesopotamians feared their rivers. Instead they sang its praises:

> Hail to thee, O Nile, that issues from the earth and comes to
>   keep Egypt alive! . . .
> He that waters the meadows which Re created,
> He that makes to drink the desert . . .
> He who makes barley and brings emmer [wheat] into being . . .
> He who brings grass into being for the cattle.
> He who makes every beloved tree to grow . . .
> O Nile, verdant art thou, who makest man and cattle to live.[15]

In the minds of the Egyptians, the Nile was the supreme fertilizer
and renewer of the land. Each September the Nile floods its valley, transforming it into a huge area of marsh or lagoon. By the
end of November the water retreats, leaving behind a thin covering of fertile mud ready to be planted with crops.

  The annual flood made the growing of abundant crops almost
effortless, especially in southern Egypt. Herodotus, used to the
rigors of Greek agriculture, was amazed by the ease with which
the Egyptians raised their crops:

> For indeed without trouble they obtain crops from the land
> more easily than all other men. . . . They do not labor to dig
> furrows with the plough or hoe or do the work which other
> men do to raise grain. But when the river by itself inundates
> the fields and the water recedes, then each man, having sown
> his field, sends pigs into it. When the pigs trample down the

seed, he waits for the harvest. Then when the pigs thresh the grain, he gets his crop.[16]

As late as 1822, John Burckhardt, an English traveler, watched nomads sowing grain by digging large holes in the mud and throwing in seeds. The extraordinary fertility of the Nile valley made it easy to produce an annual agricultural surplus, which in turn sustained a growing and prosperous population.

Whereas the Tigris and Euphrates and their many tributaries carved up Mesopotamia into isolated areas, the Nile served to unify Egypt. The river was the principal highway and promoted easy communication throughout the valley. As individual bands of settlers moved into the Nile valley, they created stable agricultural communities. By about 3100 B.C. there were some forty of these communities in constant contact with one another. This contact, encouraged and facilitated by the Nile, virtually ensured the early political unification of the country.

Egypt was fortunate in that it was nearly self-sufficient. Besides the fertility of its soil, Egypt possessed enormous quantities of stone, which served as the raw material of architecture and sculpture. Abundant clay was available for pottery, as was gold for jewelry and ornaments. The raw materials that Egypt lacked were close at hand. The Egyptians could obtain copper from Sinai and timber from Lebanon. They had little cause to look to the outside world for their essential needs, which helps to explain the insular quality of Egyptian life.

Geography further encouraged isolation by closing Egypt off from the outside world. To the east and west of the Nile valley stretch grim deserts. The Nubian Desert and the cataracts of the Nile discourage penetration from the south. Only in the north did the Mediterranean Sea leave Egypt exposed. Thus, geography shielded Egypt from invasion and from extensive immigration. Unlike the Mesopotamians, the Egyptians enjoyed centuries of peace and tranquillity, during which they could devote most of their resources to peaceful development of their distinctive civilization.

Yet Egypt was not completely sealed off. As early as 3250 B.C. Mesopotamian influences, notably architectural techniques and materials and perhaps even writing, made themselves felt in Egyptian life. Still later, from 1680 to 1580 B.C., northern Egypt was ruled by foreign invaders, the Hyksos. Infrequent though they were, such periods of foreign influence fertilized Egyptian culture without changing it in any fundamental way.

The God-King of Egypt

The geographic unity of Egypt quickly gave rise to political unification of the country under the authority of a king whom the Egyptians called "pharaoh." The details of this process have been lost. The Egyptians themselves told of a great king, Menes, who united Egypt into a single kingdom around 3100 B.C. Thereafter the Egyptians divided their history into *dynasties*, or families of kings. For modern historical purposes, however, it is more useful to divide Egyptian history into periods. The political unification of Egypt ushered in the period known as the Old Kingdom, an era remarkable for its prosperity and artistic flowering, and for the evolution of religious beliefs.

EGYPT, THE LAND OF THE PHARAOHS
(3100-1200 B.C.)

Geography

1

The Greek historian and traveler Herodotus in the fifth century B.C. called Egypt the "gift of the Nile." No other single geographical factor had such a fundamental and profound impact on the shaping of Egyptian life, society, and history as the Nile. Unlike the rivers of Mesopotamia it rarely brought death and destruction. The river was primarily a creative force. The Egyptians never feared the relatively calm Nile in the way the Mesopotamians feared their rivers. Instead they sang its praises:

> Hail to thee, O Nile, that issues from the earth and comes to
>   keep Egypt alive! . . .
> He that waters the meadows which Re created,
> He that makes to drink the desert . . .
> He who makes barley and brings emmer [wheat] into being . . .
> He who brings grass into being for the cattle.
> He who makes every beloved tree to grow . . .
> O Nile, verdant art thou, who makest man and cattle to live.[15]

In the minds of the Egyptians, the Nile was the supreme fertilizer and renewer of the land. Each September the Nile floods its valley, transforming it into a huge area of marsh or lagoon. By the end of November the water retreats, leaving behind a thin covering of fertile mud ready to be planted with crops.

1a

The annual flood made the growing of abundant crops almost effortless, especially in southern Egypt. Herodotus, used to the rigors of Greek agriculture, was amazed by the ease with which the Egyptians raised their crops:

> For indeed without trouble they obtain crops from the land more easily than all other men. . . . They do not labor to dig furrows with the plough or hoe or do the work which other men do to raise grain. But when the river by itself inundates the fields and the water recedes, then each man, having sown his field, sends pigs into it. When the pigs trample down the

seed, he waits for the harvest. Then when the pigs thresh the grain, he gets his crop.[16]

As late as 1822, John Burckhardt, an English traveler, watched nomads sowing grain by digging large holes in the mud and throwing in seeds. The extraordinary fertility of the Nile valley made it easy to produce an annual agricultural surplus, which in turn sustained a growing and prosperous population.

2   Whereas the Tigris and Euphrates and their many tributaries carved up Mesopotamia into isolated areas, the Nile served to unify Egypt. The river was the principal highway and promoted easy communication throughout the valley. As individual bands of settlers moved into the Nile valley, they created stable agricultural communities. By about 3100 B.C. there were some forty of these communities in constant contact with one another. This contact, encouraged and facilitated by the Nile, virtually ensured the early political unification of the country.

3   Egypt was fortunate in that it was nearly self-sufficient. Besides the fertility of its soil, Egypt possessed enormous quantities of stone, which served as the raw material of architecture and sculpture. Abundant clay was available for pottery, as was gold for jewelry and ornaments. The raw materials that Egypt lacked were close at hand. The Egyptians could obtain copper from Sinai and timber from Lebanon. They had little cause to look to the outside world for their essential needs, which helps to explain the insular quality of Egyptian life.

4   Geography further encouraged isolation by closing Egypt off from the outside world. To the east and west of the Nile valley stretch grim deserts. The Nubian Desert and the cataracts of the Nile discourage penetration from the south. Only in the north did the Mediterranean Sea leave Egypt exposed. Thus, geography shielded Egypt from invasion and from extensive immigration. Unlike the Mesopotamians, the Egyptians enjoyed centuries of peace and tranquillity, during which they could devote most of their resources to peaceful development of their distinctive civilization.

5   Yet Egypt was not completely sealed off. As early as 3250 B.C. Mesopotamian influences, notably architectural techniques and materials and perhaps even writing, made themselves felt in Egyptian life. Still later, from 1680 to 1580 B.C., northern Egypt was ruled by foreign invaders, the Hyksos. Infrequent though

6   they were, such periods of foreign influence fertilized Egyptian culture without changing it in any fundamental way.

The God-King of Egypt

The geographic unity of Egypt quickly gave rise to political unification of the country under the authority of a king whom the Egyptians called "pharaoh." The details of this process have been lost. The Egyptians themselves told of a great king, Menes, who united Egypt into a single kingdom around 3100 B.C. Thereafter the Egyptians divided their history into *dynasties*, or families of kings. For modern historical purposes, however, it is more useful to divide Egyptian history into periods. The political unification of Egypt ushered in the period known as the Old Kingdom, an era remarkable for its prosperity and artistic flowering, and for the evolution of religious beliefs.

READING WITH UNDERSTANDING
EXERCISE 2

LEARNING TO IMPROVE YOUR UNDERLINING SKILLS

Read the following paragraphs, in which some words are printed in italic type to help you find the major points. Read the passage a second time and underline or highlight one or two sentences in each paragraph that best summarize the paragraph's major point. Now study and review these points. Finally, close the book and on a piece of notepaper summarize the major points *with a few words* under the heading "The Success of Benedictine Monasticism." Compare your summary with that found at the end of the exercise.

The Success of Benedictine Monasticism

Why was the Benedictine form of monasticism so successful? Why did it eventually replace other forms of Western monasticism? The answer lies partly in its *spirit of flexibility and moderation*, and partly in the *balanced life* it provided. Early Benedictine monks and nuns spent part of the day in prayer, part in study or some other form of intellectual activity, and part in manual labor. The monastic life as conceived by Saint Benedict did not lean too heavily in any one direction; it struck a balance between asceticism and idleness. It thus provided opportunities for persons of entirely different abilities and talents—from mechanics to gardeners to literary scholars. Benedict's *Rule* contrasts sharply with Cassiodorus's narrow concept of the monastery as a place for aristocratic scholars and bibliophiles.

Benedictine monasticism also *suited the social circumstances of early medieval society*. The German invasions had fragmented European life: the self-sufficient rural estate replaced the city as the basic unit of civilization. A monastery too had to be *economically self-sufficient*. It was supposed to produce from its lands and properties all that was needed for food, clothing, buildings, and the liturgical service of the altar. The monastery fit in—indeed, represented—the trend toward localism.

B-1

Benedictine monasticism also succeeded partly because it was so *materially successful*. In the seventh and eighth centuries, monasteries pushed back forest and wasteland, drained swamps, and experimented with crop rotation. For example, the abbey of Saint Wandrille, founded in 645 near Rouen in northwestern Gaul, sent squads of monks to clear the forests that surrounded it. Within seventy-five years, the abbey was immensely wealthy. The abbey of Jumièges, also in the diocese of Rouen, followed much the same pattern. Such Benedictine houses made *a significant contribution to the agricultural development* of Europe. The socialistic nature of their organization, whereby property was held in common and profits pooled and reinvested, made this contribution possible.

Finally, *monasteries conducted schools* for local young people. Some learned about prescriptions and herbal remedies and went on to provide medical treatment for their localities. A few copied manuscripts and wrote books. This training did not go unappreciated in a society desperately in need of it. Local and royal governments drew on the services of *the literate men and able administrators* the monasteries produced. This was not what Saint Benedict had intended, but the effectiveness of the institution he designed made it perhaps inevitable.

ANSWER

The Success of Benedictine Monasticism

1. A flexible and balanced life

2. Economically self-sufficient

3. Economically successful, especially in agriculture

4. Provided education for young and able administrators for governments

CHAPTER 13

EUROPEAN SOCIETY IN THE AGE OF THE
RENAISSANCE

CHAPTER OBJECTIVES

After reading and studying this chapter you should be able to answer the following
questions:

Q-1. What does the term "Renaissance" mean?
Q-2. How did the Renaissance influence politics, government, and social organiza-
tion?
Q-3. Did the Renaissance cause shifts in religious attitudes?
Q-4. What developments occurred in the evolution of the nation-state?
Q-5. What were the intellectual and artistic hallmarks of the Renaissance?

CHAPTER SYNOPSIS

While the fourteenth century is often described in terms of death and violence, the
following two centuries are usually regarded as composing an era of intellectual and
artistic brilliance unsurpassed in European history. This period, which is called the
Renaissance, is difficult to define. Yet it is clear that some thinking people in this
era saw themselves living in an age more akin to that of the bright and creative ancient world than that of the recent dark and gloomy Middle Ages. Although many
of the supposedly "new" Renaissance ideas are actually found in the Middle Ages,
scholars generally agree that the Renaissance was characterized by a number of distinctive ideas about life and humanity—individualism, secularism, humanism, materialism, and hedonism.

   The Renaissance began in Florence, Italy, in the fourteenth century. It subse-
quently spread to the rest of Italy—particularly Rome—and then to northern Europe,
where it developed somewhat differently. The best-known manifestations of the bold

new Renaissance spirit can be seen in the painting, sculpture, and architecture of the period. But new attitudes were also found in education, politics, and philosophy and in Northern Europe in ideas of social reform. Although the Renaissance brought some benefits to the masses of people, such as the printing press, it was basically an elitist movement. One negative feature of the age was a deterioration in the power and position of women in society.

The political side of the Renaissance expressed itself in an approach to power and the state that historians often call the theory and practice of "new monarchies." The best known and most popular theoretician of this school was the Florentine Niccolo Machiavelli. Its most able practitioners are the fifteenth- and sixteenth-century monarchs of France, England, and Spain. In Italy, the city-state system led to wealthy and independent cities that were marvelously creative but also vulnerable to invasion and control from the outside by powerful Spanish and French kings.

STUDY OUTLINE

I. The origins and hallmarks of the Renaissance
   A. The evolution of the Italian Renaissance
      1. The "Renaissance" was a period of cultural achievement in two phases—from 1050 to 1300 and from 1300 to about 1600
      2. The wealth of the northern Italian cities was a cause of the Renaissance; it was an artistic and intellectual movement sustained by urban wealth
      3. Florence, the first city of the Renaissance, was a banking and manufacturing center
   B. Communes and republics
      1. Northern Italian "communes" were cities wherein the feudal nobility and the commercial aristocracy merged and ruled
         a. The *popolo*, or middle class was excluded from power
         b. Popolo-led republican governments failed—which led to the rule of despots or oligarchies
         c. In the fifteenth century, the princely courts of the rulers were centers of wealth and art
      2. Italy had no political unity; it was divided into city-states such as Milan, Venice, and Florence, a papal area, and a kingdom of Naples in the south
      3. The political and economic competition among the city-states was damaging
      4. After 1494 a divided Italy became a European battleground
II. Intellectual hallmarks of the Renaissance
   A. Many, like the poet and humanist Petrarch, saw the fourteenth century as a new age and a revival of ancient Roman culture
   B. Individualism

      1. Medieval people usually saw themselves as members of a group

      2. Renaissance people believed in individual will and genius

  C. The revival of antiquity

      1. Italians copied the ancient Roman lifestyle

      2. The study of the classics led to humanism, or an emphasis on human beings

         a. Humanists sought to understand human nature through a study of pagan antiquity *and* Christian thought

         b. The humanist writer Pico della Mirandola believed that there were no limits to what human beings could accomplish

      3. Ancient Latin style was considered superior to medieval Latin

  D. Secular spirit

      1. *Secularism* means a concern with materialism rather than religion

      2. Unlike medieval people, Renaissance people were concerned about money and the accumulation of wealth

      3. They were also interested in pleasure and the enjoyment of life on earth

      4. The church did little to combat secularism; in fact, many popes were Renaissance patrons and participants

  E. Art, the artist, and power in the fourteenth century

      1. The *quattrocento* and the *cinquecento* saw great artistic activity as the center of activity shifted from Florence to Rome

      2. Art served a social function during the Renaissance

         a. It was patronized by corporate groups such as guilds and religious bodies, and by rich individuals

         b. It was a means of glorifying politicians and rich families

      3. The purpose and style of art changed in the fifteenth century

         a. It became more secular

         b. Painting and sculpture became more naturalistic and realistic

         c. The human body was glorified in art—for example, by Michelangelo

         d. A new "international-style" emphasized color, decoration, and curvilinear rhythms

      4. The status and personality of the artist were affected by the Renaissance

         a. The status of the artist improved during the Renaissance; most work was done by commission from a prince

         b. The creative genius of the artist was recognized

         c. The Renaissance was largely an elitist movement that cared little for ordinary people

III. Social change during the Renaissance

  A. Education and political thought

      1. Vergerio's humanism represents the Renaissance concern for education

      2. The Renaissance man was well rounded

3. Castiglione's *The Courtier* describes the model Renaissance gentleman as a man of many talents, including intellectual and artistic skills
4. Machiavelli's *The Prince* describes how to acquire political power
   a. Machiavelli believed that the politician may use any means to gain power
   b. He viewed the state not as a utopia but as an amoral force

B. The printed word
   1. The invention of movable type by Gutenberg, Fust, and Schöffer—all at Mainz, Germany—revolutionized life
   2. Printing brought about new possibilities for propaganda, encouraged wider "common identity," and improved literacy
   3. It meant the spread of ideas—ideas that were often critical of the existing order

C. Women in Renaissance society
   1. The status of upper-class women declined during the Renaissance
   2. Nevertheless, the Renaissance meant improved educational opportunities for women
   3. Women's position declined with regard to sex and love
   4. The rape of women by upper-class men was frequent and not considered serious
   5. Infanticide and abandonment of children was frequent and eventually led to the establishment of foundling hospitals

D. Blacks in Renaissance society
   1. Beginning in the fifteenth century, black slaves were brought into Europe in large numbers
   2. Black slaves filled a variety of positions, from laborers to dancers and musicians
   3. The Europeans perceived blacks from both positive and negative religious perspectives

IV. The Renaissance in the north of Europe
   A. The Renaissance in the north began about 1475
      1. It was more Christian than the Renaissance in Italy, and it stressed social reform based on Christian ideals
      2. Christian humanists sought to create a more perfect world
         a. Humanists like Lefèvre and Colet believed in the use of the Bible by common people
         b. Thomas More, the author of *Utopia*, believed that society, not people, needed improving
         c. The Dutch monk Erasmus best represents Christian humanism in his emphasis on education and inner Christianity
      3. French humanist writers were more secular
         a. Rabelais satirized social institutions and behavior while he promoted individual instinct and enjoyment of life

    4. Northern art and architecture were more religious than in Italy and less influenced by classical themes and motifs
      a. van Eyck painted realist works based on human themes
      b. Bosch used religion and folk legends as themes

V. Politics and the state in the Renaissance (ca. 1450-1521)
  A. The "new" monarchs
    1. The fifteenth century saw the rise of many powerful and ruthless rulers interested in the centralization of power and the elimination of disorder and violence
    2. Many of them seemed to be acting according to Machiavelli's principles
    3. The ideas of the new monarchs were not entirely original—some of them had their roots in the Middle Ages
  B. France after the Hundred Years' War
    1. Charles VII ushered in an age of recovery and ended civil war
      a. He expelled the English
      b. He made the church subject to the state
    2. Louis XI expanded the French state and laid the foundations of later French absolutism
  C. England
    1. Feudal lords controlled England in the fifteenth century
    2. Edward IV and his followers began to restore royal power
    3. The English Parliament had become a power center for the aristocracy but was manipulated by Henry VII into becoming a tool of the king
      a. Henry VII used the royal council and the Court of Star Chamber to check aristocratic power
      b. He rebuilt the monarchy and restored the economy
  D. Spain
    1. The marriage of Ferdinand and Isabella united Spain into a loose confederation
    2. They used the *hermandades*, or local police forces, to administer royal justice
    3. The royal council checked aristocratic power
    4. The church was used to strengthen royal authority
    5. Ferdinand and Isabella completed the *reconquista*—the expulsion or conversion of Arabs and Jews
    6. Anti-Semitic riots, called *conversos*, were frequent

REVIEW QUESTIONS

Q-1. Describe the evolution of government and social class relations in the Italian cities from the time of the emergence of the urban nobility to the rise of the *signori*.

Q-2. Medieval people saw themselves as a part of a corporate society. Explain. How did the men and women of the Renaissance differ?

Q-3. Define the Renaissance by discussing the interests and characteristics of Renaissance people.

Q-4. How do Valla and Boccaccio illustrate and represent what Renaissance people were like?

Q-5. Do you believe that it is possible, through education, to perfect mankind? What did the Renaissance thinkers believe the keys to this process to be?

Q-6. According to Vergerio, what is the purpose of education? Was he a humanist?

Q-7. How does Castiglione's *The Courtier* define the "perfect Renaissance man"? How does this book represent the philosophy of humanism?

Q-8. In what ways does Machiavelli represent a Renaissance thinker? What were his suggestions for and philosophy of the acquisition and meaning of political power?

Q-9. Explain why the invention of movable type revolutionized European life.

Q-10. What were the similarities and differences between the Renaissance in northern Europe and that of Italy?

Q-11. Discuss Christian humanism by describing the works and ideas of Thomas More and Desiderius Erasmus.

Q-12. Describe the makeup of the Italian city-state political system. How well did it work?

Q-13. "After 1494, Italy became a battleground for the European superpowers." Explain.

Q-14. What were the obstacles to royal authority faced by the kings of France in the fifteenth century? How did Charles VII and his successors strengthen the French monarchy?

Q-15. What devices did Henry VII of England use to check the power of the aristocracy and strengthen the monarchy?

Q-16. The reign of Ferdinand and Isabella is one of the most important in Spanish history. Why? What were their achievements in the areas of national power and national expansion?

Q-17. Why were blacks valued in Renaissance society? What roles did they play in the economic and social life of the times?

STUDY-REVIEW EXERCISES

Define the following key concepts and terms.

oligarchies

signori

communes

popolo

reconquista

Renaissance

humanism

secularism

individualism

materialism

hermandades

Machiavellian

Explain the importance of each of the following.

English Royal Council and Court of Star Chamber

conquest of Granada

Habsburg-Valois wars

Brunelleschi's Foundling Hospital in Florence

Identify each of the following people and give his significance.

Pico della Mirandola

Desiderius Erasmus

Jan Van Eyck

Thomas More

Donatello

Baldassare Castiglione

Niccolo Machiavelli

Johan Gutenberg

Lefèvre d'Etaples

Saint John Chrysostom

Lorenzo Valla

Savonarola

Jerome Bosch

François Rabelais

Explain *why each of the following is often considered to be a "new monarch."*

Louis XI of France

Henry VII of England

Ferdinand and Isabella of Spain

Charles VII of France

Cesare Borgia

Test *your understanding of the chapter by answering the following questions.*

1. He was the author of a best-selling political critique called *The Prince*.

    _____

2. Renaissance humanists tended to be *more/less* concerned about religion than about people.

3. In the fifteenth century, infanticide *increased/decreased*.
4. He was an important English humorist and the author of *Utopia*.

---

5. Generally, the legal status of upper-class women *improved/declined* during the Renaissance.
6. It *is/is not* clear that the economic growth and the material wealth of the Italian cities were direct causes of the Renaissance.

MULTIPLE-CHOICE QUESTIONS

1. Which of the following statements about the earliest printed books is *false*?
   a. They dealt mainly with economic and business subjects.
   b. They encouraged literacy.
   c. Movable type was first developed in Mainz, Germany.
   d. They had an effect on the process of learning.

2. The Renaissance began in
   a. the Low Countries.
   b. Rome.
   c. France.
   d. Florence

3. The patrons of the Renaissance were mostly
   a. churchmen.
   b. the popes.
   c. the common people.
   d. merchants and bankers.

4. The frail and ugly king who began French economic and political recovery in the early fifteenth century was
   a. Henry Tudor.
   b. Charles VII.
   c. Philip the Fair.
   d. Louis XI.

5. It appears that in Renaissance society blacks were
   a. valued as soldiers.
   b. valued as servants and entertainers.
   c. considered undesirable and were not allowed in society.

6. A major difference between Northern and Italian humanism is that Northern humanism stressed
   a. economic gain and materialism.
   b. social reform.
   c. pagan virtues.

7. Local groups in Spain that were given royal authority to administer justice were the
   a. *conversos.*
   b. liberals.
   c. *hermandades.*
   d. royal tribunals.

8. The court of Star Chamber in England was
   a. a common law court.
   b. under the control of the barons in the House of Lords.
   c. done away with by the powerful Tudors.
   d. used to check aristocratic power.

9. The superiority of the French monarch over the church was the object of the
   a. Pragmatic Sanction of Bourges.
   b. Habsburg-Valois wars.
   c. Declaration of Calais.
   d. Hundred Years' War.

10. Most of the northern Renaissance thinkers agreed that
    a. democracy, not monarchy, was the only workable political system.
    b. humanity is basically sinful.
    c. Christianity is unacceptable.
    d. society is perfectable.

11. The late fifteenth-century ruler of England who ended the civil war and strengthened the crown was
    a. John I.
    b. William III.
    c. Henry II.
    d. Henry VII.

12. Which of the following statements about Florence at the time of the Renaissance is *false*?
    a. Its major industry was wool production.
    b. It lost probably half its population to the Black Death.

    c. It was a major banking center.

    d. It was an important Mediterranean port city.

13. The High Renaissance masterpiece, the dome of St. Peter's in Rome, is considered to be the greatest work of

    a. Brunelleschi.

    b. Donatello.

    c. Michelangelo.

    d. Ghiberti.

14. The term *Renaissance* means

    a. a rise in the average standard of living among the masses.

    b. a resurgence of art and culture out of a concern for individualism and study of the ancients.

    c. an increase in the population after the ravaging effects of the "Four Horsemen of the Apocalypse."

    d. the recovery of the church from economic and moral decline.

15. The financial and military strength of the towns of northern Italy was directly related to

    a. their wealth, which enabled them to hire mercenary soldiers to protect their commercial interests.

    b. their contractual and marital alliances with the rural nobility.

    c. protections provided them by the Holy Roman Emperor.

    d. their alliance with the papacy.

16. The northern Renaissance differed from the Italian Renaissance in that the former was characterized by

    a. interest in biblical scholarship.

    b. an emphasis on the use of reason.

    c. the combination of the best aspects of antiquity and Christianity.

    d. all of the above

17. Erasmus advocated

    a. paganism.

    b. Christian education for moral and intellectual improvement.

    c. monastic life of contemplation and divorce from the material world.

    d. obedience to church doctrine and ritual.

18. The Renaissance artist of talent and ability often lived a life

    a. of economic desperation.

    b. of economic security through patronage.

    c. of luxury, but without social status.
    d. like that of the masses.

19. The most influential book on Renaissance court life and behavior was
    a. Castiglione's *The Courtier*.
    b. Machiavelli's *The Prince*.
    c. Augustine's *The City of God*.
    d. Boccaccio's *Decameron*.

20. Machiavelli's *The Prince* is considered by scholars to be
    a. an accurate description of politics in Renaissance Italy.
    b. a satire on sixteenth-century politics.
    c. a call for Italian nationalism.
    d. all of the above

21. The Wars of the Roses were
    a. civil wars between the English ducal houses of York and Lancaster.
    b. between England and France.
    c. civil wars between the English king, Henry VI, and the aristocracy.
    d. minor disputes among English gentry.

22. Just before the advent of Ferdinand and Isabella, the Iberian peninsula could best be described as
    a. a homogeneous region sharing a common language and cultural tradition.
    b. a heterogeneous region consisting of several ethnic groups with a diversity of linguistic and cultural characteristics.
    c. a culturally poor and backward region.
    d. a region dominated equally by Arabs and Jews in both numbers and political powers.

UNDERSTANDING HISTORY THROUGH READING AND THE ARTS

The music of the Renaissance is introduced in the recordings *From the Renaissance* (STL-150) and *From the Renaissance-Concert* (STL-160) in the Time-Life series *The Story of Great Music* (1967), which includes a book with a good introduction to the period and its musical styles, art, and history. Another good introduction to Renaissance music is H. Brown, *Music in the Renaissance** (1976).

    One of the best ways to understand the Renaissance is to read the works of its participants. Three works dealt with in this chapter are Niccolo Machiavelli, *The*

*Available in paperback.

*Prince** (a number of paperback translations are available); Baldassare Castiglione, *The Courtier**, Charles Singleton, trans. (1959); and Thomas More, *Utopia**.

Urban and rural life, court life, war, and witchcraft are among the many aspects of Renaissance life covered in E. R. Chamberlin, *Everyday Life in Renaissance Times** (1967).

Color, genius, romance, intrigue, brilliance, energy—the Renaissance had all of these. The best portrait of the age is J. H. Plumb, *The Renaissance* (1961), which includes biographies of Michelangelo, Petrarch, Da Vinci, and others and includes hundreds of color plates and a comprehensive history of Renaissance art. One of the best sources on Renaissance music is G. Reese, *Music in the Renaissance* (1954). Among the most admired poetry of this period is that of Petrarch, the poet laureate of the Renaissance and often called the first modern man. The vanity and secularism of Renaissance life is reflected in the fascinating *Autobiography* of Benvenuto Cellini, one of the best known Renaissance craftsmen.

PROBLEMS FOR FURTHER INVESTIGATION

Students interested in women in the Renaissance should begin with M. Rose et al., *Women in the Middle Ages and the Renaissance: Literary and Historical Perspectives* (1986).

The Swiss historian Jacob Burckhardt called the Renaissance the "mother" of our modern world. Was the Renaissance as important as Burckhardt and others have claimed? Did it dramatically change the way people acted and the direction history was to take? These and other questions are considered in several historical debates on the Renaissance: D. Hay, ed., *The Renaissance Debate** (1965); B. Tierney, et al., *Renaissance Man—Medieval or Modern?** (1967); and K. H. Dannenfeldt, ed., *The Renaissance—Medieval or Modern?** (1959). What impact did Renaissance thinking have on the arts? Fine illustrations and a discussion of new directions in the arts are woven into a number of interesting essays on the age in D. Hay, *The Renaissance* (1967).

*Available in paperback.

READING WITH UNDERSTANDING
EXERCISE 3

LEARNING HOW TO IDENTIFY MAIN POINTS THAT ARE EFFECTS, RESULTS, CONSEQUENCES

In the introduction to this *Study Guide* and in Reading with Understanding Exercises 1 and 2 we noted that learning to underline properly plays an important part in college work. Underlining (or highlighting with a felt-tipped pen) provides a permanent record of what you study and learn. It helps you review, synthesize, and do your best on exams.

We suggested three simple guidelines for effective underlining or highlighting:*

1. Be selective; do not underline or highlight too much.
2. Underline or highlight the main points.
3. Consider numbering the main points.

These guidelines will help you in courses in many different subjects.

Cause and Effect in History

The study of history also requires learning to recognize special kinds of main points. These points are *explanatory* in nature. *They answer why and how questions*, thereby helping you to interpret and make sense of the historical record.

Two particularly important types of why and how questions focus on *cause* and *effect* in history. You are already familiar with questions of this nature, questions that provide much of history's fascination and excitement. "Why did the Roman Empire

---

*The guidelines for underlining are from *RSVP: The Houghton Mifflin Reading, Study, & Vocabulary Program*, second edition, by James F. Shepherd (Houghton Mifflin, 1984). We urge students to consult this very valuable book for additional help in improving their reading and study skills.

decline and fall?" That is, what *causes* explain the decline and fall of the Roman Empire? "What were the *effects* of the Black Death?" You should pay particular attention to questions of cause and effect. They give history meaning. They help you increase your ability to think and reason in historical terms.

Two other insights will help you greatly in identifying main points involving cause and effect. First, historians use a number of different words and verbal constructions to express these concepts. Thus "causes" often become "reasons" or "factors," or things that "account for," "contribute to," or "play a role in" a given development. "Effects" often become "results" or "consequences," or are "the product of an impact." In most cases students can consider such expressions as substitutes for cause and effect, although they should be aware that historians are not of one mind on these matters.

Second, cause and effect are constantly interrelated in the historical process. Yesterday's results become today's causes, which will in turn help bring tomorrow's results. To take examples you have studied, the *causes* of the fall of the Roman Empire (such as increasing economic difficulties) brought *results* (such as the self-sufficient agrarian economy) which contributed to—helped *cause*—the rise of Benedictine monasticism. In short, *a historical development can usually be viewed as a cause or an effect, depending on what question is being answered.*

Exercise A

Read the following passage once as a whole. Read it a second time to underline or highlight it in terms of main points identified as effects or results. Consider numbering the effects in the margin. Then do Exercise B at the end of the passage.

The effects of the invention of movable-type printing were not felt overnight. Nevertheless, within a half-century of the publication of Gutenberg's Bible of 1456, movable type brought about radical changes. The costs of reproducing books were drastically reduced. It took less time and money to print a book by machine than to make copies by hand. The press also reduced the chances of error. If the type had been accurately set, all the copies would be correct no matter how many were reproduced. The greater the number of pages a scribe copied, the greater the chances for human error.

Between the sixteenth and eighteenth centuries, printing brought about profound changes in European society and culture. Printing transformed both the private and the public lives of Europeans. Governments that "had employed the cumbersome methods of manuscripts to communicate with their subjects switched quickly to print to announce declarations of war, publish battle accounts, promulgate treaties or argue disputed points in pamphlet form. Theirs was an effort 'to win the psychological war.' " Printing made propaganda possible, emphasizing differences between various groups, such as crown and nobility, church and state. These differences laid the basis for the formation of distinct political parties.

Printed materials reached an invisible public, allowing silent individuals to join causes and groups of individuals widely separated by geography to form a common identity; this new group consciousness could compete with older, localized loyalties. Book shops, coffee shops, and public reading rooms gradually appeared and, together with print shops, provided sanctuaries and meeting places for intellectuals and wandering scholars. Historians have yet to assess the degree to which such places contributed to the rise of intellectuals as a distinct social class.

Printing also stimulated the literacy of lay people and eventually came to have a deep effect on their private lives. Although most of the earliest books and pamphlets dealt with religious subjects, students, housewives, businessmen, and upper- and middle-class people sought books on all subjects. Printers responded with moralizing, medical, practical, and travel manuals. Pornography as well as piety assumed new forms. Broadsides and flysheets allowed great public festivals, religious ceremonies, and political events to be experienced vicariously by the stay-at-home. Since books and printed materials were read aloud to the illiterate, print bridged the gap between written and oral cultures.

Exercise B

Study the last paragraph again. Can you see how it is a good example of the historical interaction of cause and effect? Do you see how a given development is an effect or a cause *depending on what historical question is being asked?* Be prepared for such "reversals" in the text, in lecture and class discussion, and on exams.

Hint: In the last paragraph, what is an *effect* of the invention of the printing press? (Ideas could be spread more rapidly.) What "stimulated"—helped *cause*—the spread of literacy? (The invention of the printing press. The author develops this point further in Chapter 14.)

CHAPTER 14

REFORM AND RENEWAL IN THE
CHRISTIAN CHURCH

CHAPTER OBJECTIVES

After reading and studying this chapter you should be able to answer the following questions:

Q-1. What religious developments paved the way for Protestant thought?

Q-2. What role did social and political factors play in the several reformations?

Q-3. What were the consequences of religious division?

Q-4. Why did Luther's ideas trigger political, social, and economic reactions and how did the Catholic Church respond?

CHAPTER SYNOPSIS

A great religious upheaval called the Protestant Reformation ended the centuries-long religious unity of Europe and resulted in a number of important political changes. In the sixteenth century, cries for reform were nothing new, but this time they resulted in revolution. There were a number of signs of disorder within the church, pointing to the need for moral and administrative reform. For example, it was the granting of indulgences (remissions from the penalties for sin) that propelled the German professor Martin Luther into the movement for doctrinal change in the church. Luther had come to the conclusion that salvation could not come by good works or indulgences, but only through faith. This was to be one of the fundamental tenets of Protestantism and one of the ideas that pushed Luther and the German nobility to revolt against not only Rome but Rome's secular ally, the Holy Roman Emperor.

It is important to recognize that Luther's challenge to the authority of the church and to Catholic unity in Europe invited and supported an attack on the emperor by the German nobility. The pope and the emperor, as separate powers and allies, represented religious and political unity and conformity in Germany. Thus, the victory of Luther and the nobility was a victory for decentralized authority; it meant the collapse of Germany as a unified power in Europe. This is one reason Catholic France usually supported the German Protestants in their quarrel with Rome.

Outside of Germany the Protestant reformer Calvin had a greater impact on Europe than Luther. Calvin's harsh and dogmatic religion spread from Geneva into northern Europe, England, and Scotland. It was England, in fact, that eventually became the political center of Protestantism. Initiated by Henry VIII, the English Protestant Reformation was at first motivated by the personal and political interests of the king himself. The type of Protestantism eventually adopted by the Church of England was much more moderate—and closer to Catholicism—than that of Scotland.

With the Council of Trent of 1545-1563, the Catholic church, finding the Habsburgs unable to destroy the heretical Protestantism, launched a massive and somewhat successful Counterreformation to convince dissidents to return to the church.

All in all, Protestantism developed and spread for economic and political reasons as well as religious ones. In the end Protestantism meant greater spritual freedom for some individuals, but spiritual disunity and disorganization for Europe as a whole. In England, Scotland, the Scandinavian states, and elsewhere, it contributed to the power of the nation and thus meant a further political division of Europe, while in Germany it slowed down the movement toward nationhood.

STUDY OUTLINE

I.   The condition of the church (ca. 1400-1517)
   A.   The declining prestige of the church
      1.   The Babylonian captivity and the Great Schism damaged the church's prestige
      2.   Humanists such as Erasmus and Machiavelli satirized and denounced moral corruption within the church
      3.   The exact amount of corruption is difficult to ascertain, however, because many local priests brought spiritual help to the poor
   B.   Signs of disorder in the early sixteenth century
      1.   Critics wanted moral and administrative reform in three areas
         a.   Clerical immorality created a scandal among the faithful
         b.   The lack of education of the clergy was condemned by Christian humanists
         c.   The absenteeism, pluralism (holding of several *benefices*, or offices), and wealth of the greater clergy bore little resemblance to Christian gospel

2. The prelates and popes of the period lived like secular princes; they did not set a good example

C. Signs of vitality in the late fifteenth and early sixteenth centuries
   1. Sixteenth-century Europe remained deeply religious
   2. New organizations were formed to educate and minister to the poor
   3. Thomas à Kempis and the Brethern of the Common Life urged ordinary people to achieve spiritual perfection by means of the simple life
   4. The Italian Oratorians devoted themselves to ministering to society
   5. Pope Julius II summoned an ecumenical council on reform in the church called the Lateran Council (1512-1527)

II. Martin Luther and the birth of Protestantism
   A. Luther's early years
      1. Luther was a middle-class German trained as a monk and a professor of religion
      2. Luther's search for identity and salvation led him to the religious life
      3. He concluded that faith was central to Christianity and the only means to salvation
   B. Luther's Ninety-five Theses (October 1517)
      1. Luther's opposition to the sale of indulgences (remissions of penalities for sin) prompted his fight with Rome
      2. His Ninety-five Theses, or propositions on indulgences, raised many theological issues and initiated a long period of debate in Europe
      3. Luther was excommunicated by the pope and declared an outlaw by Charles V at Worms in 1521
   C. Protestant thought (1520-1530)
      1. Protestant thought was set forth in the Confession of Augsburg, in which Luther modified four basic theological issues
         a. He believed that salvation derived through faith alone
         b. He stated that religious authority rests with the Bible, not the pope
         c. He believed that the church consists of the entire community of Christian believers
         d. And he believed that all work is sacred and everyone should serve God in his or her individual vocation
      2. Protestantism, therefore, was a reformulation of Christian beliefs and practices

III. The social impact of Luther's beliefs
   A. By 1521 Luther's religious ideas had a vast following among all social classes and eventually led to social revolt
      1. Luther's ideas were popular because of popular resentment of clerical wealth
      2. Prosperous burghers encouraged preaching of sermons while peasants found in Luther a reason to demand land

      3. In the end Luther did not support them; he believed in obedience to civil authority

      4. Widespread peasant revolts were brutally crushed but some land was returned to common use

      5. Luther's greatest weapon was his mastery of the language, and his words were spread by the advent of printing

         a. Zwingli and Calvin were greatly influenced by his writings

         b. The publication of Luther's translation of the New Testament in 1523 democratized religion

  B. Luther held enlightened views on sex and marriage—although he claimed that women should be no more than efficient wives

IV. Germany and the Protestant Reformation

  A. The Holy Roman Empire in the fourteenth and fifteenth centuries

      1. By the Golden Bull of 1356 each of the seven electors had virtual sovereignty

      2. Localism and chronic disorder allowed the nobility to strengthen their territories

  B. The rise of the Habsburg dynasty

      1. The Habsburgs gave unity to much of Europe, especially with the marriage of Maximilian I of Austria and Mary of Burgundy in 1477

      2. Charles V, their grandson, dominated Europe and was committed to the idea of its religious and political unity

  C. The political impact of Luther's beliefs

      1. The Protestant Reformation stirred nationalistic feelings in Germany against the wealthy Italian papacy

      2. Luther's appeal to patriotism earned him the support of the princes, who used religion as a means of gaining more political independence

      3. Thus, Luther's teachings prevailed, despite his condemnation by the pope and the Holy Roman Emperor

      4. Charles V did not understand or take any interest in the Luther issue

         a. The Turkish threat blocked Charles V's position in Germany

         b. He was also involved in numerous wars against France, which kept Germany a divided and weakened royal power

      5. By the Peace of Augsburg of 1555, Charles recognized Lutheranism as a legal religion with the Peace of Augsburg

V. The growth of the Protestant Reformation

  A. Calvinism

      1. Calvin believed that God selects certain people to do His work and that he was selected to reform the city of Geneva

      2. Under Calvin, Geneva became a theocracy, in which the state was subordinate to the church

    3. Calvin's central idea was his belief in the omnipotence of God and the insignificance of humanity and *predestination*
      a. People lacked free will
      b. God decided ahead of time who would be saved (predestination)
    4. Austere living and intolerance characterized Calvin's Geneva
    5. The city was the model for international Protestantism, and Calvinism became the most dynamic and influential form of Protestantism

B. The Anabaptists
    1. This Protestant sect believed in adult baptism, revelation, and the separation of church and state
    2. Their beliefs and practices were humane but too radical for the times, and they were bitterly persecuted

C. The English Reformation
    1. As early as the fourteenth century the English Lollards stressed the idea of a direct relationship between the individual and God
    2. Wolsey's career represents corruption in the English church
    3. Henry VIII desired a divorce from his queen, Catherine, daughter of Ferninand and Isabella of Spain
    4. Pope Clement VII (because he did not wish to admit papal error) and Charles V blocked the divorce
    5. The pro-Protestant Archbishop Cranmer engineered the divorce
    6. The result was the nationalization of the English church and a break with Rome as Henry used Parliament to legalize the Reformation
      a. Henry needed money so he dissolved the monasteries and confiscated their lands, but this did not lead to more equal land distribution
      b. Some traditional Catholic practices, such as confession and the doctrine of transubstantiation, were maintained, however
      c. Nationalization of the church led to new form of government
    7. Under Edward VI, Henry's heir, England shifted closer to Protestantism
    8. Mary Tudor attempted to bring Catholicism back to England
    9. Under Elizabeth I a religious settlement—mainly Protestant—was made

D. The establishment of the Church of Scotland
    1. Scotland was an extreme case of church abuse
    2. John Knox brought Calvinism to Scotland from Geneva
    3. The Presbyterian Church became the national church of Scotland

E. Protestantism in Ireland
    1. The English ruling class in Ireland adopted the new faith
    2. The Irish defiantly remained Catholic

F. Lutheranism in Scandinavia
    1. In Sweden, Norway, and Denmark the monarchy led the religious reformation

        2. The result was Lutheran state churches

VI. The Catholic and counter reformations

    A. New religious orders

        1. The Ursuline order, dedicated to combating heresy through education, spread to France and America

        2. The Jesuits were interested in fighting heresy, reforming the church, and converting pagans

    B. The slowness of institutional reform

        1. Too often the popes were preoccupied with politics or sensual pleasures

        2. Popes feared conciliarism because it would limit their authority, so they resisted calls for a council

    C. The Council of Trent

        1. Pope Paul III called the Council of Trent (1545-1563)

           a. An attempt to reconcile with the Protestants was made, but it failed

           b. International politics hindered the theological debates and attempts at reconciliation

        2. The principle of papal authority was maintained

        3. Considerable reform was undertaken, and the spiritual renewal of the church was begun

           a. Tridentine decrees forbade the sale of indulgences and outlawed pluralism and simony

           b. Attempts were made to curb clerical immorality and to encourage education

    D. The Sacred Congregation of the Holy Office

        1. The Roman Inquisition—founded in 1542 by Pope Paul III—was an arm of the Counterreformation empowered to combat heresy

        2. Under the direction of religious fanatics, it had the power to arrest, imprison, and execute

        3. Its influence was confined to Italy

VII. The significance of the Reformation

    A. The paradoxical nature of the Reformation

        1. The unity of Europe was destroyed but religious beliefs remained strong

        2. Individualism in religion won out but confusion existed

        3. The sixteenth century and the Reformation are a dividing line between the medieval and the modern world

REVIEW QUESTIONS

Q-1. Describe the condition of the church in 1517. Were the village clergy useless and corrupt?

Q-2. What were some of the signs of disorder within the early sixteenth-century church? What impact did church wealth have on the condition of the church?

Q-3. What were some of the signs of religious vitality in fifteenth- and early sixteenth-century society?

Q-4. Describe the circumstances that prompted Luther to post his Ninety-five Theses.

Q-5. Describe the practice of indulgence selling. What authority did Luther question and on what argument did he base his position?

Q-6. What were Luther's answers, as delineated in the Confession of Augsburg, to the four basic theological issues?

Q-7. What effect did Luther's concept of state authority over church authority have on German society and German history?

Q-8. Calvin's Geneva was called "the city that was a church." Explain. What is a theocracy?

Q-9. In what ways were the Anabaptists radical for their time? Why did many of their beliefs cause them to be bitterly persecuted?

Q-10. Explain the causes and results of the English Reformation.

Q-11. What was the Elizabethan Settlement?

Q-12. Compare and contrast the religious settlements made in Scotland and Ireland. Why was Protestantism in one way a source of national strength and in the other a source of national weakness?

Q-13. What were the repercussions of the marriage of Maximilian and Mary? What impact did this marriage have on France?

Q-14. Charles V has been considered a medieval emperor. In what respects is this true? What were the origins of his empire?

Q-15. Why was the condemnation of Luther in 1521 at Worms not enforced by the German nobility? What was the result?

Q-16. What were the goals and methods of the Ursuline order and the Society of Jesus?

Q-17. Why was reform within the Catholic church often unwelcome and slow in coming?

Q-18. What were the achievements of the Council of Trent? What circumstances surrounding the calling of the council to make its task difficult and its goal of reconciliation with Protestantism unattainable?

Q-19. What was the Roman Inquisition? How extensive was its power?

Q-20. Discuss the overall impact of the Reformation on European society. Do you see it as a blessing or a disaster for the people of Europe?

STUDY-REVIEW EXERCISES

Identify each of the following and give its significance.

Brethern of the Common Life

John Knox

Pope Paul III

Archbishop Cranmer

John Tetzel

Martin Luther

Angela Merici

Henry VIII

Charles V

Mary Tudor

Pope Alexander VI

Council of Trent

Counterreformation

Elizabethan Settlement

Act of Restraint of Appeals

pluralism

benefices

Peace of Augsburg

Ninety-five Theses

preacherships

Explain the subject matter and historical significance of the following books. How does each relate to the question of religion in society?

Erasmus, *The Praise of Folly*

Chaucer, *Canterbury Tales*

Thomas à Kempis, *The Imitation of Christ*

Luther, *Appeal to the Christian Nobility of the German Nation*

Calvin, *The Institutes of the Christian Religion*

Define the basic beliefs of the following Christian religions and churches.

Roman Catholicism

Lutheranism

Calvinism

Anabaptism

Church of England

Presbyterian Church of Scotland

Test your understanding of the chapter by answering the following questions.

1. The Council of Trent *did/did not* reaffirm the seven sacraments, the validity of tradition, and transubstantiation.

2. The English Supremacy Act of 1534 declared the _____ to be the Supreme Head of the Church of England.
3. For the most part, the English Reformation under Henry VIII dealt with *political/ theological* issues.
4. He wrote: "How comes it that we Germans must put up with such robbery and such extortion of our property at the hands of the pope?"

_____

5. This pope's name became a synonym for moral corruption.

_____

6. Mary Tudor, the English queen and daughter of Henry VIII, *was/was not* interested in the restoration of Catholicism in England.
7. In general, Protestantism tended to *strengthen/weaken* Germany as a political unit.
8. During the reign of Elizabeth, the English church moved in a moderately *Protestant/Catholic* direction.

MULTIPLE-CHOICE QUESTIONS

1. Under the Presbyterian form of church government, the church is governed by
   a. bishops.
   b. the king of Scotland.
   c. ministers.
   d. the people.

2. Which one of the following was not of the Anabaptist tradition?
   a. Congregationalists
   b. Puritans
   c. Quakers
   d. Jesuits

3. According to Luther, salvation comes through
   a. good works.
   b. faith.
   c. indulgences.
   d. a saintly life.

4. The cornerstone of Calvin's theology was his belief in
   a. predestination.
   b. indulgences.
   c. the basic goodness of man.
   d. religious tolerance and freedom.

5. John Knox and the Reformation movement in Scotland were most influenced by which of the following theological positions?
   a. Catholicism
   b. Calvinism
   c. Lutheranism
   d. the Church of England

6. Which of the following is *not* identified with corrupt practices in the early sixteenth-century church?
    a. pluralism
    b. the Brethren of the Common Life
    c. Pope Alexander VI
    d. absenteeism

7. Which of the following clearly did *not* support Luther?
    a. the German peasants
    b. the German nobility
    c. Charles V
    d. Ulrich Zwingli

8. Overall, Henry VIII's religious reformation in England occurred
    a. strictly for economic reasons.
    b. for religious reasons.
    c. mostly for political reasons.
    d. mostly for diplomatic reasons.

9. The Reformation in Germany resulted in
    a. a politically weaker Germany.
    b. a politically stronger Germany.
    c. no political changes of importance.
    d. a victory for imperial centralization.

10. The great Christian humanists of the fifteenth and sixteenth centuries believed that reform could be achieved through
    a. the use of violent revolution.
    b. education and social change.
    c. mass support of the church hierarchy.
    d. none of the above

11. Luther tacked his Ninety-five Theses to the door in Wittenberg as a response to
    a. the sale of indulgences and papal wealth.
    b. a revelation he experienced instructing him to start a new church.
    c. the illiteracy of the clergy.
    d. the oppressive rule of Frederick of Saxony.

12. The peasants who revolted in 1524 wanted
    a. the abolition of serfdom.
    b. the reform of the clergy.
    c. an end to taxes and tithes.
    d. all of the above

13. Luther's success was a result of
    a. a strong command of language.
    b. the development of the printing press.
    c. his appeal to the nobility and the middle classes.
    d. all of the above

14. The Holy Roman Emperor who tried to suppress the Lutheran revolt was
    a. Charles II.
    b. Henry VIII.
    c. Alexander V.
    d. none of the above

15. By 1555 the Protestant Reformation had spread to all but
    a. England.
    b. Scandinavia.
    c. Spain.
    d. Scotland.

16. The chief center of the Protestant Reformers in the sixteenth century was
    a. Paris.
    b. Geneva.
    c. Zurich.
    d. Cologne.

17. The Anabaptists appealed to
    a. the nobility.
    b. the poor, uneducated, and unemployed.
    c. the intellectuals.
    d. the merchant classes.

18. Henry VIII dissolved the monasteries largely because
    a. they were corrupt and mismanaged.
    b. they were symbolic of papal authority.
    c. he needed the wealth they would bring.
    d. they were a burden on the state.

19. The Scandinavian countries were most influenced by the religious beliefs of
    a. Martin Luther.
    b. John Knox.
    c. Roger Brown.
    d. the Jesuits.

20. A vow of the Jesuit order making it uniquely different from others was
    a. poverty.
    b. chastity.
    c. obedience to the pope.
    d. pacifism.

UNDERSTANDING HISTORY THROUGH READING AND THE ARTS

Few men in history have been the subject of more biographies than Martin Luther, the German reformer. One of the most important is a psychological study by E. Erikson entitled *Young Man Luther: A Study in Psychoanalysis and History** (1962). Other books about Luther include R. Bainton, *Here I Stand** (1950); E. Schwiebert, *Luther and His Times* (1952); G. Forel, *Faith Active in Love* (1954); and J. Atkinson, *Martin Luther and the Birth of Protestantism** (1968).

King Henry VIII of England is the subject of a number of interesting biographies. Three of the best are L. B. Smith, *Henry VIII* (1971); A. F. Pollard, *Henry VIII** (1905); and J. Scarisbrick, *Henry VIII* (1968). Henry's marital problems, as seen from his wife's side, are the subject of the fascinating and exciting *Catherine of Aragon** (1941) by G. Mattingly.

PROBLEMS FOR FURTHER INVESTIGATION

Students interested in further study of the religious revolution of the sixteenth century will find some of the problems of interpretation and investigation relative to that subject set out in L. W. Spitz, ed., *The Reformation** (1972) and K. Sessions, ed., *Reformation and Authority: The Meaning of the Peasant's Revolt** (1968). The relationship between the Protestant religion and economic growth has long interested historians. This historical problem is defined in R. Green, ed., *Protestantism, Capitalism, and Social Science* (1973). Students interested in the Counterreformation should begin with E. M. Burns, *The Counter Reformation** (1964), and those interested in the political implications of Calvinism should see R. Kingdon, *Calvin and Calvinism: Sources of Democracy** (1970).

*Available in paperback.

CHAPTER 15

THE AGE OF EUROPEAN EXPANSION
AND RELIGIOUS WARS

CHAPTER OBJECTIVES

After reading and studying this chapter you should be able to answer the following questions:

Q-1. Why and how did Europeans gain control over distant continents?

Q-2. What effect did overseas expansion have on Europe and conquered societies?

Q-3. What were the causes of religious wars in France, the Netherlands, and Germany?

Q-4. How did the religious wars affect the status of women?

Q-5. How and why did African slave labor become the dominant form of labor organization in the New World?

Q-6. What religious and intellectual developments led to the growth of skepticism?

Q-7. What literary masterpieces did this period produce?

CHAPTER SYNOPSIS

In this chapter we see how the trends in the High Middle Ages toward centralized nations ruled by powerful kings and toward European territorial expansion were revitalized. The growth of royal power and the consolidation of the state in Spain, France, and England accompanied and supported world exploration and a long period of European war.

The Portuguese were the first to push out into the Atlantic, but it was Spain, following close behind, that built a New World empire that provided the economic basis for a period of Spanish supremacy in European affairs. In the short run, Spanish gold and silver from the New World made the Spanish Netherlands the financial and manufacturing center of Europe, and Spain became Europe's greatest military power.

In the long run, however, overseas expansion ruined the Spanish economy, created massive European inflation, and brought the end of Spain's empire in Europe.

The attempts by Catholic monarchs to re-establish European religious unity and by both Catholic and Protestant monarchs to establish strong centralized states led to many wars among the European states. Spain's attempt to keep religious and political unity within her empire led to a long war in the Netherlands—a war that pulled England over to the side of the Protestant Dutch. There was bitter civil war in France, which finally came to an end with the reign of Henry of Navarre and the Edict of Nantes in 1598. The Thirty Years' War in Germany from 1618 to 1648 left that area a political and economic shambles.

The sixteenth century also saw a vast increase in witch-hunting and the emergence of modern racism, sexism, and skepticism. Generally, the power and status of women in this period did not change. Protestantism meant a more positive attitude toward marriage, but the revival of the idea that women were the source of evil and the end of the religious orders for women caused them to become increasingly powerless in society. North American slavery and racism had their origins in the labor problems in America and in Christian and Muslim racial attitudes. Skepticism was an intellectual reaction to the fanaticism of both Protestants and Catholics and a sign of things to come, while the Renaissance tradition was carried on by Shakespeare's work in early sixteenth-century England.

STUDY OUTLINE

I. Discovery, reconnaissance, and expansion (1450-1650)
    A. Overseas exploration and conquest
        1. The spread of the Ottoman Turks frightened the Europeans and overshadowed their international exploits at first
        2. Political centralization in Spain, France, and England prepared the way for expansion
        3. The Portuguese, under the leadership of Prince Henry the Navigator, pushed south from North Africa
            a. Da Gama, Diaz, and Cabral set routes to India
            b. The Portuguese gained control of the Indian trade by overpowering Muslim forts in India
        4. Spain began to play a leading role in exploration and exploitation
            a. Columbus sailed under the Spanish flag and discovered the Caribbean
            b. Spanish exploitation in the Caribbean led to the destruction of the Indian population
            c. Magellan sailed southwest across the Atlantic for Charles V of Spain, and his expedition circumnavigated the earth

        d. Pizarro crushed the Inca empire in Peru and opened the Potosi mines to Spanish use

        e. New Spain brought great wealth to Spain

    5. The Low Countries, particularly the cities of Antwerp and Amsterdam, became the center of European trade

        a. The Dutch East India Company became the major organ of Dutch imperialism

        b. The Dutch West India Company gained control of much of the African and American trade

    6. France and England made sporadic efforts at exploration and settlement

B. The explorers' motives

    1. The desire to Christianize the Muslims and pagan peoples played a central role in European expansion

    2. Limited economic and political opportunity for upper class men in Spain led to emigration

    3. Government encouragement was also important

    4. Renaissance curiosity caused people to seek out new worlds

    5. The economic motive—the quest for material profit—was the basic reason for European exploration and expansion

C. Technological stimuli to exploration

    1. The development of the cannon aided European expansion

    2. New sailing and navigational developments—such as the caravel ship and the compass—also aided the expansion

D. The economic effects of Spain's discoveries in the New World

    1. Enormous amounts of American gold and silver poured into Spain

    2. It is probable that population growth and not empire building caused inflation in Spain

    3. Spanish gold caused European inflation, which hurt the poor the most

E. Colonial administration

    1. The Spanish monarch divided his new world into four viceroyalties, each with a viceroy and *audiencia*

    2. Spanish economic policy toward its colonies was that of mercantilism

    3. Portuguese administration and economic policy was similar

II. Politics, religion, and war

  A. The Spanish-French wars ended in 1559 with a Spanish victory, thus leading to a variety of wars centering on religious and national issues

    1. These wars used bigger armies, with gun powder, and with a need for better financial administration

    2. Governments had to use various propaganda devices, including the printing press, to arouse public opinion

    3. The Peace of Westphalia (1648) ended religious wars but also ended the idea of a unified Christian society

B. The origins of difficulties in France (1515-1559)
   1. By 1500, France was recovering from plague and disorder, and the nobility began to lose power
   2. The French kings, such as Francis I and Henry II, continued the policies of centralization but spent more money than they raised
   3. The wars between France and Emperor Charles V—the Habsburg-Valois wars—were costly
   4. To raise money, Francis signed the Concordat of Bologna (1516), in which he recognized the supremacy of the papacy in return for the right to appoint French bishops
      a. This settlement established Catholicism as the national religion
      b. It also perpetuated corruption within the French church
      c. The corruption made Calvinism attractive to Christians eager for reform: some clergy and members of the middle and artisan classes
C. Religious riots and civil war in France (1559-1589)
   1. The French nobility, many of them Calvinist, attempted to regain power
   2. Frequent religious riots symbolized the struggle for power
   3. The Saint Bartholomew's Day massacre of Calvinists led to the War of the Three Henrys, a conflict for secular power
   4. King Henry IV's Edict of Nantes (1598) saved France from further civil war by allowing Protestants to worship
D. The Netherlands under Charles V
   1. The Low Countries were part of the Habsburg empire and enjoyed relative autonomy
   2. Charles V divided his empire between his brother Ferdinand and his son, King Philip of Spain
E. The revolt of the Netherlands (1556-1587)
   1. Regent Margaret attempted to destroy Protestantism by establishing the Inquisition in the Netherlands
   2. Popular support for Protestantism led to the destruction of many Catholic churches
   3. The Duke of Alva and his Spanish troops were sent by Philip II to crush the disturbances in the Low Countries
   4. Alva's brutal actions only inflamed the religious war, which raged from 1568 to 1578
   5. The Low Countries were finally split into the Spanish Netherlands in the south and the independent United Provinces of the Netherlands in the north
      a. The north was Protestant and ruled by the commercial aristocracy
      b. The south was Catholic and ruled by the landed nobility
   6. Elizabeth I of England supported the northern, or Protestant, cause as a safeguard against Spain's attacking England

        a. This was for economic reasons

        b. She had her rival Mary Queen of Scots beheaded

F. Philip II and the Spanish Armada

    1. Philip II planned war on England for several reasons

        a. He wanted to keep England in the Catholic fold

        b. He believed he would never conquer the Dutch unless he defeated England first

    2. The failure of the Spanish invasion of England—the armada of 1598—did not mean the end of the war, but it did prevent Philip from forcibly unifying western Europe

    3. In 1609, Philip III agreed to a truce, recognizing the independence of the United Provinces

G. The Thirty Years' War (1618-1648)

    1. Protestant Bohemian revolt over religious freedom led to war in Germany

    2. The Bohemian phase was characterized by civil war in Bohemia for religious liberty and political independence from the Habsburgs; the Catholics won

    3. The Danish phase led to further Catholic victory

    4. The Swedish phase ended the Habsburg plan to unite Germany

    5. The French phase ended with a destroyed Germany and an independent Netherlands

H. Germany after the Thirty Years' War

    1. The war was economically disastrous for Germany

    2. The war led to agricultural depression in Germany, which in turn encouraged a return to serfdom for many peasants

III. Changing attitudes

A. The status of women

    1. Literature on women and marriage called for a subservient wife with the household as her first priority and a protective, firm-ruling, and loyal husband

        a. Catholic marriages could not be dissolved while Protestants held that divorce and remarriage were possible

        b. Women did not lose their identity or meaningful work, but their subordinate status did not change—although a few women (like Bess of Hardwick) gained wealth and power

    2. Sexual indulgence was popular and widespread

        a. Prostitution was common—as brothels were licensed—but Protestant Moralists fought it

    3. Protestant reformers believed that convents were antifeminist and that women should be free to marry and enjoy sex

      a. However, it was understood even by Protestants that religious orders for women provided upper class women with an outlet for their talents

B. The great European witch-hunt

    1. Growth in religion and advent of religious struggle led to a rise in the belief in the evil power of witches

    2. The thousands of people executed as witches represent society's drift toward social and intellectual conformity

    3. Reasons varied but all in all witch hunting reflects widespread misogyny

C. European slavery and the origins of American racism

    1. Black slavery originated with the end of white slavery (1453) and the widespread need for labor, particularly in the new sugar-producing settlements

    2. Africans were brought to America to replace the Indians

    3. A few, like Las Casas, called for the end of slavery

    4. North American racist ideas originated in Christian and Muslim ideas

D. The origins of modern skepticism

    1. Skeptics doubt whether definitive knowledge is ever attainable

    2. Montaigne is the best representative of early modern skepticism

        a. He was a humanist graced with open-mindedness and tolerance

        b. He believed that the beginning of wisdom lies in the confession of ignorance

    3. Montaigne's skepticism represents a sharp break with the past; it is a forerunner of modern attitudes

IV. Elizabethan and Jacobean literature

A. The golden age of English literature: the late sixteenth and early seventeenth centuries

    1. Shakespeare reflects the Renaissance in that his great plays express national consciousness and human problems

    2. The Authorized Bible of King James I is a masterpiece of English vernacular writing

REVIEW QUESTIONS

Q-1. Describe the Portuguese explorations. Who were the participants and what were their motives?

Q-2. Describe the American-Spanish-Dutch economic arrangement. How did it work? Who were the winners and who were the losers?

Q-3. The sixteenth century was a century of money inflation. Why?

Q-4. What role did technology play in European expansion?

Q-5. Overall, what do you believe to be the major reasons for European expansion in the fifteenth and sixteenth centuries?

Q-6. What impact did Protestantism have on the economic and political development of France? Why is the Edict of Nantes an important event in French history?

Q-7. What were the causes and consequences of the French civil war of 1559-1589? Was it chiefly a religious or a political event?

Q-8. Discuss the origins and the outcome of the war between the Netherlands and Spain in the late sixteenth and early seventeenth centuries.

Q-9. What were the circumstances surrounding Elizabeth's decision to aid the United Netherlands in their war against Spain? What was the Spanish reaction?

Q-10. Why did Catholic France side with the Protestants in the Thirty Years' War?

Q-11. What were the political, religious, and economic consequences of the Thirty Years' War in Europe?

Q-12. Describe the social status of women between 1560 and 1648.

Q-13. What were the origins of North American racism?

Q-14. What is skepticism? Why did faith and religious certainty begin to come to an end in the first part of the seventeenth century?

Q-15. What were the major literary masterpieces of this age? In what ways can the English playwright Shakespeare be regarded as a true Renaissance man?

Q-16. What do the witch hunts tell us about social attitudes toward women?

STUDY-REVIEW EXERCISES

Identify each of the following.

politiques

Elizabeth I of England

Huguenots

Philip II of Spain

Prince Henry the Navigator

Michel de Montaigne

Christopher Columbus

Bartholomew Diaz

Hernando Cortez

Elizabeth Hardwick

Council of Blood

Habsburg-Valois wars

quinto

audiencia

corregedores

Thirty Years' War

defeat of the Spanish Armada

Concordat of Bologna

Peace of Westphalia

Saint Bartholomew's Day massacre

War of the Three Henrys

Edict of Nantes

Define the following key concepts and terms.

mercantilism

inflation

sexism

racism

skepticism

misogyny

Test your understanding of the chapter by answering the following questions.

1. The war that brought destruction and ensured division in Germany.

   _____

2. The Spanish explorer who conquered the Aztecs. _____

3. The Spanish priest and defender of the American Indians.

   _____

4. The law of 1598 that granted religious freedom to French Protestants.

   _____

5. Spain's golden century. _____

6. The king of Sweden who intervened in the Thirty Years' War.

   _____

7. After 1551, the seven northern provinces of the Netherlands were called

   _____ .

8. The city that became the financial capital of Europe by 1600.

   _____

9. The monarch of Britain at the time of the Spanish Armada.

   _____

10. The idea that nothing is completely knowable.

    _____

11. The emperor who divided the Habsburg empire into two parts.

    _____

12. The 1516 compromise between church and state in France.

    _____

13. The first European country to establish sea routes to the east.

    _____

MULTIPLE-CHOICE QUESTIONS

1. Which of the following was *not* a motive for Portuguese exploration in the late fifteenth and sixteenth centuries?
   a. the search for gold
   b. Christianizing the Muslims
   c. the discovery of sea routes to India
   d. the conquest of Constantinople

2. Beginning in 1581, the northern Netherlands revolted against their political overlord,
   a. France.
   b. Spain.
   c. Elizabeth I of England.
   d. Florence.

3. North American racist attitudes toward African blacks originated in
   a. South America.
   b. Spain.
   c. France.
   d. England.

4. In the Thirty Years' War, France supported
   a. the German Catholics.
   b. the Holy Roman Emperor.
   c. Spain.
   d. the German Protestants.

5. Which of the following statements about the Spanish Armada of 1588 is *false*?
   a. It was the beginning of a long war with England.
   b. It failed in its objective.
   c. It prevented Philip II from reimposing unity on western Europe by force.
   d. It made possible Spanish conquest of the Netherlands.

6. The nation that considered itself the international defender of Catholicism was
   a. France.
   b. Spain.
   c. Italy.
   d. England.

7. Columbus, like many of his fellow explorers, was principally motivated by
   a. a desire to discover India.
   b. a desire to Christianize the Americans.
   c. the desire of Spain to control the New World.
   d. the Spanish need to control the Mediterranean.

8. The earliest known explorers of North America were
   a. the Spanish.
   b. the Vikings.
   c. the Italians.
   d. the English.

9. Select the one which was *not* a feature of Spanish colonial administration:
   a. The New World was divided into four vice-royalties.
   b. Each territory had an *audiencia*, or judicial council.
   c. Each territory had royal officials, or intendants, responsible to the crown.
   d. The crown had only indirect and limited control over colonies.

10. In order to gain control of the spice trade of the Indian Ocean, the Portuguese were thrown into direct competition with
    a. Spain.
    b. England.
    c. the Muslims.
    d. France.

11. The main contribution of Cortez and Pizzaro to Spain was
    a. the tapping of the rich silver resources of Mexico and Peru.
    b. the Christianizing of the New World peoples.
    c. the further exploration of the Pacific Ocean.
    d. the discovery of South Africa.

12. The flow of huge amounts of gold and silver from the New World caused
    a. serious inflation in Spain and in the rest of Europe.
    b. the Spanish economy to become dependent on New World gold and silver.
    c. the suffering of the poor because of the dramatic rise in food prices.
    d. all of the above

13. Of the following, which was not a technological improvement that facilitated the "Age of Expansion"?

a. the galley
b. the magnetic compass
c. the cannon
d. the caravel

14. France was saved from religious anarchy when religious principles were set aside for political necessity by the new king,
    a. Henry III.
    b. Francis I.
    c. Henry IV of Navarre.
    d. Charles IX.

15. Calvinism was appealing to the middle classes for each of the following reasons *except*
    a. its heavy moral emphasis.
    b. its stress on leisure and ostentatious living.
    c. its intellectual emphasis.
    d. its approval of any job well done, hard work, and success.

16. The vast palace of the Spanish monarchs, built under the direction of Philip II, was called
    a. Versailles.
    b. the Escorial.
    c. Tournai.
    d. Hampton Court.

17. The Treaty of Westphalia, which ended the Thirty Years' War (1618-1648),
    a. further strengthened the Holy Roman Empire.
    b. completely undermined the Holy Roman Empire as a viable state.
    c. maintained that only Catholicism and Lutheranism were legitimate religions.
    d. refused to recognize the independence of the United Provinces of the Netherlands.

18. Of the following, the best representative of early modern skepticism is
    a. Las Casas.
    b. James I.
    c. Calvin.
    d. Montaigne.

19. The Spanish missionary Las Casas convinced Charles V to import Africans to Brazil because

a. church law did not strictly forbid the use of black slavery.
b. blacks were better able to withstand the rigors of hard work in a hot climate.
c. the native Indians were not durable enough under such harsh conditions.
d. all of the above

20. The Portuguese explorer who first reached India was
    a. Bartholomew Diaz.
    b. Prince Henry the Navigator.
    c. Vasco da Gama.
    d. Hernando Cortez.

21. The origin of racial attitudes found in North America was
    a. England.
    b. Spain.
    c. Catholic teaching.
    d. the Dutch.

22. The appearance of gunpowder in Europe
    a. put a common soldier on equal footing with a gentleman soldier.
    b. changed the popular belief that warfare bettered the individual.
    c. created the need for governments to use propaganda to convince their people to support war.
    d. all of the above

GEOGRAPHY

A. Using Map 15.1 in the text as a guide:
   1. Show on the outline map the exploration routes of da Gama, Columbus, and Magellan.
   2. Mark the location of the Aztec and Inca empires and locate and label the following places.

Cueta	Cape of Good Hope	Amsterdam	Guinea Coast of Africa
Calicut	Cape Horn	London	Lisbon
Goa	Antwerp	Mexico City	Moluccas

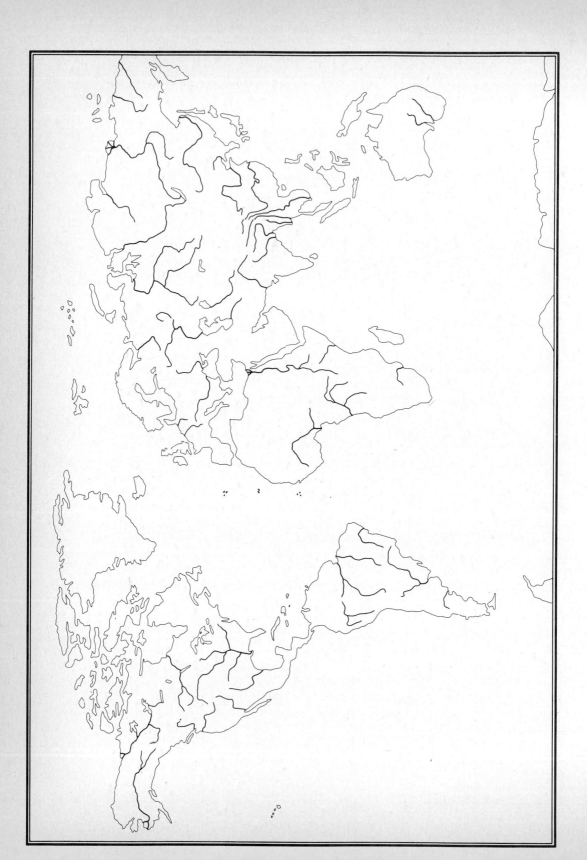

3. Why did the Spanish and Portuguese gain an early lead in European expansion? What were the goals of the early explorers, such as Columbus?

4. Explain, in geographic and economic terms, the reasons for the growth of the Flemish (Netherland) towns such as Antwerp and Amsterdam.

5. Explain the important economic relationship that developed among Spain, the Americas, and the Netherlands.

B. Using Map 15.4 in the text as a reference, list below the areas that were the main sources of African slaves and the main areas of slave importation into the New World. Do the latter areas illustrate the economic origins of the slave trade?

UNDERSTANDING HISTORY THROUGH READING AND THE ARTS

Those interested in skepticism and the life of its finest representative will want to read M. Lowenthal, ed., *Autobiography of Michel de Montaigne** (1935). There were a number of extremely important and powerful women of the sixteenth century whose biographies make for fascinating reading: R. Roeder, *Catherine de Medici and the Lost Revolution** (1937); J. E. Neal, *Queen Elizabeth I** (1934, 1966); and A. Fraser, *Mary Queen of Scots** (1969). An interesting seventeenth-century woman is Gustavus Adolphus's daughter, whose life is told in G. Masson, *Queen Christina* (1968); N. Harvey, *The Rose and the Thorn* (1977) is an account of the lives and times of Mary and Margaret Tudor.

*Available in paperback.

PROBLEMS FOR FURTHER INVESTIGATION

Those interested in doing work in the area of European expansion should begin with
D. L. Jensen, ed., *The Expansion of Europe: Motives, Methods, and Meaning* (1967).
A discussion of some of the problems faced in studying the religious conflict in France
is found in J. H. M. Salmon, *The French Wars of Religion** (1967), and anyone interested in research on the Thirty Years' War should begin with S. H. Steinberg, *The
Thirty Years' War and the Conflict for European Hegemony, 1600-1660** (1966) and
T. K. Rabb, *The Thirty Years' War** (1964). Those interested in understanding how
the vast Spanish Empire worked will want to see C. H. Haring, *The Spanish Empire
in America** (1947, 1963). This book includes an excellent bibliography on the subject.

*Available in paperback.

CHAPTER 16

ABSOLUTISM AND CONSTITUTIONALISM
IN WESTERN EUROPE (CA 1589-1715)

CHAPTER OBJECTIVES

After reading and studying this chapter you should be able to answer the following questions:

Q-1. How did absolute monarchy and constitutionalism differ from the feudal and dynastic monarchies of earlier centuries?
Q-2. Which countries best represent absolutism and constitutionalism?

CHAPTER SYNOPSIS

This chapter examines how the political system of absolutism succeeded gloriously in France and failed dismally in England in the seventeenth century. Few kings have been as successful in establishing complete monarchial sovereignty as the great Sun King of France, Louis XIV. Louis gave Europe a masterful lesson on how to reduce the power of the class that historically had been a constant competitor of the monarchy, the nobility. He was a superb actor and propagandist, who built on the earlier achievements of Henry IV and Richelieu and used his magnificent palace of Versailles to imprison the French nobility in a beautiful golden cage. He succeeded in expanding France at the expense of the Habsburgs, and his patronage of the arts helped form the great age of French classicism. However, the economic progress he first made was later checked by his policy of revoking religious toleration.

While the France of Louis was the classic model of modern absolutism, Spain was the classic case of imperial decline. By 1600 Spain was in trouble, and by 1700 it was no longer a major European power. Not only did the silver and labor of America run out, but this great American wealth ruined the Spanish economic and social structure.

War with the Dutch, the English, and the French also helped turn Spain into a back-water of Europe.

England and the United Provinces of the Netherlands provide a picture of con-stitutionalism triumphing over absolutism. For England, the seventeenth century was a long period of political conflict, complete with a bitter civil war and a radical experiment with republicanism. The causes of this era of conflict were varied, but it is clear that by 1689 the English army and Parliament had destroyed the Stuart quest for divine-right absolutism. The period that followed witnessed some important changes in the way the state is managed.

The Netherlands was important not only because it became the financial and com-mercial center of Europe, but also because it provided the period's third model of political development—a loosely federated, middle-class constitutional state.

STUDY OUTLINE

I. Absolutism
   A. Absolutism defined
      1. Under absolutism, sovereignty resided in kings—not the nobility or the parliament—who considered themselves responsible to God alone
      2. Absolute kings created new state bureaucracies and armies, and they regulated all the institutions
      3. However, the ambitions of absolute monarchs were limited and not the same as those of leaders of modern totalitarian states
   B. Henry IV and the foundations of French absolutism
      1. Henry IV achieved peace and curtailed the power of the nobility
      2. His minister, Sully, brought about financial stability and economic growth
   C. The cornerstone of French absolutism: Louis XIII and Richelieu
      1. Cardinal Richelieu, the ruler of France under King Louis XIII, broke the power of the French nobility
      2. He also brought about administrative reform that helped centralize the state's power
      3. However, his financial actions were unsound and created problems for the future
      4. Richelieu regarded the Protestant Huguenots as a source of aristocratic power
      5. Under Richelieu, France sought to break the Habsburg power
      6. Mazarin's policies gave rise to the *Fronde*
II. The absolutism of Louis XIV
   A. Louis the "Sun King" was selfish, an insatiable eater, a great actor, and fear-ful of the nobility

    B. He made the court at Versailles a fixed institution and used it as a means of preserving royal power and as the center of French absolutism
        1. The court at Versailles was a device to ruin the power of the aristocracy
        2. The architecture and art of Versailles was a means of carrying out state policy
        3. The French language and culture became the international style
    C. Economic management under Louis XIV: Colbert and mercantilism
        1. Mercantilism is a collection of governmental policies for the regulation of the economy by the state
        2. Louis XIV's finance minister, Colbert, tried to achieve a favorable balance of trade and make France self-sufficient so the flow of gold to other countries would be halted
            a. Colbert encouraged French industry, enacted high tariffs, and created a strong merchant marine
            b. He hoped to make Canada part of a French empire
            c. Though France's industries grew, its agricultural economy declined
    D. The revocation of the Edict of Nantes
        1. In 1685, Louis revoked the Edict of Nantes, which had given religious freedom to French Protestants
        2. This revocation caused many Protestants to flee the country; but it had little effect on the economy and it caused fear and hatred abroad

III.   French classicism in art and literature
    A. French classicism imitated and resembled the arts of the ancients and the Renaissance
    B. Poussin best illustrates classical idealism in painting, while Le Nain is an important realistic painter
    C. Louis XIV was a patron to the music composers Lully, Couperin, and Charpentier
    D. The comedies of Molière and the tragedies of Racine best illustrate the classicism in French theater

IV.   Louis XIV's wars
    A. The French army under Louis XIV was modern because it employed mercenaries rather than nobles
    B. Louis XIV's foreign policy was expansionist
    C. The height of French expansion was reached in 1678 with victory over Spain and the Holy Roman Empire
    D. Louis then fought the new Dutch king of England, William III and the League of Augsburg
    E. The War of the Spanish Succession (1701-1713) involved the issue of the succession to the Spanish throne: Louis claimed Spain but was opposed by the Dutch, English, Austrians, and Prussians

    1. The war was also an attempt to check French economic growth in the world

    2. The war was concluded by the Peace of Utrecht in 1713, which forbade the union of France and Spain

    3. The war left France on the brink of bankruptcy with widespread misery

V. The decline of absolutist Spain in the seventeenth century

  A. Factors contributing to Spain's decline:

    1. Fiscal disorder, political incompetence, population decline, intellectual isolation, and psychological malaise contributed to the decline

    2. The defeat of the "Invincible Armada" in 1588 was a crushing blow to Spain's morale

    3. Spain's economy began to decline by 1600

      a. Royal expenditure increased, but income from the Americas decreased

      b. Business and agriculture suffered

    4. Spanish kings lacked force of character and could not deal with all these problems

    5. Spain could not escape from her past: military glory, Roman Catholicism, and easy money from America

VI. Constitutionalism in England and the Netherlands

  A. Constitutionalism defined

    1. Under constitutionalism, the state must be governed according to law, not royal decree

      a. It implies a balance between the power of the government and the rights of the subjects

      b. A nation's constitution may be written or unwritten, but the government must respect it

    2. Constitutional government is not the same as full democracy because not all of the people have the right to participate

  B. The decline of royal absolutism in England (1603-1649)

    1. The Stuart kings of England lacked the political wisdom of Elizabeth I

    2. James I was devoted to the ideal of rule by divine right

    3. His absolutism ran counter to English belief

    4. James I faced a new, educated merchant-gentry class that opposed absolutism

    5. This new class controlled the House of Commons, which the Stuarts attempted to control

  C. The Protestant or "capitalist ethic" and the problem of religion in England

    1. Many English people were attracted by the values of hard work, thrift, and self-denial implied by Calvinism; these people were called Puritans

    2. The Puritans, who were dissatisfied with the Church of England, saw James I as an enemy

    3. Charles I and his archbishop, Laud, appeared to be pro-Catholic

D. The English Civil War (1642-1649)
    1. Charles I had ruled without Parliament for eleven years
    2. A revolt in Scotland over the religious issue forced him to call a new Parliament into session to finance an army
        a. The Commons passed an act compelling the king to summon Parliament every three years
        b. It also impeached Archbishop Laud
        c. Religious differences in Ireland led to a revolt there, but Parliament would not trust Charles with an army
    3. Charles initiated military action against Parliament
        a. The Civil War revolved around the issue of whether sovereignty should reside in the king or in Parliament
        b. The problem was not resolved, but Charles was beheaded in 1649

E. Puritanical absolutism in England: Cromwell and the Protectorate
    1. Kingship was abolished in 1649 and a commonwealth proclaimed
    2. In actuality, the army—led by Cromwell—controlled the government
    3. Cromwell's Protectorate became a military dictatorship—absolutist and puritanical
        a. Cromwell allowed religious toleration for all Christians, except Roman Catholics, and savagely crushed the revolt in Ireland
        b. He censored the press and closed the theaters
        c. He regulated the economy according to mercantilist principles

F. The restoration of the English monarchy (1660-1688)
    1. The restoration of the Stuart kings failed to solve the problems of religion and authority in society
    2. Charles II's Cabal was the forerunner of the cabinet system, and it helped create good relations with the Parliament
    3. Charles's pro-French policies led to a Catholic scare
    4. James II violated the Test Act, which prevented Catholics from holding government posts
    5. Fear of Catholicism led to the expulsion of James II and the Glorious Revolution
    6. The Bill of Rights of 1689 stated that sovereignty henceforth resided with Parliament
        a. Locke argued that all people have natural rights—including that of rebellion
        b. Locke's ideas served as the foundation of English and American liberalism
    7. The cabinet system, which developed in the eighteenth century, reflects the victory of aristocratic government over absolutism

G. The Dutch republic in the seventeenth century
  1. The Dutch republic emerged from the sixteenth-century struggle against Spain
  2. Power in the republic resided in the local Estates
    a. The republic was a confederation: a weak union of strong provinces
    b. The republic was based on middle-class ideas and values
  3. Religious toleration fostered economic growth
  4. The province of Holland became the commercial and financial center of Europe

REVIEW QUESTIONS

Q-1. In what way does the French minister Richelieu symbolize absolutism? What were his achievements?

Q-2. It has been said that the palace of Versailles was a device to ruin the nobility of France. Explain. Was Versailles a palace or a prison?

Q-3. Define mercantilism. What were the mercantilist policies of the French minister Colbert?

Q-4. The revocation of the Edict of Nantes has been considered a great error on the part of Louis XIV. Why?

Q-5. What were the reasons for the fall of the Spanish Empire?

Q-6. Discuss the foreign policy goals of Louis XIV. Was he successful?

Q-7. Define absolutism. How does it differ from totalitarianism?

Q-8. What was the impact of Louis XIV's wars on the French economy and French society?

Q-9. What were the causes of the War of the Spanish Succession? What impact did William III of England have on European events after about 1689?

Q-10. What was constitutionalism? How does it differ from democratic form of government?

Q-11. Discuss John Locke's political theory. Why is it said that Locke was the spokesman for the liberal English Revolution of 1689 and for representative government?

Q-12. What were the attitudes and policies of James I that made him so unpopular with his subjects?

Q-13. Who were the Puritans? Why did they come into conflict with James I?

Q-14. What were the immediate and the long-range causes of the English Civil War of 1642-1649? What were the results?

Q-15. Why did James II flee from England in 1688? What happened to the kingship at this point?

Q-16. Were the events of 1688-89 a victory for English democracy? Explain.

Q-17. Compare and contrast constitutionalism and absolutism. Where does sovereign power reside in each system?

Q-18. What accounts for the phenomenal economic success and political stability of the Dutch republic?

STUDY-REVIEW EXERCISES

Define the following key concepts and terms.

mercantilism

absolutism

totalitarianism

republicanism

constitutionalism

cabinet government

French classicism

sovereign power

quixotic

commonwealth

Identify each of the following and give its significance.

Molière

Poussin

Versailles

Dutch Estates General

intendants

Peace of Utrecht

Cabal of Charles II

Instrument of Government

Puritans

Oliver Cromwell

Cardinal Richelieu

Louis XIV of France

James II of England

English Bill of Rights

John Churchill

Philip II of Spain

Thomas Hobbes

Richelieu's *Dictionary*

Explain what each of these men believed about the placement of authority within society.

James I of England

Thomas Hobbes

Louis XIV of France

John Locke

Sully

<u>*Explain what the following events were and why they were important.*</u>

revocation of the Edict of Nantes

Scottish revolt of 1640

War of the Spanish Succession

Glorious Revolution

English Civil War of 1642-1646

Treaty of the Pyrenees

<u>*Test your understanding of the chapter by answering the following questions.*</u>

1. The highest executive office of the Dutch republic. _____

2. Louis XIV's able minister of finance was _____ .
3. During the age of economic growth in Spain, a vast number of Spaniards *entered/ left* religious orders.
4. For Louis XIV of France the War of the Spanish Succession was a *success/disaster*.
5. The Englishman who inflicted defeat on Louis XIV at Blenheim was

    _____ .

6. The archbishop whose goal was to enforce Anglican unity in England and Scot-

    land was _____ .

MULTIPLE-CHOICE QUESTIONS

1. Mercantilism
    a. was a military system.
    b. insisted on a favorable balance of trade.
    c. was adopted in England but not in France.
    d. claimed that state power was based on land armies.

2. French Protestants tended to be
   a. poor peasants.
   b. the power behind the throne of Louis XIV.
   c. a financial burden for France.
   d. clever business people.

3. The War of the Spanish Succession began when Charles II of Spain left his territories to
   a. the French heir.
   b. the Spanish heir.
   c. Eugene of Savoy.
   d. the archduke of Austria.

4. This city was the commercial and financial capital of Europe in the seventeenth century.
   a. London
   b. Hamburg
   c. Paris
   d. Amsterdam

5. Of the following, the country most centered on middle-class interests was
   a. England.
   b. Spain.
   c. France.
   d. the Netherlands.

6. Which of the following Englishmen was a Catholic?
   a. James II
   b. Oliver Cromwell
   c. Archbishop Laud
   d. William III

7. Which of the following is *not* a characteristics of an absolute state?
   a. sovereignty embodied in the person of the ruler
   b. bureaucracies solely accountable to the king
   c. a strong voice expressed by the nobility
   d. permanent standing armies

8. Cardinal Richelieu's most notable accomplishment was
   a. the creation of a strong financial system for France.
   b. the creation of a highly effective administration system.
   c. winning the total support of the Huguenots.
   d. allying the Catholic church with the government.

9. The statement "There are no privileges and immunities which can stand against a divinely appointed king" forms the basis of the
   a. Stuart notion of absolutism.
   b. Stuart notion of constitutionalism.
   c. English Parliament's notion of democracy.
   d. English Parliament's notion of constitutionalism.

10. The English Long Parliament
    a. enacted legislation supporting absolutism.
    b. supported the Catholic tendencies of Charles I.
    c. supported Charles I as a military leader.
    d. enacted legislation against absolutism.

11. Cromwell's government is best described as a
    a. constitutional state.
    b. democratic state.
    c. military dictatorship.
    d. monarchy.

12. Absolute monarchs secured mastery over the nobility by
    a. the creation of a standing army.
    b. the creation of a state bureaucracy.
    c. the use of war.
    d. all of the above

13. Cardinal Richelieu consolidated the power of the French monarchy by each of the following *except* for
    a. destroying the castles of the nobility.
    b. ruthlessly treating conspirators who threatened the monarchy.
    c. keeping nobles from gaining high government offices.
    d. eliminating the "intendant" system of local government.

14. One way in which Louis XIV controlled the French nobility was by
    a. maintaining standing armies in the countryside to crush noble uprisings.
    b. requiring the presence of the major noble families at Versailles for at least part of the year.
    c. periodically visiting the nobility in order to check on their activities.
    d. none of the above

15. Features of the French army under Louis XIV included the following *except* for

a.   standarized uniforms and weapons.
b.   living off the countryside.
c.   the ambulance corps caring for the troops.
d.   a system of recruitment, training, and promotion.

16. The Peace of Utrecht in 1713
a.   enlarged the British Empire significantly.
b.   reflected the balance-of-power principle.
c.   ended Spain's role as a major power in Europe.
d.   all of the above

17. The downfall of Spain in the seventeenth century from being a major European
power can be blamed on
a.   a weak monarchy.
b.   a decline in industry and trade.
c.   a contraction of slave labor.
d.   all of the above

18. When Archbishop Laud tried to make the Presbyterian Scots accept the Anglican Book of Common Prayer, the Scots
a.   revolted.
b.   reluctantly accepted the archbishop's directive.
c.   ignored the directive.
d.   none of the above

19. Acting as spokesman for the landowning class and proponent of the idea that
the purpose of government is to protect life, liberty, and property was
a.   Thomas Hobbes.
b.   William of Orange.
c.   John Locke.
d.   Edmund Burke.

20. After the United Provinces of the Netherlands won independence from Spain,
their structure of government was
a.   a strong monarchy.
b.   a centralized parliamentary system.
c.   a weak union of strong provinces.
d.   a democracy.

21. The Dutch economy was based on
a.   fishing and the merchant marine.
b.   silver mining in Peru.
c.   export of textiles.
d.   all of the above

GEOGRAPHY

1. Using Map 16.1 in the text as a guide, on the outline map shade in the territory added to France as a result of the wars and foreign policy of King Louis XIV.
2. Explain how each of the territories was acquired and from whom.

3. Louis XIV declared in 1700 that "the Pyrenees no longer exist." What did he mean?

4. What changes in the balance of power came about as a result of the Treaty of Utrecht in 1713?

UNDERSTANDING HISTORY THROUGH READING AND THE ARTS

Louis XIV and the magnificence of his court at Versailles are re-created with color and spirit in W. H. Lewis, *The Splendid Century** (1953), and a vivid picture of life of the English upper classes—how they ran their estates, entertained, and when possible ran the country—is found in Mark Girouard, *Life in the English Country House: A Social and Architectural History* (1979).

The seventeenth century was a period of architectural splendor in France and in England. Some of the great achievements of this period are discussed in Chapter 7 of N. Pevsner, *An Outline of European Architecture* (7th ed., 1963). The splendor of Versailles and French and British baroque painting and architecture are the subjects of Chapter 7, "The Baroque in France and England," in H. W. Janson, *History of Art* (1962).

Much good reading is found in the literature of the seventeenth century. The great comic writer of the age was Molière, whose *Tartuffe* is still a source of entertainment. LaFontaine's *Fables* are a lively reworking of tales from antiquity and Cervantes's *Don Quixote* continues to inspire its readers. The greatest writer to emerge from the Puritan age in England was John Milton, whose *Paradise Lost* is a classic.

*Available in paperback.

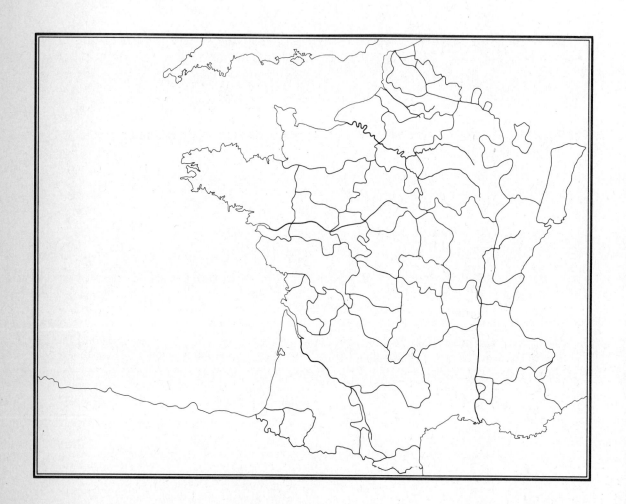

PROBLEMS FOR FURTHER INVESTIGATION

James Stuart was a successful king in Scotland but a failure in England. Why? See D. Willson, *King James VI and I** (1956). Was the Glorious Revolution of 1688-89 in England a victory for modern political democracy or a palace revolution by a group of aristocrats? This and other problems surrounding this political event are discussed in G. M. Straka, ed., *The Revolution of 1688 and the Birth of the English Political Nation** (rev. ed., 1973). Some of the problems in interpretation of the crucial period 1642 to 1649 in Britain are considered in P. A. M. Taylor, ed., *The Origins of the English Civil War** (1960), L. Stone, ed., *Social Change and Revolution in England, 1540-1640** (1965)—and B. Manning deals with popular participation in the wars and revolution in *The English People and the English Revolution* (1976).

Students interested in research on absolutism and Louis XIV in France will want to consider H. G. Judge, ed., *Louis XIV* (1965); William F. Church, ed., *The Greatness of Louis XIV: Myth or Reality?** (rev. ed., 1972); and R. F. Kierstead, ed., *State and Society in Seventeenth-Century France** (1975). The best biography of Louis XIV is *Louis XIV* (1968) by J. Wolf.

*Available in paperback.

CHAPTER 17

ABSOLUTISM IN EASTERN EUROPE
TO 1740

CHAPTER OBJECTIVES

After reading and studying this chapter you should be able to answer the following questions:

Q-1. Why did the basic structure of society in eastern Europe move away from that in western Europe?

Q-2. How and why did the rulers of Austria, Prussia, and Russia manage to build more durable absolute monarchies than that of Louis XIV of France?

Q-3. How did the absolute monarchs' interactions with artists and architects contribute to the achievements of baroque culture?

CHAPTER SYNOPSIS

This chapter discusses why monarchial absolutism developed with greater lasting strength in eastern Europe than in western Europe. In Russia, Prussia, and Austria monarchs became more powerful as the peasants were pushed back into serfdom. That is, peasants gradually lost the personal and economic freedoms they had built up over several hundred years during the Middle Ages. At the same time that eastern nobles gained greater social and economic control over the enserfed peasants, they lost political power to the rising absolute monarchs. The author concludes that while there were some economic reasons for the re-emergence of serfdom in the east, it was essentially for political reasons that this strong authoritarian tradition emerged. As opposed to western Europe, it was the common people—the peasants—who were the great losers in the power struggle between nobility and monarchy.

Absolutism in Russia, Austria, and Prussia emerged because of war, foreign invasion, and internal struggle. For example, the Austrian monarchs solved the problems arising from external conflicts and a multicultural state by building a strong, central-ized military state. Prussian absolutism—intended to check the power of the nobility—was achieved by the Hohenzollern monarchs, while Russian absolutism was largely the outgrowth of the Mongol conquest and internal power struggles.

Some of the absolute monarchs were enlightened reformers, but their good in-tentions were often thwarted by internal problems. But if reform from above was not overly effective, the absolute monarchs' use of architecture and urban planning—much of which was in the so-called baroque form—to enhance their images was a noteworthy success. They created buildings and cities that reflected their growing power, and they hired baroque painters and musicians such as Rubens and Bach to glorify them and to fill their palaces with paintings and music.

STUDY OUTLINE

I. Lords and peasants in eastern Europe
   A. The medieval background (1400-1650)
      1. Personal and economic freedom for peasants increased between 1050 and 1300
      2. Thus, living conditions improved and serfdom was reduced
      3. After 1300, powerful lords in eastern Europe reinstituted serfdom to combat their economic problems
      4. Laws restricted freedom, and labor obligations were increased in eastern Europe
   B. The consolidation of serfdom
      1. The re-establishment of hereditary serfdom took place in Poland, Prussia, and Russia between 1500 and 1650
      2. This was a result of the growth of estate agriculture
         a. Lords seized peasant land for their own estates
         b. They then demanded unpaid serf labor on those estates
   C. Political reasons for changes in serfdom in eastern Europe
      1. Serfdom increased because of political, not economic, reasons
      2. Weak monarchs could not resist the demands of the powerful noble land-lords
      3. The absence of the Western concept of sovereignty meant that the king did not think in terms of protecting the people of the nation
      4. Overall, the peasants of the East were weaker than those of the West, and the urban middle class was undermined by the landlords
II. The rise of Austria and Prussia (1650-1750)
   A. Austria and the Ottoman Turks
      1. After the end of the Thirty Years' War in 1648, the Austrian Habsburgs, having failed to destroy Protestantism, turned inward and eastward to unify their holdings

    2. Austria became absorbed in a war against the Turks for the conquest of Hungary and Transylvania

    3. Under Suleiman the Magnificent the Turks built the most powerful empire in the world, which included part of central Europe

        a. The Turkish sultan was the absolute head of the state

        b. There was little private property, and a bureaucracy staffed by slaves

    4. The Turkish attack on Austria in 1683 was turned back, and the Habsburgs conquered all of Hungary and Transylvania

    5. The Habsburg possessions consisted of Austria, Bohemia, and Hungary, which were joined in a fragile union

        a. The Pragmatic Sanction (1713) stated that the possessions should never be divided

        b. The Hungarian nobility resisted accepting Habsburg rule

  B. Prussia in the seventeenth century

    1. The Hohenzollern family ruled the electorate of Brandenburg but had little real power

    2. The Thirty Years' War weakened the representative assemblies of the realm and allowed the Hohenzollerns to consolidate their absolutist rule

    3. Frederick William (the Great Elector) used military force and taxation to unify his holdings into a strong state

  C. The consolidation of Prussian absolutism

    1. Frederick William I encouraged Prussian militarism and created the best army in Europe plus an efficient bureaucracy

    2. The nobility—the Junker class—became the military elite

III. The development of Russia

  A. The Vikings and the Kievan principality

    1. Eastern Slavs moved into Russia between the fifth and ninth centuries

    2. Slavic-Viking settlements grew up in the ninth century

    3. The Vikings unified the eastern Slavs politically and religiously, creating a ruling dynasty and accepting Eastern Orthodox Christianity for themselves and the Slavs

    4. A strong aristocracy (the boyars) and a free peasantry made it difficult to strengthen the state

  B. The Mongol yoke and the rise of Moscow

    1. The Mongols conquered the Kievan state in the thirteenth century and unified it under their rule

    2. The Mongols used Russian aristocrats as their servants

        a. The princes of Moscow served the Mongols well and became the hereditary great princes

        b. Ivan I served the Mongols while using his wealth and power to strengthen the principality of Moscow

      c. Ivan III stopped acknowledging the Mongol Khan and assumed the headship of Orthodox Christianity

C. Tsar and people to 1689
1. By 1505, the prince of Moscow—the tsar—had emerged as the divine-right ruler of all the lands of the eastern Slavs
2. The tsars and the boyars struggled over who would rule the state, and the tsars won
3. Ivan the Terrible was an autocratic tsar who expanded Muscovy and further reduced the power of the boyars
    a. He murdered leading boyars and confiscated their estates
    b. Many peasants fled his rule to the newly conquered territories, forming groups called Cossacks
    c. Businessmen and artisans were bound to their towns and jobs
4. The Time of Troubles (1598-1613) was a period characterized by internal struggles and invasions
    a. There was no heir
    b. Cossack bands slaughtered many nobles and officials
    c. Swedish and Polish armies invaded
5. Michael Romanov was elected tsar by the nobles (1613), and he reestablished tsarist autocracy
6. The Romanovs brought about the total enserfment of the people
7. A split in the church over religious reforms led to mass protests by the peasants, and the church became dependent on the state for its authority

D. The reforms of Peter the Great
1. Peter wished to create a strong army for protection and expansion
    a. He forced the nobility to serve in the army or in the civil service
    b. He created schools to train technicians for his army
2. Army and government became more efficient and powerful as an interlocking military-civilian bureaucracy was created and staffed by talented people
3. Russian peasant life under Peter became more harsh
4. Modest territorial expansion took place under Peter, and Russia became a European Great Power
5. Peter borrowed many western ideas

IV. Absolutism and the Baroque
A. Baroque art and music
1. Baroque art fulfilled the needs of the Catholic Church and the absolute rulers
2. In painting, the baroque is best seen in the work of Rubens; in music, it reached its height with Bach

B. Palaces and power

1. Architecture played an important role in politics because it was used by kings to enhance their image and awe their subjects
2. The royal palace was the favorite architectural expression of absolutist power
3. The dominant artistic style of the age of absolutism was baroque—a dramatic and emotional style

C. Royal cities and urban planning
   1. The new St. Petersburg is an excellent example of the tie among architecture, politics, and urban development
      a. Peter the Great wanted to create a modern, baroque city from which to rule Russia
      b. The city became a showplace for the tsar paid for by the Russian nobility and built by the peasants

D. The growth of St. Petersburg
   1. During the eighteenth century, St. Petersburg became one of the world's largest and most influential cities
   2. The new city was modern or "baroque" in its layout and design
   3. All social groups, including the peasants, paid heavily in the construction of the city
   4. Tsarina Elizabeth and architect Rastrelli crowned the city with great palaces

REVIEW QUESTIONS

Q-1. What were the reasons for the re-emergence of serfdom in eastern Europe in the early modern period (1400-1650)? Build a case for either an economic or a political explanation.

Q-2. In western Europe the conflict between the king and his vassals resulted in gains for the common man. Why did this not happen in eastern Europe?

Q-3. Why would the reign of the Great Elector be regarded as "the most crucial constitutional struggle in Prussian history for hundreds of years"? What did he do to increase royal authority? Who were the losers?

Q-4. Prussia has traditionally been considered one of the most militaristic states in Europe. How do you explain this development? Who or what was responsible?

Q-5. How did war (the Thirty Years' War) and invasion (by the Ottoman Turks) help the Habsburgs consolidate power?

Q-6. What was the Pragmatic Sanction and why were the Hungarian and Bohemian princes opposed to it?

Q-7. What role, if any, did war play in the evolution of absolutism in eastern Europe?

Q-8. Use the following to illustrate the relationship between baroque architecture and European absolutism: St. Petersburg, Karlesruhe, Upper and Lower Belvedere, Schönbrunn. Was it simply that "every fool likes his own hat"? Explain.

Q-9. It has been said that the common man benefited from the magnificent medieval cathedrals as much as the princes. Can the same be said about the common man and the building projects of the absolute kings and princes? Explain.

Q-10. Discuss the influence of the Vikings and the Mongols on Russian history.

Q-11. Why do you think the history of Russia is more a history of servitude than of freedom? How do you account for the enormous amount of violence in Russian history?

Q-12. Why was territorial expansion "the soul of tsardom"?

Q-13. Trace the fortunes and political power of the boyar class in Russia from the time of the Kievan state to the death of Peter the Great.

Q-14. Peter the Great of Russia and Frederick William I of Prussia are often viewed as heroes and "reformers" in the histories of their own countries. How valid is this assessment in terms of the peasants of the early eighteenth century?

STUDY-REVIEW EXERCISES

Identify the following people and explain their importance.

Bartolomeo Rastrelli

Suleiman the Magnificent

Frederick the Great

Charles VI of Austria

Jenghiz Khan

Ivan the Terrible

J. S. Bach

Peter the Great

Frederick William the Great Elector

Ivan III

Peter Paul Rubens

Define the following key concepts and terms.

absolutism

baroque

Prussian Junkers

Hohenzollern

kholops

Romanov

boyar

autocracy

Vikings

Hapsburg

Mongol Yoke

Pragmatic Sanction

Explain and describe baroque architecture by referring to the pictures in the textbook.

Explain what the following events were, who participated in them, and why they were important.

Building of the Winter Palace of St. Petersburg

Siege of Vienna, 1683

War of the Austrian Succession

Time of Troubles

Battle of Poltava

Test your understanding of the chapter by answering the following questions.

1. He was the founder of the new Russian city on the coast of the Baltic Sea.

    _____

2. He is the unsurpassed master of baroque music. _____
3. After 1500, serfdom in eastern Europe *increased/decreased.*
4. The Ottoman Turkish leader who captured Vienna in 1529 was

    _____ .
5. In the struggle between the Hungarian aristocrats and the Austrian Habsburgs, the Hungarian aristocrats *maintained/lost* their traditional privileges.
6. This Prussian monarch doubled the size of Prussia in 1740 by taking Silesia from

    Austria. _____
7. Number the following events in correct chronological order.

    _____ The election of the first Romanov tsar

    _____ The establishment of the Kievan state

    _____ The Time of Troubles

    _____ Invasion by the Mongols

    _____ The building of St. Petersburg

    _____ The battle of Poltava
8. The monarchs of eastern Europe in the sixteenth and seventeenth centuries were generally *stronger/weaker* than the kings of western Europe.

MULTIPLE-CHOICE QUESTIONS

1. The unifiers and first rulers of the Russians were the
   a. Mongols.
   b. Turks.
   c. Romanovs.
   d. Vikings.

2. By the seventeenth century, in Russia commercial activity, manufacturing, and mining were owned or controlled by the
   a. rising urban capitalists.
   b. Cossacks.
   c. Tsar.

3. The monarchs of eastern Europe used their increased power after 1600 to do all of the following *except*
   a. impose taxes without consent.
   b. maintain standing armies.
   c. control the treatment of serfs by their lords.
   d. conduct foreign affairs independently.

4. The principality called the "sandbox of the Holy Roman Empire" was
   a. Brandenburg-Prussia.
   b. Hungary.
   c. Sweden.
   d. Austria.

5. Ivan the Terrible
   a. failed to conquer Kazan.
   b. was afraid to call himself tsar.
   c. monopolized a great deal of mining and business activity.
   d. abolished the system of compulsory service for noble landlords.

6. Peter the Great's reforms included all but which one of the following?
   a. Compulsory education away from home for the higher classes
   b. A lessening of the burdens of serfdom for Russian peasants
   c. A fourteen-rank merit-system bureaucracy
   d. A strengthening of the Russian army

7. The dominant artistic style of the seventeenth and early eighteenth centuries was

    a. Gothic.
    b. Romantic.
    c. impressionistic.
    d. baroque.

8. The noble landowners of Prussia were known as
    a. Boyars.
    b. Junkers.
    c. Vikings.
    d. Electors.

9. Apparently the most important reason for the return to serfdom in eastern Europe from about 1500 to 1650 was
    a. political.
    b. economic.
    c. military.
    d. religious.

10. The eastern European nobility gained power from struggling monarchs during the late Middle Ages because of
    a. the many wars that occurred during the period.
    b. disputed royal successions.
    c. the absence of a well-developed concept of sovereignty.
    d. all of the above

11. After the disastrous defeat of the Czech nobility by the Habsburgs at the battle of White Mountain in 1618, the
    a. old Czech nobility in great numbers accepted Catholicism.
    b. majority of Czech noble land was given to soldiers who had fought for the Habsburgs.
    c. conditions of the enserfed peasantry improved.
    d. Czech nobility continued their struggle effectively for many years.

12. After the Thirty Years' War and the creation of a large standing army, Austria turned its attention to control of
    a. northern Italy.
    b. Prussia.
    c. Hungary.
    d. Poland.

13. The result of the Hungarian nobility's struggle against Habsburg oppression was that

    a. they suffered a fate similar to the Czech nobility.

    b. they gained a great deal of autonomy compared with the Austrian and Bohemian nobility.

    c. they won their independence.

    d. their efforts were inconclusive.

14. In 1742, as a result of the War of Austrian Succession, Maria Theresa
    a. was forced to abdicate.
    b. was forced to give up the province of Silesia to Prussia.
    c. gained Prussian possessions.
    d. was unable to keep Hungary in the Austrian Empire.

15. The Viking invaders in early Russian history were principally interested in
    a. controlling vast new lands politically.
    b. spreading their religion.
    c. establishing and controlling commercial interests.
    d. none of the above

16. The Muscovite princes gained their initial power through
    a. services rendered to the Vikings.
    b. strategic marriages.
    c. services rendered to the Mongols.
    d. none of the above

17. The rise of the Russian monarchy was largely a response to the external threat of the
    a. French monarchy.
    b. Asiatic Mongols.
    c. Prussian monarchy.
    d. English monarchy.

18. The Time of Troubles was caused by
    a. a dispute in the line of succession.
    b. Turkish invasions.
    c. Mongol invasions.
    d. severe crop failures resulting in starvation and disease.

19. In order to strengthen the Russian military, Peter the Great
    a. made the nobility serve in the civil administration or army for life.
    b. established schools and universities to train Russian youth.
    c. searched out and brought talented foreigners into his service.
    d. all of the above

20. The real losers in the growth of eastern Europe absolutism were the
    a. peasants.
    b. peasants and middle classes.
    c. nobility.
    d. nobility and the clergy.

GEOGRAPHY

1. Show on the outline map the area covered by the principality of Moscow in 1300. Was the principality of Moscow an important state at that time?

2. Shade in with different colors the territories acquired by the principality of Moscow from 1300 to 1689. How successful was Moscow in expanding before 1689?

3. Shade in the acquisitions of Peter the Great. How do these acquisitions suggest that Russia was becoming more western and European and less eastern and Asiatic during Peter the Great's reign?

4. Using your knowledge of Russian geography and the information in the textbook, explain how Russia's history has been influenced by its geography. For example, does Russia's geographic setting contribute to its absolutism?

5. Looking at Map 17.1 in the text, identify the three territorial parts of the Habsburg (Austrian) state and explain how they came to be united. Do these geographic facts help explain the development of absolutism and militarism in Austria?

UNDERSTANDING HISTORY THROUGH READING AND THE ARTS

For centuries the Moscow Kremlin was the axis of Russian culture—that is, it was the place where works of great historical and artistic significance were amassed. Many examples of painting and applied art of the Kremlin are discussed and illustrated in *Treasures of the Kremlin** published by the Metropolitan Museum of Art, New York (1979). See also, T. Froncek, ed., *The Horizon Book of the Arts of Russia* (1970), and G. Hamilton, *The Art and Architecture of Russia* (1975). For the greatest architectural symbol of absolutism in France the student should turn to G. Walton, *Louis XIV's Versailles** (1986).

Baroque music, the dominant musical style in the age of absolutism, was often written for a particular monarch or princely court. The mathematical and harmonic emphasis of baroque music and its aristocratic patronage are illustrated in the six Brandenburg Concertos by Johann Sebastian Bach, written for the margrave of Brandenburg in the early eighteenth century, and in George F. Handel's *Water Music*, written for George I of England at about the same time. Both of these are available on numerous recordings. For the history of baroque music see M. F. Bukofzer, *Music in the Baroque Era* (1947).

PROBLEMS FOR FURTHER INVESTIGATION

The personality and reign of Tsar Peter the Great have generated considerable controversy for many years. Many ideas for further research can be found in M. Raeff, *Peter the Great* (rev. ed., 1972), and in L. J. Oliva, ed., *Russia and the West from Peter to Khrushev* (1965).

*Available in paperback.

CHAPTER 18

TOWARD A NEW WORLD-VIEW

CHAPTER OBJECTIVES

After reading and studying this chapter you should be able to answer the following questions:

Q-1. Why did the world-view of the educated classes change from a primarily religious one to one that was primarily secular and scientific?
Q-2. How did this new outlook on life affect society and politics?

CHAPTER SYNOPSIS

This chapter shows how the educated classes moved from a world-view that was basically religious to a world-view that was primarily secular in the course of the seventeenth and eighteenth centuries. The development of scientific knowledge was the key cause of this intellectual change. This change was momentous because it laid the groundwork for both enlightened absolutism and the spirit of revolution.

Until about 1500, scientific thought reflected the Aristotelian-medieval world-view, which taught that a motionless earth was at the center of a universe made up of planets and stars in ten crystal spheres. These and many other beliefs showed that science was primarily a branch of religion. Beginning with Copernicus, who taught that the earth revolved around the sun, Europeans slowly began to reject Aristotelian-medieval scientific thought. They developed a new conception of a universe based on natural laws, not on a personal God. Isaac Newton, standing on the shoulders of earlier mathematicians, physicists, and astronomers, formulated the great scientific synthesis: the law of universal gravitation. Newton's work was the culminating point of the scientific revolution.

The chapter examines the causes of the scientific revolution, its relationship to religion, and its impact on nonscientific thought. The new science was more important for intellectual development than for economic activity or everyday life, for above all it promoted critical thinking. Nothing was to be accepted on faith; everything was to be submitted to the rational, scientific way of thinking. This critical examination of everything, from religion and education to war and politics, was the program of the Enlightenment and the accomplishment of the philosophes, a group of thinkers who propagandized the new world-view across Europe and the North American colonies.

The philosophes were reformers, not revolutionaries. Yet reform of society from the top down—that is, by the absolute monarchs through what is called "enlightened absolutism"—proved to be impossible because the enlightened monarchs could not ignore the demands of their conservative nobilities. In the end, it was revolution, not enlightened absolutism, that changed and reformed society.

STUDY OUTLINE

I.   The scientific revolution: the origin of the modern world
  A.   Historians now recognize that the history of science and the history of society must be brought together
  B.   Scientific thought in 1500
    1.   Until the early 1500s, European ideas about the universe were based on Aristotelian-medieval ideas
      a.   Central to this view was the belief in a motionless earth fixed at the center of the universe
      b.   Around the earth moved ten crystal spheres
      c.   Beyond the spheres was heaven
    2.   Aristotle's scheme fit into Christianity because it made human beings the center of the universe and established a home for God
  C.   The Copernican hypothesis
    1.   Copernicus, a Polish astronomer, claimed that the earth revolved around the sun—that the sun was the center of the universe
    2.   This heliocentric theory was a great departure from the medieval system
    3.   Copernicus's theory created doubts about traditional religion
  D.   From Tycho Brahe to Galileo
    1.   Brahe set the stage for the modern study of astronomy by building an observatory and collecting data
    2.   His assistant, Kepler, formulated three laws of planetary motion that proved the precise relationships among planets in a sun-centered universe
    3.   Galileo discovered the laws of motion using the experimental method— the cornerstone of modern science

       4. Galileo was tried by the Inquisition for heresy and forced to recant his views

  E. Newton's synthesis

       1. Newton integrated the astronomy of Copernicus and Kepler with the physics of Galileo

          a. He formulated a set of mathematical laws to explain motion and mechanics

          b. The key feature in his synthesis was the law of universal gravitation

       2. Henceforth, the universe could be explained through mathematics

  F. Causes of the scientific revolution

       1. Medieval universities provided the framework for the new science

       2. The Renaissance stimulated science by rediscovering ancient mathematics

       3. The navigational problems of sea voyages generated scientific research

       4. New ways of obtaining knowledge improved scientific methods

          a. Bacon advocated empirical, experimental research

          b. Descartes stressed mathematics and deductive reasoning

       5. After the Reformation the Catholic church discouraged science while Protestantism tended to favor it

  G. Some consequences of the scientific revolution

       1. There arose a scientific community whose primary goal was the expansion of knowledge

       2. A modern scientific method arose that rejected traditional knowledge and logic

       3. Because the link between pure science and applied technology was weak, the scientific revolution was more an intellectual than material revolution

II. The Enlightenment

  A. Enlightenment ideas

       1. Natural science and reason can explain all aspects of life

       2. The scientific method can explain the laws of human society

       3. It is possible to create better societies and better people

  B. The emergence and results of the Enlightenment

       1. The French philosophes popularized Enlightenment ideas

       2. The Enlightenment and the scientific revolution were directly connected—the former popularized the latter

       3. The Enlightenment encouraged the growth of uncertainty about religious truth, cultural superiority, and the role of experience in learning

  C. The philosophes and their ideas

       1. The philosophes acquainted the elite of western Europe with the ideas of the new world-view

       2. They were committed to the reformation of society and humanity, although they often had to cloak attacks on church and state in satire

a. Montesquieu used social satire to criticize existing practices
b. He proposed that power be divided and shared by all classes by adopting the principle that "power checks power"
c. Voltaire challenged traditional Catholic theology and exhibited a characteristic philosophe belief in a distant God who let human affairs take their own course
d. Diderot and d'Alembert edited a great encyclopedia that examined all of human knowledge and attempted to teach people how to think critically and rationally
   (1) The *Encyclopedia* exalted science and knowledge over religion
   (2) As a summary of the Enlightenment world-view it was extremely influential
D. The later Enlightenment built rigid and dogmatic systems
  1. D'Holbach argued that humans were completely controlled by outside forces
  2. Hume's skepticism argued that the mind can produce only empirical knowledge
  3. Rousseau attacked rationalism and civilization and claimed that children needed to be protected from society
  4. His *Social Contract* centered on the idea of the general will of the people
E. The social setting of the Enlightenment
  1. Enlightenment ideas were spread by salons of the upper classes
  2. The salons were often presided over by women like the brilliant Geoffrin and Deffand
III. The evolution of the "Greats": absolutism
A. Many believed that "enlightened" reform would come by way of "enlightened" monarchs
B. Frederick II and Catherine II of Russia
  1. Frederick II used the War of the Austrian Succession to expand Prussia into a Great Power
  2. Renewed conflict in 1756 (the Seven Years' War, 1756-1763) saw Prussia aligned against Austria and Russia
  3. Frederick allowed religious freedom and promoted education
  4. He reformed the legal system and bureaucracy and encouraged agriculture and industry to improve the life of his subjects
  5. Catherine imported Western culture to Russia and corresponded with the philosophes
    a. Her ideas about reforming serfdom changed after Pugachev's uprising in 1773, however, and she restricted the serfs even more
    b. Catherine also succeeded in annexing Poland
C. Absolutism in France and Austria

   1. With the duke of Orleans and the Parliament of Paris the French nobility enjoyed a revival of power following the death of Louis XIV, and the monarchy lost the power of taxation
   2. The French minister began the restoration of royal absolutism under Louis XV
   3. With the reign of Louis XVI royal absolutism once again declined and noble power revived
   4. The Austrian emperor Joseph II was a dedicated reformer who abolished serfdom, taxed all his subjects equally, and granted religious freedom
   5. Joseph failed, however, because of aristocratic opposition; his reforms were short-lived
D. An overall evaluation
   1. In France, the rise of judicial and aristocratic opposition combined with a public educated in liberalism put absolutism on the defensive
   2. In eastern Europe, however, the results of "enlightened absolutism" were modest and therefore absolutism remained entrenched
   3. By combining state-building with the Enlightenment these absolutists underscored the long tradition of the role of the state in society

REVIEW QUESTIONS

Q-1. Contrast the old Aristotelian-medieval world-view with that of the new science of the sixteenth and seventeenth centuries. What were the contributions of Copernicus, Brahe, Kepler, Galileo, and Newton? What is meant by Newton's "synthesis"?

Q-2. How did the new scientific theory and discoveries alter the concept of God and religion? Did science, in fact, come to dictate humanity's concept of God?

Q-3. The author tells us that Copernicus hit upon "an old Greek idea being discussed in Renaissance Italy." How does this help explain the origins of the new science?

Q-4. Discuss the origins and the momentum of the scientific revolution in terms of (a) its own "internal logic" and (b) external and nonscientific causes.

Q-5. How did Bacon and Descartes contribute to the development of the modern scientific method?

Q-6. Did the Catholic and Protestant churches retard or foster scientific investigation? Explain.

Q-7. What are the consequences of the rise of modern science?

Q-8. Were the philosophes interested in popular rule by or the political education of the people? Were their dreams of reform from above utopian?

Q-9. What was the effect of Catherine's reign on (a) the Russian nobility, (b) the Russian serfs, and (c) the position of Russia in the European balance of power?

Q-10. Describe the nature of the power struggle in France following the death of Louis XIV in 1715.

Q-11. Discuss: "Joseph II [of Austria] was a heroic but colossal failure."
Q-12. Since the enlightened absolutists tried but failed to make life better for common men and women, who were the real enemies of the people? Why was the system of absolutism resistant to change?

STUDY-REVIEW EXERCISES

Define the following key concepts and terms.

deductive reasoning

rationalism

the idea of progress

skepticism

Parlement of Paris

Enlightenment

enlightened absolutism

Aristotelian world-view

empirical method

Identify each of the following and give its significance.

Gresham College

Diderot

Bayle

Kepler

Galileo

Newton

Montesquieu

Voltaire

Copernicus

Brahe

Catherine the Great

Frederick the Great

Louis XV

Joseph II

philosophes

Bacon

Descartes

D'Holbach

Explain the general significance of the following books and indicate how these works and their authors influenced one another.

On the Revolutions of the Heavenly Spheres, Copernicus

New Astronomy or Celestial Physics, Kepler

Two New Sciences, Galileo

Principia, Newton

Explain the new ideas of the following books introduced into Enlightenment society and some of the consequences of these ideas.

Conversations on the Plurality of Worlds of 1686, Fontenelle

Historical and Critical Dictionary, Bayle

The Spirit of the Laws, Montesquieu

Essay Concerning Human Understanding, Locke

· *Philosophical Dictionary*, Voltaire

Encyclopedia: The Rational Dictionary of the Sciences, the Arts, and the Crafts,
D'Alembert, Diderot

Social Contract, Rousseau

Test your understanding of the chapter by answering the following questions.

1. According to Aristotle, the sublunar world was made up of four elements: air,

   fire, _____, and _____ .
2. Copernicus *did/did not* attempt to disprove the existence of God.
3. Galileo claimed that *motion/rest* is the natural state of all objects.

4. The key feature in Newton's synthesis was the law of _____ .
5. In the medieval universities, science emerged as a branch of

   _____ .

6. The method of finding latitude came out of study and experimentation in the

   country of _____ .
7. The idea of "progress" *was/was not* widespread in the Middle Ages.
8. In the seventeenth and eighteenth centuries a close link between pure (theoretical) science and applied technology *did/did not* exist.

9. A _____ is one who believes that nothing can ever be known beyond all doubt.

10. Voltaire believed that _____ was history's greatest man because he gave humanity truth.
11. Overall, Joseph II of Austria *succeeded/failed* as an enlightened monarch.

MULTIPLE-CHOICE QUESTIONS

1. Catherine the Great did all but which one of the following?
   a. Annexed part of Poland
   b. Freed the Russian serfs
   c. Allowed limited religious tolerations
   d. Supported the philosophes of France

2. "Enlightened" monarchs believed in
   a. reform.
   b. democracy.
   c. urbanization.
   d. all of the above

3. Geoffrin and Deffand were
   a. scientific writers.
   b. religious leaders.
   c. "enlightened" women.
   d. leaders of the serf uprising.

4. The philosophes were
   a. mainly university professors.
   b. generally hostile to monarchial government.
   c. enthusiastic supporters of the Catholic church.
   d. satirist writers who wished to reform society and humanity.

5. The social setting of the Enlightenment
   a. excluded women.
   b. was characterized by poverty and boredom.
   c. was dominated by government officials.
   d. was characterized by witty and intelligent conversation.

6. Catherine the Great
   a. believed the philosophes were dangerous revolutionaries.
   b. freed the serfs to satisfy Diderot.
   c. increased the size of the Russian Empire.
   d. established a strong constitutional monarchy.

7. According to medieval thought, the center of the universe was the
   a. sun.
   b. earth.
   c. moon.
   d. heaven.

8. The Aristotelian world-view lasted two thousand years because
   a. it provided understandable answers for what people could see happening around them.
   b. its ideas were workable within the realm of Christian theology.
   c. its ideas placed human beings at the center of the universe.
   d. all of the above

9. Copernicus' theory of a sun-centered universe
   a. suggested the universe was small and closed.
   b. challenged the idea that crystal spheres moved the stars around the earth.
   c. ruled out the belief that the worlds of heaven and earth were different.
   d. suggested an enormous and possibly infinite universe.

10. The first astronomer to prove his theories through the use of mathematical equations was
    a. Galileo.
    b. Johannes Kepler.
    c. Tycho Brahe.
    d. Isaac Newton.

11. D'Holbach, Hume, and Rousseau are examples of the later Enlightenment trend toward
    a. rigid systems.
    b. social satire.
    c. religion.
    d. the idea of absolutism.

12. The French philosopher who rejected his contemporaries and whose writings influenced the romantic period was
    a. Rousseau.
    b. Voltaire.
    c. Diderot.
    d. Condorcet.

13. The gathering ground for many who wished to discuss the ideas of the French Enlightenment was the
    a. salon.
    b. lecture hall.
    c. palace at Versailles.
    d. the University of Paris.

14. Frederick II was considered an enlightened despot because he
    a. freed the serfs.
    b. wrote poetry, allowed religious freedom, and improved the legal and bureaucratic systems.
    c. kept the Junkers in a dominant position socially and politically.
    d. avoided war.

15. Catherine the Great of Russia hardened her position on serfdom after the _____ rebellion.
    a. Pugachev
    b. Moscow
    b. Polish
    c. "Five Year"

16. After Louis XIV's death,
    a. the nobility made a drastic comeback in power.
    b. the nobility secured judicial positions in the Parlements.
    c. the French government struggled with severe economic difficulties.
    d. all of the above

17. He used the War of the Austrian Succession to expand Prussia into a great power.
    a. Joseph II
    b. Frederick II
    c. William I
    d. None of the above

18. The imperialist aggressiveness of Prussia, Austria, and Russia led to the disappearance of this eastern European kingdom from the map after 1795.
    a. Hungary
    b. Sweden
    c. Brandenburg
    d. Poland

19. Francis Bacon's great contribution to scientific methodology was
    a. the geocentric theory.
    b. the notion of logical speculation.
    c. the philosophy of empiricism.
    d. analytic geometry.

20. This man set the stage for the modern study of astronomy by building an observatory and collecting data.
    a. Darwin
    b. Hume
    c. Newton
    d. Brahe

UNDERSTANDING HISTORY THROUGH READING AND THE ARTS

The upsurge of creativity in the arts in the seventeenth and eighteenth centuries, which was greatly influenced by the Enlightenment, is known as the age of the baroque. The meaning of this highly creative and dynamic style and the achievements of its great artists are discussed in M. Kitson, *The Age of the Baroque* (1966). See also Chapter 6 in N. Pevsner, *An Outline of European Architecture* (7th ed., 1963). Few artists captured English life as well as did the painter Hogarth, whose *Rake's Progress* and *Harlot's Progress* point to the consequences of moral decay. Hogarth's paintings can be seen and studied in W. Gaunt, *The World of William Hogarth* (1978), and D. Bindman, *Hogarth** (1981).

The two greatest philosophes of the age of Enlightenment were Rousseau and Voltaire. Rousseau's ideas on education and natural law are interestingly set forth in his *Emile*, and Voltaire's most-praised work is *Candide*, a funny and sometimes bawdy parody on eighteenth-century life and thought. Much of the new fiction writing of the eighteenth century reflects, often in satire, the spirit of the new world-view—Jonathan Swift, *Gulliver's Travels*; Daniel Defoe, *Moll Flanders*; and Henry Fielding, *Tom Jones*, are just a few. In Germany, the *Sturm und Drang* (storm and stress) movement, which produced works such as Lessing's *Nathan the Wise* which stressed a universal religion, was devoted to the ideas of the Enlightenment and romanticism.

PROBLEMS FOR FURTHER INVESTIGATION

Those interested in pursuing the topic of the Enlightenment will want to begin with two books that set forth some of the major issues and schools of interpretation on the subject: B. Tierney, et al., eds., *Enlightenment—The Age of Reason** (1967), and R. Wines, ed., *Enlightened Despotism** (1967).

Why was it not until the seventeenth century that rational science emerged? What has been the relationship between science and religion in Western society? What ideas did Darwin and modern biology draw from the Scientific Revolution of 1500-1800? These are just a few of the questions asked by scholars of the subject. Begin your

*Available in paperback.

investigation with a general reference and bibliography such as G. Sarton, *Introduction to the History of Science* (1927-1948, 5 vols.), and L. Thorndike, *History of Magic and Experimental Science* (1923-1958). On particular figures in science see F. S. Taylor, *Galileo and the Freedom of Thought* (1938), A. Armitage, *Copernicus, the Founder of Modern Astronomy* (1938), M. Casoar, *Johannes Kepler* (1959, trans. C. Hellman), L. T. More, *Isaac Newton* (1934), and I. Cohen, *Franklin and Newton* (1956).

READING WITH UNDERSTANDING
EXERCISE 4

LEARNING TO CLASSIFY INFORMATION ACCORDING TO SEQUENCE

As you know, a great deal of historical information is classified by sequence, in which things follow each other in time. This kind of *sequential order* is also known as *time order* or *chronological order*.

Attention to time sequence is important in the study of history for at least two reasons.

1. It helps us organize historical information effectively.

2. It promotes historical understanding. If the student knows the order in which events happened, he or she can think intelligently about questions of cause and effect. The student can begin to evaluate conflicting interpretations.

Since time sequences are essential in historical study, the authors have placed a number of timelines in the text to help you organize the historical information.

Two Fallacies Regarding Time Sequences

One common fallacy is often known by the famous Latin phrase *post hoc, ergo propter hoc:* "after this, therefore because of this." This fallacy assumes that one happening that follows another *must* be caused by the first happening. Obviously, some great development (such as the Protestant Reformation) could come after another (the Italian Renaissance) without being caused by it. *Causal relationships must be demonstrated, not simply assumed on the basis of the "after this, therefore because of this" fallacy.*

A second common, if old-fashioned, fallacy assumes that time sequences are composed only of political facts with precise data. But in considering social, intellectual, and economic developments, historians must often speak with less chronological exactitude—in terms of decades or even centuries, for example. Yet they still use time sequences, and students of history must recognize them. For example, did you realize that the sections on "The Scientific Revolution" and "The Enlightenment" in Chapter 18 are very conscientious about time sequence, even though they do not deal with political facts?

Exercise

Reread the large section in Chapter 18 on "The Scientific Revolution" with an eye for dates and sequential order. Then take a sheet of notebook paper and with the book open make a "Timeline for the Scientific Revolution." Pick out at least a dozen important events and put them in the time sequence, with a word or two to explain the significance when possible.

Suggestion: Do not confine yourself solely to specific events with specific dates. Also, integrate some items from the subsection on the causes of the Scientific Revolution into the sequence. You may find that constructing timelines helps you organize your study.

After you have completed your timeline, compare it with the one on the following page, which shows how one of the authors of the text did this assignment.

Timeline on the Scientific Revolution

(1300-1500)	Renaissance stimulates development of mathematics
early 1500s	Aristotle's ideas on movement and universe still dominant
1543	Copernicus publishes *On the Revolution of the Heavenly Spheres*
1572, 1577	New star and comet create more doubts about traditional astronomy
1546-1601	Tycho Brache—famous astronomer, creates mass of observations
1571-1630	Johannes Kepler—his three laws prove Copernican theory and demolish Aristotle's beliefs
1589	Galileo Galilei (1564-1642) named professor of mathematics
1610	Galileo Galilei studies moon with telescope and writes of experience
1561-1626	Francis Bacon—English scientific enthusiast, advocates experimental (inductive) method
1596-1650	René Descartes—French philosopher, discovers analytical geometry in 1619 and advocates theoretical (deductive) method
to about 1630	All religious authorities oppose Copernican theory
about 1632	Galileo tried by papal inquisition
1622	Royal Society of London founded—brings scientists and practical men together
1687	Isaac Newton publishes his *Principia*, synthesizing existing knowledge around idea of universal gravitation
to late 1700s	Consequences of Scientific Revolution primarily intellectual, not economic

CHAPTER 19

THE EXPANSION OF EUROPE IN THE
EIGHTEENTH CENTURY

CHAPTER OBJECTIVES

After reading and studying this chapter you should be able to answer the following questions:

Q-1. How did the European economy expand and change in the eighteenth century?
Q-2. What were the causes of this expansion?
Q-3. How did these changes affect people and their work?

CHAPTER SYNOPSIS

How did our "modern" world begin? This chapter discusses the important economic and demographic changes of the eighteenth century, which led up to the Industrial Revolution. It also prepares us for understanding the life of ordinary people in the eighteenth century, which is the subject of the following chapter.

The chapter covers four important and interrelated subjects. First, the centuries-old open-field system of agricultural production, a system that was both inefficient and unjust, is described. This system was gradually transformed into a more productive system of capitalistic farming, first in the Low Countries and then in England. Some English peasants suffered in the process, but on the whole the changes added up to a highly beneficial agricultural revolution. The second topic is the explosive growth of European population in the eighteenth century. This growth, still imperfectly understood, was probably due largely to the disappearance of the plague and to new and better foods, such as the potato. Doctors and organized medicine played a very minor role in the improvements in health. Third, the chapter discusses the movement of manufacturing from urban shops to cottages in the countryside. Rural families worked there as units in the new domestic system, which provided employment for many in the growing population. The domestic system was particularly effective in the textile industry, which this chapter examines in detail.

Finally, the chapter shows how the mercantilist economic philosophy of the time resulted in world wars for trade and colonies. Mercantilism also led to the acquisition of huge markets for British manufactured goods, especially cloth. The demand from these new markets fostered the continued growth of the domestic system and put pressure on it. This eventually led to important inventions and the development of the more efficient factory system. Thus the modern world was born. It is important to look for the interrelatedness of these changes and to keep in mind that it was in only one country, Great Britain, that all of these forces were fully at work.

STUDY OUTLINE

I. Agriculture and the land
    A. The hazards of an agrarian economy
        1. The agricultural yields in seventeenth-century Europe were not much higher than in ancient Greece
        2. Frequent poor harvests and bad weather led to famine and disease
    B. The open-field system
        1. The open-field system divided the land into a few large fields, which were then cut up into long, narrow strips
        2. The fields were farmed jointly by the community, but a large portion of the arable land was always left fallow
        3. Common lands were set aside for community use
        4. The labor and tax system throughout Europe was unjust, but eastern European peasants suffered the most
        5. By the eighteenth century most peasants in western Europe were free from serfdom and many owned some land
    C. The agricultural revolution of the late seventeenth and eighteenth centuries
        1. Crop rotation eliminated the need for fallowing and broke the old cycle of scarcity; more fodder meant more animals, which meant more food
        2. Enclosure of the open fields to permit crop rotation also meant the disappearance of common land
    D. The leadership of the Low Countries and England
        1. By the middle of the seventeenth century, the Low Countries led in intensive farming
        2. Dutch engineers such as Vermuyden helped England drain its marshes to create more arable land
        3. Population pressure, the growth of towns, and economic freedom in the Low Countries led to agricultural expansion

    4. Tull and Townsend in England advocated new crops and new methods

E. The debate over enclosure

    1. The fencing of open fields probably did not harm the poor people who lived off the land, as some historians have claimed

    2. Enclosure resulted in more, not less, agricultural employment for wage workers

II. The beginning of the population explosion

A. The limitations on population growth up to 1700

    1. The traditional checks on growth were famine, disease, and war

    2. Quarantine of ports and the victory of the brown rat helped reduce the plague

    3. These checks kept Europe's population growth rate fairly low

B. The new pattern of population growth in the eighteenth century

    1. The basic cause of population growth was fewer deaths, partly owing to the disappearance of the plague

    2. Advances in medicine, such as inoculation against smallpox, did little to reduce the death rate

    3. An increase in the food supply meant fewer famines and epidemics

    4. The growing population often led to overpopulation and increased rural poverty

III. The growth of cottage industry

A. Rural industry

    1. The rural poor took in manufacturing work to supplement their income

    2. This cottage industry challenged the monopoly of the urban craft guilds

B. The putting-out system

    1. It was based on rural workers producing cloth in their homes for merchant-capitalists, who supplied the raw materials and paid for the finished goods

    2. This system reduced the problem of rural unemployment and provided cheap goods

    3. England led the way in the conversion from urban to rural textile production

C. The textile industry in England as an example of the putting-out system

    1. The English textile industry was a family industry: the women would spin and the men would weave

    2. A major problem was that there were not enough spinners to make yarn for the weaver

    3. Strained relations often existed between workers and capitalist employers

    4. The capitalist found it difficult to control the worker and the quality of the product

IV. Building the Atlantic economy in the eighteenth century

A. Mercantilism and colonial wars

1. Mercantilism is an economic system whereby the state uses a variety of means to regulate the economy
2. The mercantilists claimed that a favorable balance of trade was necessary for the nation's survival
3. The Navigation Acts were a form of economic warfare
   a. They required that goods exported to England be carried mostly on British ships
   b. These acts gave Britain a virtual trade monopoly with its colonies
4. The French quest for power in Europe and North America led to international wars
   a. The loss of the War of the Spanish Succession forced France to cede parts of Canada to Britain
   b. The Seven Years' War was the decisive struggle in the French-British competition for colonial empire, and France ended by losing all its North American possessions; Spain's empire expanded
B. Land and wealth in North America
   1. Colonies helped relieve European poverty and surplus population as settlers eagerly took up farming on the virtually free land
   2. The English mercantilist system benefited American colonists
   3. The population of the North American colonies grew very quickly during the eighteenth century
C. The growth of foreign trade
   1. The English colonists made up for a decline in English trade on the Continent
   2. These colonies also encouraged industrial growth in England
D. Revival in colonial Latin America
   1. Spain's political success was matched by economic involvement in its colonies
   2. In much of Latin America Creole landowners dominated the economy and the Indian population
   3. Compared to North America, racial mixing was more frequent in Spanish America

REVIEW QUESTIONS

Q-1. How did the open-field system work? Why was much of the land left uncultivated while the people sometimes starved?

Q-2. What changes brought the open-field system to an end?

Q-3. Where did the modern agricultural revolution originate? Why?

Q-4. What is meant by "enclosure"? Was this movement a great swindle of the poor by the rich, as some have claimed?

Q-5. Was the dramatic growth of population in the eighteenth century due to a decreasing death rate or an increasing birthrate? Explain.

Q-6. How did the "revolution in the animal kingdom" break the force of the deadly bubonic plague?

Q-7. What improvements in the eighteenth century contributed to the decline of disease and famine?

Q-8. The movement of production from town to country is commonly known as the growth of the domestic or putting-out system. Using textile production as an example, explain how the system worked and why it grew.

Q-9. What were the advantages and disadvantages of the putting-out system for the merchant-capitalist? For the worker?

Q-10. What was mercantilism? How could it have been a cause of war? Of economic growth?

Q-11. How do the careers of English businessmen like Mun and Child illustrate the theory of mercantilism?

Q-12. The eighteenth century witnessed a large number of expensive and drawn-out wars. Who was attempting to alter the balance of power? Were the causes of these wars economic or political?

Q-13. Did the American colonists and the American colonial economy benefit or suffer from the British mercantilistic colonial system?

Q-14. "The Spanish settlers strove to become a genuine European aristocracy, and they largely succeeded." Explain.

Q-15. What was the cause of the Spanish War of Succession and who won?

STUDY-REVEW EXERCISES

Define the following key concepts and terms.

famine foods

common land

open-field system

enclosure

mercantilism

cottage industry

putting-out system

fallow fields

asiento

crop rotation

mestizos

primogeniture

Creole elite

Identify each of the following and give its significance.

the Asiatic brown rat

Jethro Tull

Charles Townsend

Cornelius Vermuyden

Navigation Acts

Treaty of Paris

Peace of Utrecht

spinning jenny

turnips

Explain the following wars in the age of mercantilism by providing the appropriate information.

Name of War	Dates	Participants	Causes	Outcome
Anglo-Dutch wars				

War of the Spanish Succession

War of the Austrian Succession

Seven Years' War

Fill in the blank with the letter of the correct answer.

_____ 1. Disappearance of this encouraged population growth

_____ 2. Agricultural land set aside for general village use

_____ 3. The area with highest average standard of living in the world

_____ 4. After 1763 the major power in India

_____ 5. West African slave trade

_____ 6. Led Europe in agricultural improvement

_____ 7. Products of racial miscegenation

_____ 8. The most important new eighteenth-century food

a. Low Countries
b. mestizos
c. commons
d. Thirty Years' War
e. American colonies
f. potato
g. *asiento*
h. France
i. bubonic plague
j. Britain

MULTIPLE-CHOICE QUESTIONS

1. All but which one of the following is a reason for Dutch agricultural success in the eighteenth century?
    a. The nature of the people themselves
    b. Their excellent teachers, the British
    c. The extensive urbanization of the lowlands
    d. The dense population of the lowlands

2. Which of the following was *not* a shortcoming of the cottage textile industry?
    a. An imbalance between spinning and weaving
    b. Strained labor relations
    c. Difficulty in controlling the quality of the product
    d. Not enough demand for the product

3. All but which one of the following is a characteristic of eighteenth-century economic change?
   a. Increased world trade
   b. The switch from the cottage system of production to the factory system
   c. The creation of more common lands and open fields for production
   d. The increase in both population and food supply

4. The battle in England against the enclosure movement has often been exaggerated. Proof of this is the fact that
   a. no English land at all had been enclosed by 1750.
   b. parliamentary actions after 1760 initiated the enclosure movement.
   c. the proportion of landless laborers was very large after 1830.
   d. enclosure actually created jobs.

5. The agricultural improvements of the mid-eighteenth century were based on the elimination of
   a. livestock farming.
   b. the open-field system.
   c. rotation of fields.
   d. nitrogen-producing plants, such as peas and beans.

6. Which of the following prevented eighteenth-century peasants from gaining a profit on their land?
   a. The combination of oppressive landlords and poor harvests
   b. The plague
   c. The relatively light taxes imposed on them by landlords
   d. Their reliance on crop rotation

7. The mercantilist attitude toward the state was that
   a. the government should regulate the economy.
   b. governmental power should be increased at the expense of private profit.
   c. using governmental economic power to help private interests is unethical.
   d. the economy should be left to operate according to its natural laws.

8. The new farming system consisting of crop rotation and the use of nitrogen-sorting crops caught on quickly in
   a. the Low Countries and England.
   b. Russia.
   c. eastern Europe as a whole.
   d. Scandinavia.

9. The rapid development of Dutch farming was the result of
   a. a dense population.
   b. the increasing number of cities and towns.
   c. an unencumbered political and economic system.
   d. all of the above

10. A fair description of population fluctuation figures before 1700 in Europe would be that the
    a. population was remarkably uniform in its growth.
    b. population increased steadily on account of very young marriages and large families.
    c. population decreased slightly on account of war, famine, and disease.
    d. population grew slowly and erratically.

11. After 1720, the plague did not reappear because of
    a. quarantining in Mediterranean ports.
    b. the practice of isolating carriers of the dread disease.
    c. the invasion of the Asiatic brown rat.
    d. all of the above

12. In the mid-seventeenth century, England's major maritime competitor was
    a. France.
    b. the Netherlands.
    c. Spain.
    d. Denmark.

13. The Seven Years' War (1756-1763) between France and Britain resulted in
    a. British dominance in North America and India.
    b. French dominance in North America and India.
    c. a stalemate.
    d. British dominance only in North America.

14. The slow growth of industry in America during the colonial period was caused by
    a. excessive availability of land and the high cost of labor.
    b. a lack of capital for investment.
    c. a scorn for industry.
    d. none of the above

15. The black-to-white ratio in America by 1774 was
    a. one to four.
    b. one to eight.
    c. one to ten.
    d. one to two.

16. The abundance of land in the American colonies encouraged
    a. increased population through natural increase and immigration.
    b. a higher standard of living.
    c. economic equality.
    d. all of the above

17. Which of the following did not result from the British mercantile system?
    a. It reduced sales on the continent caused by the closing of French markets.
    b. It further exploited British colonial markets.
    c. It balanced and diversified English exports.
    d. It stagnated the British foreign trade economy.

18. The group that used the new farming methods to the fullest in England was
    a. independent farmers.
    b. well-financed, profit-minded tenant farmers.
    c. large landowners.
    d. small landowning wage laborers.

19. The dominant political and economic group in Spanish America was the
    a. Creoles.
    b. Indians.
    c. mestizos.
    d. none of the above

20. The landowners who dominated the economy and the Indian population of Spain's Latin American empire are known as
    a. mestizos.
    b. Creoles.
    c. mercantilists.
    d. warlords.

GEOGRAPHY

1. Locate on the outline map and shade in with different colors the four main European countries that had large holdings in the New World in 1701.

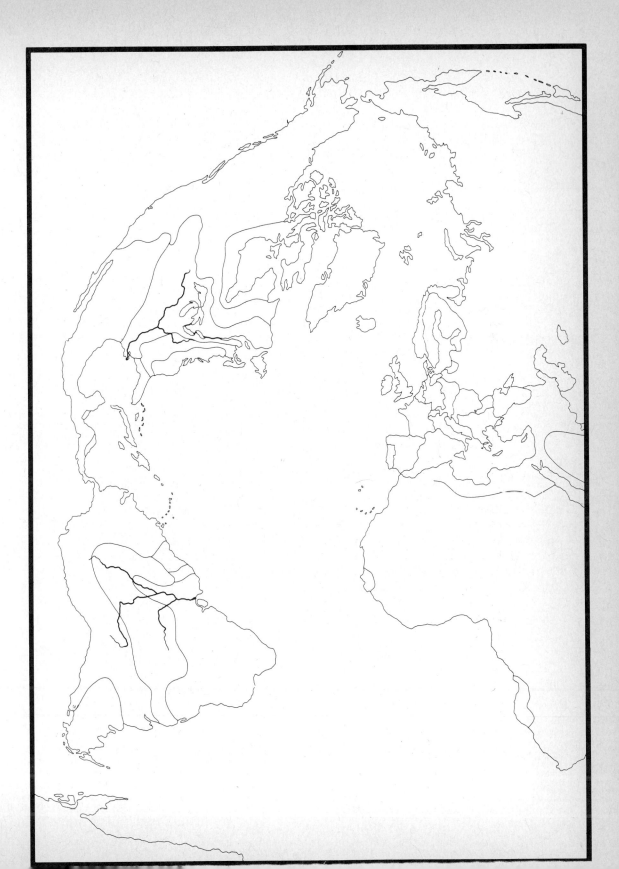

2. Using the same shading scheme, shade in the respective colonial holdings in North and South America, referring to Map 19.1 if necessary. Did the largest colonial holdings go to the largest European countries? Or was a position on the Atlantic the key factor?

3. Redraw the outline map to show territorial changes in the Americas after 1763. Which European country was the big winner? The big loser?

4. Draw in and label arrows that show the main paths of trade in the Atlantic Basin in the eighteenth century. In what ways do these trade routes illustrate the doctrines of mercantilism at work?

UNDERSTANDING HISTORY THROUGH READING AND THE ARTS

The relationship between people and agriculture makes for interesting reading. For more on the agricultural life in Britain the reader should start with J. D. Chambers and G. E. Mingay, *The Agricultural Revolution (1750-1880)* (1966), and on the subject of soil, climate, land tenure, and the routine of peasant life in Russia before 1917 turn to R. Pipes, *Russia Under the Old Regime** (1974, 1982). For Europe in general, F. Huggett, *The Land Question and European Society Since 1650** (1975), presents a picture of how agricultural changes have affected the development of European society.

PROBLEMS FOR FURTHER INVESTIGATION

Was the enclosure a blessing or a great swindle for the British farmer? This question has been debated by historians and social commentators since the movement toward

*Available in paperback.

business agriculture began in sixteenth-century England. The general argument against enclosure was first set out in the sixteenth century by Sir Thomas More, who claimed (in his book *Utopia*) that it resulted in rural unemployment and rural crime. It is the enclosures between 1750 and 1850, however, that are the most controversial. The best contemporary coverage of the debate is G. E. Mingay, *Enclosure and the Small Farmer in the Age of the Industrial Revolution** (1968), which also contains a useful bibliography.

*Available in paperback.

CHAPTER 20

THE LIFE OF THE PEOPLE

CHAPTER OBJECTIVES

After reading and studying this chapter you should be able to answer the following questions:

Q-1. Why did traditional marriage and sex practices begin to change in the late eighteenth century?
Q-2. What was it like to be a child in preindustrial society?
Q-3. How adequate was the diet and health care of the people of the eighteenth century? Were there any signs of improvement?
Q-4. What influence did religion hold in everyday life and what was *pietism*?

CHAPTER SYNOPSIS

Until recently scholars have not been very interested in how men and women lived in preindustrial society. The aspects of everyday life, such as family relations, sex, marriage, health, and religion, took a secondary place in history. As a result, much of our understanding of these subjects is often based on myth rather than on solid historical research and interpretations. This chapter corrects some of the long-standing myths and provides a close look at the life of the people.

Contrary to early belief, for example, it appears that in western Europe the nuclear family was very common among preindustrial people. Furthermore, preindustrial people did not marry in their early teens, and illegitimacy was not as common as usually thought, and certainly less so than today. The concept of childhood as we know it hardly existed. The author also shows that the diet of poor people was probably almost as nutritionally sound as that of rich people—when the poor got enough to eat. As for medical science, it probably did more harm than good in the eighteenth

269

century. Also explained in this chapter are the reasons for a kind of "sexual revolution" beginning in the mid-eighteenth century—with young people engaging in sex at an earlier age and with illegitimacy on the rise.

In the area of religion the eighteenth century witnessed a tug of war between the Enlightenment's attempt to demystify Christianity and place it on a more rational basis and a popular movement to retain traditional ritual, superstition, and religious mysteries. In Protestant and Catholic countries alike, rulers and religious leaders sought to purify religion by eliminating many ritualistic practices. The response to this "reform" by the common people in Catholic countries was a resurgence of religious ritual and mysticism, while in Protestant Germany and England there occurred a popular religious revival based on piety and emotional "conversion." Meanwhile, most of Europe—Catholic and Protestant—saw the state increase its control over the church.

STUDY OUTLINE

I.   Marriage and the family in preindustrial society
    A. Extended and nuclear families
       1. Contrary to popular belief, the extended family was not common in western Europe
       2. Also, early marriage was not common prior to 1750, and many people never married at all
       3. Marriage was commonly delayed because of poverty and/or local law and tradition
    B. Work away from home
       1. Many boys left home to work as craftsmen or laborers
       2. Girls left to work as servants
    C. Premarital sex and birth-control practices
       1. Illegitimate children were not common in preindustrial society
       2. Premarital sex was common, but marriage usually followed
       3. Coitus interruptus was the most common form of birth control
    D. New patterns of marriage and illegitimacy after about 1750
       1. The growth of cottage industry resulted in people marrying earlier—and for love
       2. The explosion of births and the growth of prostitution from about 1750 to 1850 had several causes
          a. Increasing illegitimacy signified rebellion against laws that limited the right of the poor to marry
          b. Pregnant servant girls often turned to prostitution, which also increased illegitimacy

    E. The question of sexual emancipation for women
        1. Women in cities and factories had limited economic independence
        2. Poverty kept many people single—leading to premarital sex and illegitimate births

II. Women and children in preindustrial society
    A. Child care and nursing
        1. Infant mortality was very high
        2. Breast-feeding of children was common among poor women
        3. Middle- and upper-class women hired wet nurses
        4. The occupation of wet-nursing was often exploitative of lower-class women
    B. Foundlings and infanticide
        1. "Killing nurses" and infanticide were forms of population control
        2. Foundling hospitals were established but could not care for all the abandoned babies
    C. Attitudes toward children
        1. Attitudes toward children in preindustrial society were different from those of today
            a. Parents and doctors were generally indifferent to children
            b. Children were often neglected or treated brutally
        2. The Enlightenment brought about more humane treatment of children
    D. Schools and education
        1. The beginnings of education for common people lie in the seventeenth and eighteenth centuries
        2. Protestantism encouraged popular education
        3. Literacy increased, especially in France and Scotland, between 1700 and 1800

III. The Europeans' food
    A. Life expectancy
        1. The life span of Europeans increased from twenty-five years to thirty-five years between 1700 and 1800
        2. Life expectancy increased because diet improved and plagues and economic crises decreased
    B. Diet and nutrition
        1. The diet of ordinary people improved
            a. Poor people ate mainly grains and vegetables
            b. Milk and meat were rarely eaten
        2. Rich people ate quite differently from the poor
            a. Their diet was rich in meat and wine
            b. They spurned fruits and vegetables
    C. The impact of diet on health

    1. There were nutritional advantages and disadvantages to the diet of the poor
        a. Their breads were very nutritious
        b. Their main problem was getting enough green vegetables and milk
    2. The rich often ate too much rich food
  D. New foods and new knowledge about diet
    1. The potato substantially improved the diet of the poor
    2. There was a growth in market gardening and an improvement in food variety in the eighteenth century
    3. There was some improvement in knowledge about diet, although Europeans did not entirely cast off their myths
    4. Greater affluence caused many to turn to less nutritious food such as white bread and sugar

IV. Medical science and the sick
  A. The medical professionals
    1. The demonic view of disease was common, and faith healers were used to exorcise the demons
    2. Pharmacists sold drugs that were often harmful to their patients
    3. Surgeons often operated without anesthetics and in the midst of dirt
    4. Physicians frequently bled or purged people to death
  B. The terrible conditions at hospitals
    1. Patients were crowded together, often several to a bed
    2. There was no fresh air or hygiene
  C. Mental illness
    1. Mental illness was misunderstood and treated inhumanely
    2. Some attempts at reform occurred in the late eighteenth century
  D. Medical experiments and research
    1. Much medical experimentation was creative quackery
    2. The conquest of smallpox was the greatest medical triumph of the eighteenth century
        a. Jenner's vaccination treatment, begun in 1796, was a great medical advance
        b. Smallpox soon declined drastically in Europe

V. Religion and Christian churches
  A. The institutional church
    1. Despite the critical spirit of the Enlightenment, the local parish church remained important in daily life
    2. The Protestant belief in individualism in religion was tempered by increased state control over the church and religion
  B. Catholic piety
    1. In Catholic countries the old religious culture of ritual and superstition remained popular

    2. Catholic clergy reluctantly allowed traditional religion to survive

C. Protestant revival

    1. Pietism stressed religious enthusiasm and individualism

    2. In England, Wesley was troubled by religious corruption, decline, and uncertainty

    3. His "Methodist" movement rejected Calvinism and stressed salvation through faith

    4. Wesley's ministry brought on a religious awakening, particularly among the lower classes

REVIEW QUESTIONS

Q-1. It is often believed that the typical preindustrial family consisted of an extended family. Do you agree? Define "extended" and "nuclear" family.

Q-2. In *Romeo and Juliet*, Juliet was just fourteen and Romeo was not too many years older. Is this early marriage typical of preindustrial society? Why did so many people not marry at all?

Q-3. When did the custom of late marriage begin to change? Why?

Q-4. Did preindustrial men and women practice birth control? What methods existed?

Q-5. How do you explain that prior to 1750 there were few illegitimate children but that there was a growth of illegitimacy thereafter?

Q-6. It is often claimed that factory women, as opposed to their rural counterparts, were sexually liberated. Is this claim correct? Explain.

Q-7. How and why did life expectancy improve in the eighteenth century?

Q-8. What were the differences in the diets of the rich and the poor in the eighteenth century? What nutritional deficiencies existed?

Q-9. How important was the potato in the eighteenth century? Is it important enough to merit more attention from historians?

Q-10. How important were the eighteenth-century advances in medical science in extending the life span?

Q-11. What was the demonic view of disease?

Q-12. It is said that when it came to medical care, the poor were better off than the rich because they could not afford doctors or hospitals. Why might this have been true?

Q-13. Why was there so much controversy over the smallpox inoculation? Was it safe? What contribution did Edward Jenner make to the elimination of this disease?

Q-14. How was mental illness regarded and treated in the eighteenth century?

Q-15. What effect did changes in church-state relations have on the institutions of the Church?

Q-16. Describe the forms in which popular religious culture remained in Catholic Europe.

Q-17. Define *pietism* and describe how it is reflected in the work and life of John Wesley.

STUDY-REVIEW EXERCISES

Define the following key concepts and terms.

extended family

demonic view of disease

nuclear family

preindustrial childhood

illegitimacy explosion

Methodists

coitus interruptus

purging

"killing nurses"

Jesuits

Identify each of the following and give his or her significance.

Saint Vincent de Paul

Lady Mary Montague

Edward Jenner

James Graham

Joseph II

John Wesley

Test your understanding of the chapter by answering the following questions.

1. It is apparent that the practice of breast-feeding *increased/limited* the fertility of lower-class women.
2. The teenage bride *was/was not* the general rule in preindustrial Europe.
3. Prior to about 1750, premarital sex usually *did/did not* lead to marriage.

4. In the eighteenth century, the _____ was the primary new food in Europe.
5. People lived *longer/shorter* lives as the eighteenth century progressed.
6. The key to Jenner's inoculation discovery was the connection between immun-

   ity from smallpox and _____ , a mild and not contagious disease.
7. In Catholic countries it was largely *the clergy/the common people* who wished to hold on to traditional religious ritual and superstition.
8. The Englishman who brought religious "enthusiasm" to the common folk of

   England was _____ .

MULTIPLE-CHOICE QUESTIONS

1. One of the chief deficiencies of the diet of both rich and poor Europeans was the absence of sufficient
   a. meat.
   b. fruit and vegetables.
   c. white bread.
   d. wine.

2. A family in which three or four generations live under the same roof under the direction of a patriarch is known as a(n)
   a. nuclear family.
   b. conjugal family.
   c. industrial household.
   d. extended family.

3. Prior to about 1750, marriage between two persons was more often than not
   a. undertaken freely by the couple.
   b. controlled by law and parents.
   c. based on romantic love.
   d. undertaken without economic considerations.

4. The establishment of foundling hospitals in the eighteenth century was an attempt to
   a. prevent the spread of the bubonic plague.
   b. isolate children from smallpox.
   c. prevent willful destruction and abandonment of newborn children.
   d. provide adequate childbirth facilities for rich women.

5. All but which one of the following is true about preindustrial society's attitudes toward children?
   a. Parents often treated their children with indifference and brutality.
   b. Poor children were often forced to work in the early factories.
   c. Doctors were the only people interested in the child's welfare.
   d. Killing of children by parents or nurses was common.

6. It appears that the role of doctors and hospital care in bringing about improvement in health in the eighteenth century was
   a. very significant.
   b. minor.
   c. helpful only in the area of surgery.

7. In the seventeenth and early eighteenth centuries people usually married
   a. surprisingly late.
   b. surprisingly early.
   c. almost never.
   d. with enormous frequency.

8. Which of the following was *not* a general characteristic of the European family of the eighteenth century?
   a. The nuclear family
   b. Late marriages
   c. Many unmarried relatives
   d. The extended family

9. The overwhelming reason for postponement of marriage was
   a. that people didn't like the institution of marriage.
   b. lack of economic independence.
   c. the stipulation of a legal age.
   d. that young men and women valued the independence of a working life.

10. In the second half of the eighteenth century, the earlier patterns of marriage and family life began to break down. Which of the following was *not* a result of this change?
    a. A greater number of illegitimate births
    b. Earlier marriages
    c. Marriages *exclusively* for economic reasons
    d. Marriages for love

11. The "illegitimacy explosion" of the late eighteenth century was encouraged by all but which one of the following?
    a. The laws, especially in Germany, concerning the poor's right to marry
    b. The mobility of young people needing to work off the farm
    c. The influence of the French Revolution, which repressed freedom in sexual and marital behavior
    d. The exploitation of girls in the servant class

12. Which of the following statements best describes the attitude toward children in the first part of the eighteenth century?
    a. They were protected and cherished.
    b. They were never disciplined.
    c. They were treated as they were—children living in a child's world.
    d. They were ignored, often brutalized, and often unloved.

13. Most of the popular education in Europe of the eighteenth century was sponsored by
    a. the church.
    b. the state.
    c. private individuals.
    d. parents, in the home.

14. Which of the following would most likely be found in an eighteenth-century hospital?
    a. Isolation of patients
    b. Sanitary conditions
    c. Uncrowded conditions
    d. Uneducated nurses and poor nursing practices

15. The greatest medical triumph of the eighteenth century was the conquest of
    a. starvation.
    b. smallpox.
    c. scurvy.
    d. cholera.

16. The practice of sending one's newborn baby to be cared for by a poor woman in the countryside was known as
    a. the cottage system.
    b. infanticide.
    c. wet-nursing.
    d. all of the above

17. Which of the following was not a common food for the European poor?
    a. Vegetables
    b. Beer
    c. Dark bread
    d. Milk

18. It appears that the chief dietary problem of European society was the lack of an adequate supply of
    a. vitamins A and C.
    b. vitamin B complex.
    c. meat.
    d. sugar.

19. Most probably the best thing an eighteenth-century sick person could do with regard to hospitals would be to
    a. enter only if an operation was suggested by a doctor.
    b. enter only if in need of drugs.
    c. enter only a hospital operating under Galenic theory.
    d. stay away.

20. The country that led the way in the development of universal education was
    a. Britain.
    b. Prussia.
    c. France.
    d. none of the above

UNDERSTANDING HISTORY THROUGH READING AND THE ARTS

Painting is one of the major sources of information for the history of childhood. Preindustrial childhood is the subject of *Children's Games*, by Pieter Brueghel the Elder. It is a lively and action-packed painting of over two hundred children engaged in more than seventy different games, and it is the subject of an interesting article by A. Eliot, "Games Children Play," *Sports Illustrated* (January 11, 1971): 48-56.

Tom Jones, eighteenth-century England's most famous foundling, was the fictional hero of Henry Fielding's *Tom Jones* and the subject and title of director Tony Richardson's highly acclaimed, award-winning film version of Fielding's novel. Starring Albert Finney, Susannah York, and Dame Edith Evans, the film re-creates, in amusing and satirical fashion, eighteenth-century English life. A more recent film adaptation is Richardson's *Joseph Andrews*, based on another Fielding novel.

London was the fastest-growing city in the eighteenth century. How people lived in London is the subject of two highly readable and interesting books: M. D. George, *London Life in the Eighteenth Century** (3rd ed., 1951), and R. J. Mitchell and M. D. R. Leys, *A History of London Life** (1963).

Few men in preindustrial society earned enough to support a family. This, in part, explains why and when women married, and why most women worked. The preindustrial woman, therefore, was not in any modern sense a homemaker. The subject of women and the family economy in eighteenth-century France is discussed by O. Hufton in *The Poor of Eighteenth-Century France* (1974).

PROBLEMS FOR FURTHER INVESTIGATION

Did medical science contribute to an improvement in eighteenth-century life? Until about twenty years ago, it was fashionable to believe that the population explosion was due to improvements made by medical science. Although this theory is generally disclaimed today, it appears to be enjoying a slight revival. For both sides, read the following journal articles (which also have bibliographies): T. McKeown and R. G. Brown, "Medical Evidence Related to English Population Change," *Population Studies* 9 (1955); T. McKeown and R. G. Record, "Reasons for the Decline in Mortality in England and Wales During the Nineteenth Century," *Population Studies* 16 (1962); and P. Razzell, "Population Change in Eighteenth-Century England: A Reinterpretation," *Economic History Review*, 2nd series, 18-2 (1965); and on the history of disease see D. Hopkins, *Princes and Peasants: Smallpox in History* (1977).

*Available in paperback.

CHAPTER 21

THE REVOLUTION IN POLITICS,
1775-1815

CHAPTER OBJECTIVES

After reading and studying this chapter you should be able to answer the following questions:

Q-1. What were the causes of the political revolutions between 1775 and 1815 in America and France?

Q-2. What were the ideas and objectives of the revolutionaries in America and France?

Q-3. Who won and who lost in these revolutions?

CHAPTER SYNOPSIS

The French and American revolutions were the most important political events of the eighteenth century. They were also a dramatic conclusion to the Enlightenment, and both revolutions, taken together, formed a major turning point in human history. This chapter explains what these great revolutions were all about.

The chapter begins with liberalism, the fundamental ideology of the revolution in politics. Liberalism had deep roots and called for freedom and equality at a time when monarchs and aristocrats took their great privileges for granted. The author sees the immediate origins of the American Revolution in the British effort to solve the problem of war debts, which was turned into a political struggle by the American colonists, who already had achieved considerable economic and personal freedom. The American Revolution stimulated reform efforts throughout Europe.

It was in France that the ideas of the Enlightenment and liberalism were put to their fullest test. The bankruptcy of the state gave the French aristocracy the chance to grab power from a weak king. This move backfired, however, because the middle class grabbed even harder. It is significant that the revolutionary desires of the middle class depended on the firm support and violent action of aroused peasants and poor urban workers. It was this action of the common people that gave the revolution its driving force.

In the first two years of the French Revolution, the middle class, with its allies from the peasantry and urban poor, achieved unprecedented reforms. The outbreak of an all-European war against France in 1792 then resulted in a reign of terror and a dictatorship by radical moralists, of whom Robespierre was the greatest. By 1795, this radical patriotism wore itself out. The revolutionary momentum slowed and the Revolution deteriorated into a military dictatorship under the opportunist Napoleon. Yet until 1815 the history of France was that of war, and that war spread liberalism to the rest of Europe. French conquests also stimulated nationalism. The world of politics was turned upside down.

STUDY OUTLINE

I. The new ideas of liberty and equality
  A. Liberty
    1. In the eighteenth century, liberty meant human rights and freedoms and the sovereignty of the people
  B. Equality
    1. This meant equal rights and equality of opportunity
  C. The roots of liberalism
    1. The Judeo-Christian tradition of individualism, reinforced by the Reformation, supported liberalism
    2. Liberalism's modern roots are found in the Enlightenment's concern for freedom and legal equality
    3. Liberalism was attractive to both the aristocracy and the middle class, but it lacked the support of the masses
II. The American Revolution (1775-1789)
  A. Some argue that the American Revolution was not a revolution at all but merely a war for independence
  B. The origins of the Revolution are difficult to ascertain
    1. The British wanted the Americans to pay their share of imperial expenses
      a. Parliament passed the Stamp Act (1765) to raise revenue
      b. Vigorous protest from the colonies forced the act's repeal (1766)
    2. Many Americans believed they had the right to make their own laws
    3. The issue of taxation and representation ultimately led to the outbreak of fighting
  C. The independence movement was encouraged by several factors

      1. The British refused to compromise, thus losing the support of many colonists

      2. The radical ideas of Thomas Paine, expressed in the best-selling *Common Sense*, greatly influenced public opinion in favor of independence

      3. The Declaration of Independence, written by Thomas Jefferson and passed by the Second Continental Congress (1776), further increased the desire of the colonists for independence

      4. Although many Americans remained loyal to Britain, the independence movement had wide-based support from all sections of society

      5. European aid, especially from the French government and from French volunteers, contributed greatly to the American victory in 1783

D. The Constitution and Bill of Rights consolidated the revolutionary program of liberty and equality

      1. The federal, or central, government was given important powers, the right to tax, the means to enforce its laws, the regulation of trade—but the states had important powers too

      2. The executive, legislative, and judicial branches of the government were designed to balance one another

      3. Some people (the Anti-Federalists) feared that the central government had too much power; to placate them, the Federalists wrote the Bill of Rights, which spells out the rights of the individual

E. The American Revolution encouraged European revolution

III. The French Revolution: the revolution that began the modern era in politics

A. The influence of the American Revolution

      1. Many French soldiers, such as Lafayette, served in America and were impressed by the ideals of the Revolution

      2. The American Revolution influenced the French Revolution, but the latter was more violent and more influential

B. The breakdown of the old order

      1. By the 1780s, the government was nearly bankrupt

      2. The French banking system could not cope with the fiscal problems, leaving the monarchy with no choice but to increase taxes

C. Legal orders and social realities: the three estates

      1. The first estate, the clergy, had many privileges and much wealth, and it levied an oppressive tax on the peasantry

      2. The second estate, the nobility, also had great privileges, wealth, and power, and it too taxed the peasantry

      3. The third estate, the commoners, was a mixture of a few rich members of the middle class, urban workers, and the mass of peasants

D. The formation of the National Assembly of 1789

      1. Louis XVI's economic reform plan to tax landed property was opposed by the notables

    2. Louis called for a meeting of the Estates General, the representative body of the three estates

       a. Traditionally, historians have viewed the bourgeoisie's class and economic interests as pushing it into a revolutionary role

       b. Revisionist historians, however, claim that the bourgeoisie's interests did not differ from the interests of the upper class

       a. The nobility represented both conservative and liberal viewpoints

       b. The third estate representatives were largely lawyers and government officials

       c. The third estate wanted the three estates to meet together so the third estate would have the most power

    3. The dispute over voting in the Estates General led the third estate to break away and form the National Assembly

    4. Louis tried to reassert his monarchial authority and assembled an army

  E. The revolt of the poor and the oppressed

    1. Rising bread prices in 1788-89 stirred the people to action

    2. Fearing attack by the king's army, angry Parisians stormed the Bastille (July 14, 1789)

       a. The people took the Bastille, and the king was forced to recall his troops

       b. The uprising of the masses saved the National Assembly

    3. The peasants revolted, forcing the National Assembly to abolish feudal dues, and won a great victory

  F. A limited monarchy established by the bourgeoisie

    1. The National Assembly's Declaration of the Rights of Man (1789) proclaimed the rights of all citizens and guaranteed equality before the law and a representative government

    2. Meanwhile, the poor women of Paris forced the king and government to move to Paris

    3. The National Assembly established a constitutional monarchy and passed major reforms of France's laws and institutions

    4. The National Assembly attacked the power of the church by seizing its land and subjugating the church to the state

    5. This attack on the church turned many people against the Revolution

IV. World war and republican France (1791-1799)

  A. War began in April 1792

    1. The European attitude toward the French Revolution was mixed

       a. Liberals and radicals such as Priestly and Paine praised it as the triumph of liberty

       b. Others such as Burke and Gentz predicted it would lead to tyranny

2. Fear among European kings and nobility that the revolution would spread resulted in the Declaration of Pillnitz (1791), which threatened the invasion of France by Austria and Prussia
3. In retaliation, the patriotic French deputies declared war on Austria in 1792, but France was soon retreating before the armies of the First Coalition
4. In 1792 a new assembly (the National Convention) proclaimed France a republic

B. The "second revolution" and rapid radicalization in France
   1. Louis XVI was tried and convicted of treason by the National Convention and guillotined in early 1793
   2. French armies continued the "war against tyranny" by declaring war on nearly all of Europe
   3. In Paris, the republicans—divided between the Girondists and the Mountain—struggled for political power
   4. The sans-culottes—the laboring poor—allied with the Mountain and helped Robespierre and the Committee of Public Safety gain power

C. Total war and the Reign of Terror (1793-94)
   1. Robespierre established a planned economy to wage total war and aid the poor
   2. The Reign of Terror was instituted to eliminate opposition to the revolution, and many people were jailed or executed
   3. The war became a national mission against evil within and outside of France

D. The "Thermidorian reaction" and the Directory (1795-1799)
   1. Fear of the Reign of Terror led to the execution of its leader, Robespierre
   2. The period of the "Thermidorian reaction" following Robespierre's death was marked by a return to bourgeois liberalism
      a. Economic controls were abolished
      b. The Directory, a five-man executive body, was established
      c. Riots by the poor were put down
   3. The poor lost their fervor for revolution
   4. A military dictatorship was established in order to prevent a return to peace and monarchy

V. The Napoleonic era (1799-1815)
A. Napoleon's rule
   1. Napoleon appealed to many, like abbé Sieyés who looked for authority from above
   2. Napoleon became the center of a plot to overturn the weak Directory and was named first consul of the republic in 1799
   3. He maintained order and worked out important compromises

        a. His civil code of 1804 granted the middle-class equality under the law and safeguarded their right to own property

        b. He confirmed the gains of the peasants

        c. He centralized the government, strengthened the bureaucracy, and granted amnesty to nobles

        d. He signed the Concordat of 1801, which guaranteed freedom of worship for Catholics

    4. He betrayed the ideals of the Revolution by violating the rights of free speech and press, and free elections

  B. Napoleon's wars and foreign policy

    1. He defeated Austria (1801) and made peace with Britain (1802)

    2. Another war (against the Third Coalition—Austria, Russia, Sweden, and Britain) resulted in British naval dominance at the battle of Trafalgar (1805)

    3. Napoleon used the fear of a conspiracy to return the Bourbons to power to get himself elected emperor

    4. The Third Coalition collapsed at Austerlitz (1805), and Napoleon gained much German territory

    5. In 1806, Napoleon defeated Prussia and gained even more territory

    6. Napoleon's Grand Empire meant French control of continental Europe

    7. The beginning of the end for Napoleon came with the Spanish revolt and the British blockade

    8. The French invasion of Russia in 1812 was a disaster for Napoleon

    9. He was defeated by the Fourth Coalition and abdicated his throne in 1814—only to be defeated again at Waterloo in 1815

VI. Was the French Revolution a success?

  A. Yes, the liberal revolution in France succeeded in giving great benefits to the people

  B. Although the Revolution brought the Reign of Terror and a dictatorship, the old order was never re-established, and thus a substantial part of the liberal philosophy survived

REVIEW QUESTIONS

Q-1. Define liberalism. What did it mean to be a "liberal" in the eighteenth and nineteenth centuries? How does this compare to twentieth-century liberalism?

Q-2. Were great differences in wealth contradictory to the revolutionaries' idea of equality? Explain.

Q-3. How did the writers of the Enlightenment differ on the method of establishing liberty?

Q-4. According to Locke, what is the function of government?

Q-5. Think back to the English Revolution of 1688 (Chapter 16). How does Locke's theory justify the English action of getting rid of their king and contracting for a new one?

Q-6. Which side, American or British, had the better argument with regard to the taxation problem? How do the Seven Years' War, the Stamp Act, and the Boston Tea Party fit into your explanation?

Q-7. Why is the Declaration of Independence sometimes called the world's greatest political editorial?

Q-8. What role did the European powers play in the American victory? Did they gain anything?

Q-9. What was the major issue in the debate between the centralists and the Anti-Federalists?

Q-10. How did Americans interpret "equality" in 1789? Has it changed since then? Are the definitions of liberalism and equality unchangeable, or do they undergo periodic redefinition?

Q-11. Did the American Revolution have any effect on France?

Q-12. Why was there fear in France that the tax-reform issue would have "opened a Pandora's box of social and political demands"?

Q-13. Describe the three estates of France. Who paid the taxes? Who held the wealth and power in France?

Q-14. With the calling of the Estates General, "the nobility of France expected that history would repeat itself." Did it? What actually did happen?

Q-15. Discuss the reforms of the National Assembly. Do they display the application of liberalism to society?

Q-16. What were the cause and the outcome of the peasants' uprising of 1789?

Q-17. What role did the poor women of Paris play in the Revolution?

Q-18. Why were France and Europe overcome with feelings of fear and mistrust?

Q-19. Why did the Revolution turn into war in 1792?

Q-20. What effect did the war have on the position of the French king and aristocracy?

Q-21. Were the French armies conquerors or liberators?

Q-22. Who were the sans-culottes? Why were they important to radical leaders such as Robespierre? What role did the common people play in the Revolution?

Q-23. Why did the Committee of Public Safety need to institute a Reign of Terror?

Q-24. What event led to the takeover by Napoleon?

Q-25. Was Napoleon a son of the Revolution or just another tyrant? Explain.

Q-26. Describe the Grand Empire of Napoleon. Was he a liberator or a tyrant?

Q-27. What caused Napoleon's downfall?

STUDY-REVIEW EXERCISES

Define the following key concepts and terms.

liberalism

Montesquieu's "checks and balances"

natural or universal rights

republican

popular sovereignty

tithe

Identify each of the following and give its significance.

Stamp Act

battle of Trafalgar

American Bill of Rights

American Loyalists

American Constitutional Convention of 1787

Jacobins

Reign of Terror

National Assembly

Declaration of the Rights of Man

Bastille

sans-culottes

Girondists

the Mountain

Explain who the following people were and give their significance.

"the baker, the baker's wife, and the baker's boy"

Lord Nelson

Thomas Paine

Edmund Burke

Marie Antoinette

Marquis de Lafayette

Thomas Jefferson

Robespierre

John Locke

abbé Sieyés

Test your understanding of the chapter by answering the following questions.

1. Napoleon's plan to invade England was made impossible by the defeat of the French and Spanish navies in the battle of

   _____ in 1805.

2. Overall, the common people of Paris played *a minor/an important* role in the French Revolution.

3. The author of the best-selling radical book *Common Sense* was

   _____ .

4. Prior to the crisis of the 1760s, American colonists had exercised *little/a great deal of* political and economic independence from Britain.

5. The peasant uprising of 1789 in France ended in *victory/defeat* for the peasant class.

6. By the mid 1790s, people like Sieyés were increasingly looking to *the people/ a military ruler* to bring order to France.

MULTIPLE-CHOICE QUESTIONS

1. Eighteenth-century liberals laid major stress on
   a. economic equality.
   b. equality in property holding.
   c. equality of opportunity.
   d. racial and sexual equality.

2. Which came first?
   a. Formation of the French National Assembly
   b. Execution of King Louis XVI
   c. American Bill of Rights
   d. Seven Years' War

3. The French Jacobins were
   a. aristocrats who fled France.
   b. monarchists.
   c. priests who supported the Revolution.
   d. revolutionary radicals.

4. The French National Assembly was established by
   a. the middle class of the Third Estate.
   b. King Louis XVI.
   c. the aristocracy.
   d. the sans-culottes.

5. The National Assembly did all but which one of the following?
   a. Nationalized church land
   b. Issued the Declaration of the Rights of Man
   c. Established the metric system of weights and measures
   d. Brought about the Reign of Terror

6. In 1789 the influential abbé Sieyés wrote a pamphlet in which he argued that France should be rule by the

    a. nobility.
    b. clergy.
    c. people.

7. In the first stage of the Revolution the French established
    a. a constitutional monarchy.
    b. an absolutist monarchy.
    c. a republic.
    d. a military dictatorship.

8. Edmund Burke's *Reflections on the Revolution in France* is a defense of
    a. the Catholic church.
    b. Robespierre and the Terror.
    c. the working classes of France.
    d. the English monarchy and aristocracy.

9. Generally, the people who did *not* support eighteenth-century liberalism were the
    a. elite.
    b. members of the middle class.
    c. masses.
    d. intellectuals.

10. Most eighteenth-century demands for liberty centered on
    a. the equalization of wealth.
    b. a classless society.
    c. better welfare systems.
    d. equality of opportunity.

11. Americans objected to the Stamp Act because the tax it proposed
    a. was exorbitant.
    b. was required of people in Britain.
    c. would have required great expense to collect.
    d. was imposed without their consent.

12. The American Revolution
    a. had very little impact on Europe.
    b. was supported by the French monarchy.
    c. was not influenced by Locke or Montesquieu.
    d. was supported by almost everyone living in the United States.

13. Which of the following was *not* a cause of the outbreak of revolution in France in 1789?
   a. An enormous national debt
   b. An economic crisis and a bad harvest
   c. The demand of the nobility for greater power and influence
   d. The invasion of France by foreign armies

14. The first successful revolt against Napoleon began in 1808 in
   a. Spain.
   b. Russia.
   c. Germany.
   d. Italy.

15. Napoleon appealed to
   a. French peasants.
   b. French businessmen.
   c. French soldiers.
   d. all of the above

16. Prior to about 1765, the American people were
   a. fairly independent of the British government.
   b. subject to heavy and punitive British controls.
   c. paying a majority share of British military costs.
   d. under the direct control of the East India Company.

17. The major share of the tax burden in France was carried by the
   a. peasants.
   b. bourgeoisie.
   c. clergy.
   d. nobility.

18. The participation of the common people of Paris in the revolution was initially attributable to
   a. their desire to be represented in the Estates General.
   b. the soaring price of food.
   c. the murder of Marat.
   d. the large number of people imprisoned by the king.

19. For the French peasants, the Revolution of 1789 meant
   a. a general movement from the countryside to urban areas.
   b. greater land ownership.
   c. significant political power.
   d. few, if any, gains.

20. The group that announced that it was going to cut off Marie Antoinette's head, "tear out her heart, [and] fry her liver" was the
    a. National Guard.
    b. Robespierre radicals.
    c. revolutionary committee.
    d. women of Paris.

21. The group that had the task of ridding France of any internal opposition to the revolutionary cause was the
    a. Revolutionary Army.
    b. secret police.
    c. republican mob of Paris.
    d. Committee of Public Safety.

GEOGRAPHY

1. Show on the outline map the boundaries of France before the outbreak of war in 1792. Now shade in the areas acquired by France by 1810. Was Napoleon successful in 1810 in expanding the boundaries of France? Who inhabited the territories newly acquired by France?

2. Shade in the dependent states in 1810. What nationalities inhabited these states? Were these large, powerful states?

3. Look closely at Map 21.1. Can you find the four small British fortified outposts scattered throughout Europe? How were these outposts necessary to and a reflection of Britain's military power? What did these outposts mean for smugglers and Napoleon's efforts to stop British trade with continental countries?

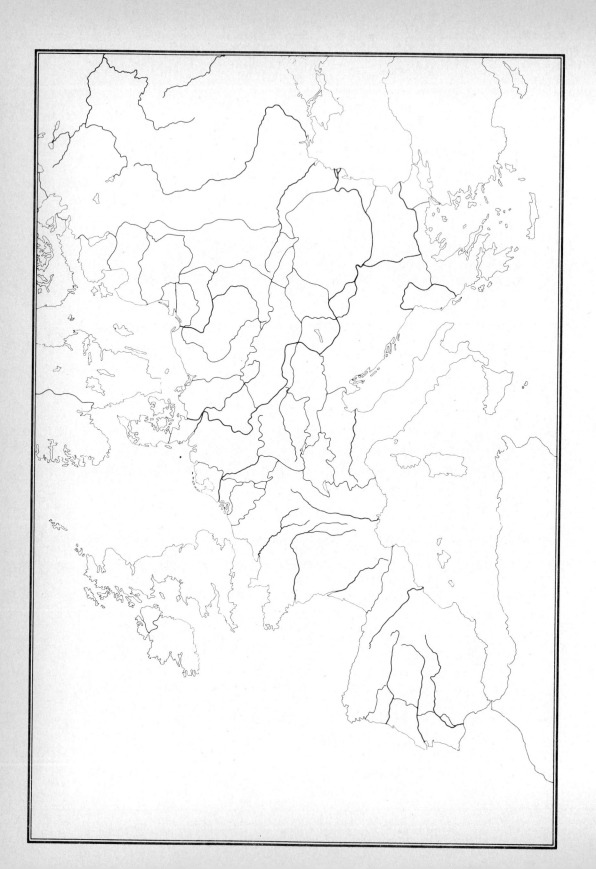

PROBLEMS FOR FURTHER INVESTIGATION

This era of revolution is ideal for the study of both individual and group actions. The various arguments of scholars over the motives and contributions of Napoleon are brought together in D. H. Pinkney, ed., *Napoleon: Historical Enigma** (1969), and the story of Admiral Lord Nelson, Britain's hero and victor of great sea battles, is interestingly told in R. Hough, *Nelson, A Biography* (1980). King George III of England has often been viewed, in American history, as the arch-enemy of liberty and constitutionalism. Is this a fair assessment? The debate over his role has gone on for a number of years and is the subject of a book of collected opinions, *George III: Tyrant or Constitutional Monarch?** (1964), edited by E. A. Reitan.

Group action in a revolution makes for an equally interesting study. The role of women in the revolution in France (and in other times) is well handled in Elise Boulding, *The Underside of History: A View of Women Through Time* (1976). The "people" (which includes the Paris mob) who participated in the revolution in France are the subject of the interesting study by George Rude, *The Crowd in the French Revolution** (1959).

Students interested in the origins of the French revolution will want to check R. W. Greenlaw, ed., *The Economic Origins of the French Revolution** (1958), and those interested in political theory may want to consider a study of liberalism beginning with H. Schultz, ed., *English Liberalism and the State—Individualism or Collectivism?** (1972).

*Available in paperback.

CHAPTER 22

THE REVOLUTION IN ENERGY
AND INDUSTRY

CHAPTER OBJECTIVES

After reading and studying this chapter you should be able to answer the following questions:

Q-1. What was the Industrial Revolution and what caused it?
Q-2. How did the Industrial Revolution affect people and society? Was it a blessing or a disaster?

CHAPTER SYNOPSIS

The world we live in today is largely a product of a revolution in industry and energy that began in England in the 1780s and lasted until about 1850. A number of important problems of interpretation relating to the revolution—the Industrial Revolution—are discussed in this chapter.

The chapter first considers why the Industrial Revolution occurred when it did and why it began in England. Important causes of English industrialization, some of which were discussed in detail in Chapter 19, were foreign and home demand for manufactured goods, agricultural improvements, a large free-trade area, good transportation, and a fairly advanced banking system. The pressure of a growing demand for textiles led to better spinning and weaving machinery which, in turn, led to the creation of the world's first modern factories. In addition, a severe energy crisis presented the challenge that resulted in new production methods: abundant coal replaced scarce wood in the all-important iron industry and fueled Watt's magnificent new steam engine. For the first time, the English people had almost unlimited energy for useful work.

The chapter next considers the gradual spread of the new industrial methods from England to continental Europe. It was not easy for continental countries to copy the English achievement, but with the coming of the railroad rapid progress was made by the 1840s. The difficult problem of assessing the impact of the Industrial Revolution on the lives of the men and women of the working class is then examined. Was industrialization mainly a blessing or a disaster for the workers? After evaluating working conditions, family ties, wages, food, clothing, and health, the author concludes, with qualifications, that the lot of ordinary men and women improved as a result of industrialization. To carry this question of the standard of living one step further, the author takes a comparative look at what happened in Ireland, a poor agricultural country that did not industrialize. There, overpopulation and the potato famine combined to produce mass starvation and disease in the 1840s. One terrible alternative to industrial development was poverty and disaster.

STUDY OUTLINE

I.   The Industrial Revolution in England
     A. The eighteenth-century origins of the Industrial Revolution
         1. The expanding Atlantic trade and a strong home market provided demand for English manufactured goods
         2. Cheap food also increased this demand
         3. Available capital, stable government, economic freedom, and mobile labor in England encouraged growth
         4. The Industrial Revolution began in England in the 1780s and on the Continent after 1815
     B. The first factories in the cotton textile industry
         1. Growing demand for textiles led to new textile inventions created a need for larger workshops—that is, factories
         2. The factory system meant cheaper clothing and more jobs
         3. But factories were often oppressive, and they utilized child labor
     C. The problem of energy
         1. The search for a solution to the energy crisis was a cause of industrialization
         2. From prehistoric to medieval times the major energy sources were plants and animals, and human beings and animals did most of the work
         3. Energy from the land was limited
             a. By the eighteenth century, England's major source of fuel, wood, was nearly gone
             b. A new source of power and energy was needed, so people turned to coal

D. The development of steam power
1. Before about 1700, coal was used for heat but not to produce mechanical energy or to run machinery
2. Early steam engines, such as those of Savery (1698) and Newcomen (1705), were inefficient but revolutionary converters of coal into energy
3. In the 1760s, James Watt increased the efficiency of steam engines, and with Matthew Boulton began to produce them
4. Steam power was used in many industries, and it encouraged other breakthroughs
   a. It enabled the cotton industry to expand
   b. The iron industry was transformed as steam power made coke available
E. The coming of the railroads
1. Stephenson's *Rocket* (1825) was Europe's first locomotive; it was powered by a steam engine
2. The railroad boom (1830-1850) meant lower transportation costs, larger markets, and cheaper goods
3. Railroad building took workers from their rural life and transported them to an urban setting
4. The railroad changed the outlook and values of the entire society
F. Prosperous Britain at mid-century
1. The 1851 Crystal Palace fair reflected the growth of industry and population in Britain and confirmed that Britain was the workshop of the world
2. Real income per person nearly doubled between 1801 and 1851
II. The spread of the Industrial Revolution
A. The challenge of industrialization
1. Revolutions and wars on the Continent retarded economic growth
2. Continental countries found it difficult to compete with Britain after 1815 because it was so economically and technologically advanced
3. But continental countries had two advantages
   a. Britain had done the developmental pathbreaking, so other countries could simply copy the British way of doing things
   b. The power of strong central governments could be used to promote industry
B. Agents of industrialization in continental Europe
1. Cockerill, in Belgium, was one of many Englishmen who brought British industrial secrets to other parts of Europe
2. In Germany, Harkort's business failure showed the problems of early industrialization and the need for government support
3. Governments aided industrialists by erecting tariffs, building roads and canals, and financing railroads

      4. Many thinkers and writers, such as List in Germany, believed that industrialization would advance the welfare of the nation

      5. A tariff policy was established in Germany in 1834 with the Zollverein

        a. Goods could move among the German member states without tariffs

        b. Goods from other nations were subject to a tariff

      6. Banks played a more important role in industrialization on the Continent than in Britain

III. Capital and labor in the age of the Industrial Revolution

  A. The new class of factory owners

      1. Capitalist owners were locked into a highly competitive system

      2. The early industrial period offered opportunities for upward economic mobility, so owners came from a variety of backgrounds

      3. But by the later nineteenth century there was less mobility

  B. The new factory workers and their working conditions

      1. Overall, industrialization meant improvement of life

      2. Many observers claimed that the Industrial Revolution brought misery to the workers

        a. The romantic poets Blake and Wordsworth protested the life of the workers and the pollution of the land and water

        b. Engels believed that the owners exploited the workers

      3. Others, such as Ure and Chadwick, claimed that life was improving

      4. The statistics with regard to wages, diet, and clothing paint a picture of overall improvement for the workers, with some qualifications

      5. On the negative side, unemployment may have risen, hours of labor increased, and there was no improvement in housing

      6. Working in the factory meant more discipline and less personal freedom

      7. The refusal of men to work in factories led to child labor

      8. As factories moved to urban areas, they attracted whole families and tended to preserve kinship ties

      9. Factory acts limited child labor

  C. A mature working class

      1. By 1850, workers were accustomed to factory discipline

      2. Workers created a labor union movement despite anti-union laws—such as the Combination Acts

        a. Robert Owen formed a national union in 1834 in Britain, but it was short-lived

        b. The "new model," or craft union movement began about 1851 in Britain

      3. Chartism was a political movement among British workers which sought universal male suffrage, shorter hours, and cheap bread

IV. The alternative to industrialization

A. The growth of population
  1. European population increased by nearly 40 percent between 1800 and 1850
  2. Overpopulation led to underemployment, poverty, and migration in search of work
B. The potato famine in Ireland (1845-1851)
  1. Irish peasants lived under the rule of English Protestant landlords who did little to improve conditions
  2. Poverty among the Irish peasants was widespread
  3. Because of the introduction of potato farming the Irish population grew from 3 to 8 million between 1725 and 1845
  4. The potato crop failures in 1845, 1846, 1848, and 1851 resulted in widespread famine and migration
  5. The famine affected Ireland's growth and development
      a. People were forced to migrate or marry late, and the country's population declined
      b. Ireland's economy remained agricultural and impoverished; this, then, was the probable alternative to industrialization

REVIEW QUESTIONS

Q-1. Why did the Industrial Revolution begin in England? Was this a planned revolution? Explain.

Q-2. Describe the energy crisis in England. How was it solved?

Q-3. What was the relationship between the steam engine and the coal mine? The railroad and the coal mine?

Q-4. What impact did the railroad have on (a) the factory system, (b) the rural workers, and (c) the outlook and values of society?

Q-5. What did James Watt and Matthew Boulton do to multiply the uses of steam power?

Q-6. How did the change in textile production affect employment in spinning and weaving for adults and children?

Q-7. What effect did the French Revolution and the wars of 1792-1815 have on the economics of the continental states?

Q-8. What disadvantages and advantages were felt by countries that industrialized *after* Great Britain?

Q-9. What do the careers of Cockerill, Harkort, and List tell us about the problems and methods of industrialization on the Continent?

Q-10. What was the purpose of the Zollverein? Of the Crédit Mobilier?

Q-11. Did Britain's new industrial middle class ruthlessly exploit the workers?

Q-12. Did real wages increase or decrease between 1790 and 1850? What about other factors such as diet and working conditons?

Q-13. It has often been argued that the factory system in Britain caused a breakup of the family, especially as an economic unit. Explain why you agree or disagree.

Q-14. What was the subcontract system and how did it work?

Q-15. What were the goals and accomplishments of the Chartists?

Q-16. How did the Irish land system work? What impact did the potato have on Irish economic and family life?

Q-17. What was the result of the 1845-1851 potato blight in Ireland?

Q-18. "The Industrial Revolution was the salvation rather than the curse of England and Europe." Defend or refute this statement.

STUDY-REVIEW EXERCISES

Define the following key concepts and terms.

cottage workers

domestic system

Industrial Revolution

protective tariff

the Chartist movement

the energy crisis of the eighteenth century

Identify each of the following and give its significance.

Andrew Ure

Irish potato famine

Crystal Palace

Cartwright's power loom

spinning jenny

Zollverein

Factory Act of 1833

Crédit Mobilier

Combination Acts

parish "apprentices" in cotton mills

Henry Cort

James Hargreaves

Robert Owen

James Watt

Friedrich List

Edwin Chadwick

George Stephenson

Grand National Consolidated Trades Union

Emile and Isaac Pereire

Friedrich Engels

craft union

Test your understanding of the chapter by answering the following questions.

1. The Industrial Revolution began in England about _____

   in the _____ industry.
2. A decrease in food prices led to an *increased/decreased* demand for manufactured goods.

3. The Scots instrument maker who improved the steam engine was

   _____ .

4. In Ireland, a single acre of _____ could support a family of six for a year.

5. The first railroad line was the _____ line, and the

   first effective locomotive was Stephenson's _____ .
6. The railroads tended to *increase/decrease* the number of cottage workers.
7. The architectural wonder of the 1851 industrial fair in London was the building

   called the _____ .
8. Between 1801 and 1851, real income in Britain *increased/decreased*.
9. The role of the government in bringing about industrialization was *greater/less* in continental countries than in Britain.
10. The economic and trade agreement that allowed goods to move among German member states without tariffs was formed in 1834 and was called the

    _____ .

11. The possibility of a worker's becoming a big industrialist *increased/decreased* as the nineteenth century wore on.

12. With the _____ Act of 1833, the employment of children in British factories tended to *increase/decrease*.

MULTIPLE-CHOICE QUESTIONS

1. In the 1830s, the most technologically advanced country in the world was
   a. Belgium.
   b. the United States.
   c. France.
   d. Britain.

2. Which of the following was a period of falling real wages for English workers?
   a. 1750-1790
   b. 1792-1815
   c. 1815-1850
   d. 1850-1890

3. Which of the following was *not* used by continental countries to meet British competition?
   a. The adoption of free trade
   b. The importation of skilled British workers
   c. Stealing secrets of technology
   d. Government grants and loans

4. Which of the following was *least* likely to be a characteristic of a prefactory (cottage or agricultural) laboring person?
   a. Observed Holy Monday
   b. Worked alongside other members of his or her family
   c. Worked hard but in spurts
   d. Would probably prefer factory work to railroad construction

5. Which of the following did *not* contribute to England's early industrialization?
   a. Colonial trade
   b. An effective central banking system
   c. High food prices due to inadequate crops
   d. A free domestic market

6. The energy crisis of the eighteenth and nineteenth centuries was solved by reliance on
   a. wood.
   b. coal and steam.
   c. electricity.
   d. water power.

7. According to Friedrich List, the promotion of industry
   a. was dangerous for the well-being of the peasants.
   b. was vital for the defense of the nation.
   c. increased the poverty of the population.
   d. required free trade between nations.

8. The first steam railways were built in the
   a. 1790s.
   b. 1830s.
   c. 1850s.
   d. none of the above

9. Legislation passed by the British Parliament outlawing unions and strikes was
   a. the Labor Law of 1834
   b. the Combination Acts.
   c. the Artisans Bill.
   d. none of the above

10. The birth of the Industrial Revolution in England was stimulated by
    a. central banking.
    b. a laissez-faire economic approach.
    c. stable government after the Glorious Revolution.
    d. all of the above

11. The invention of the railroad and its growth caused
    a. a reduction in the cost of overland freight.
    b. the widening of markets.
    c. the growth of urban centers.
    d. all of the above

12. The first continental country to industrialize was
    a. Belgium.
    b. France.
    c. Italy.
    d. Germany.

13. The industrial development of continental Europe was delayed by
    a. a lack of resources.
    b. the French Revolution and Napoleonic wars.
    c. the plague.
    d. a labor shortage.

14. To understand more fully the impact of the Industrial Revolution, historians think it best to concentrate their studies on
    a. England.
    b. France.
    c. Ireland.
    d. Belgium.

15. Before the 1830s, the
    a. family continued to work as a unit in the factories.
    b. factory employed only the females.

c. mother and father worked together while their children went to factory schools.

d. factory employed only the males.

16. The British workers' campaign to gain the franchise between 1838 and 1848 was called the
   a. Ten-Hours' movement.
   b. Luddite movement.
   c. Chartist movement.
   d. democratic movement.

17. The reformer Robert Owen
   a. tried to improve the working conditions of his workers.
   b. experimented with cooperative and socialist communities.
   c. organized one of Britain's first national unions.
   d. all of the above

18. All but one of the following led to the population explosion in Ireland:
   a. Earlier marriage
   b. The widespread cultivation of the potato
   c. Children and security in old age
   d. The widespread cultivation of wheat

19. Because of their economic problems, the Irish resorted to mass migration, primarily settling in
   a. Great Britain and Belgium.
   b. America and Canada.
   c. America and Great Britain.
   d. Wales and Scotland.

20. Those workers who smashed the machines that put them out of work were known as
   a. Luddites.
   b. anti-Modernists.
   c. Chartists.
   d. apprentices.

GEOGRAPHY

1. In the space below, compare Maps 22.1 and 22.2 in the text in terms of their major industrial areas and their transportation networks. How do these maps

explain why an ever-greater portion of the English population lived in the north as time passed? What different stages in the development of English transportation are illustrated by these maps?

2.   Referring to Maps 22.2 and 22.3 in the text, use the space below to compare British and continental industrialization by 1850 in terms of (a) railroads, (b) coal deposits, and (c) industrial centers. What role did geography play in Britain's early industrial lead?

3.   Four of Europe's most important centers of modern industry are (a) the large Manchester-Sheffield area, (b) the Ruhr valley, (c) the Liège region, and (d) the Roubaix region. Locate these regions on Maps 22.2 and 22.3. What countries are they in? What do they have in common?

UNDERSTANDING HISTORY THROUGH READING AND THE ARTS

Few nineteenth-century inventions had as great an impact on society as did the invention of the camera in 1839. Photography allowed society to examine itself with a fullness never before experienced. In the late 1860s, for example, Thomas Annan took a series of photographs of the slums of Glasgow, and thus encouraged interest in sanitary reform and urban improvement. Annan's photographs have been reproduced by Dover Press as T. Annan, *Photographs of the Old Closes and Streets of Glasgow, 1868-1877** (1977), and M. Hiley, *Victorian Working Women* (1980), is a view of the habits and life of Victorian women through photography.

Emile Zola's *Germinal** is a powerful novel about life and conditions in Belgian and French coal mines. Popular novels by Charles Dickens and Elizabeth Gaskill are among the suggested readings in the text.

The machine breakers in England (1811-1817) are the subject of M. I. Thomis's *The Luddites** (1970-1972). Those interested in reading about the new industrial working class may want to begin with J. Kuczynski, *The Rise of the Working Class* (1967), or two collections of essays on the subject—M. L. McDougal, ed., *The Working Class in Modern Europe* (1975), and E. J. Hobsbawm, ed., *Labouring Men: Studies in the History of Labour** (1964).

An unrivaled source of visual material associated with Britain's early industrial history is A. Briggs, *Iron Bridge to Crystal Palace, Impact and Images of the Industrial Revolution* (1979).

PROBLEMS FOR FURTHER INVESTIGATION

Some historians do not agree with the traditional interpretation that the Industrial Revolution began in the late eighteenth century. One such historian is John Nef, who argues that it actually began in the sixteenth century. He places considerable emphasis on the importance of the coal industry and the early energy crisis. Some of his ideas are found in J. Nef, "The Early Energy Crisis and Its Consequences," *Scientific American* (November 1977), and "The Progress of Technology and the Growth of Large-scale Industry in Great Britain, 1540-1640," *Economic History Review* 5 (October 1934).

Students interested in the causes of the Industrial Revolution will want to see a series of debates by six historians in R. M. Hartwell, ed., *The Causes of the Industrial Revolution in England** (1967).

No facet of the Industrial Revolution has been as controversial and long-lasting as the debate over whether it was a blessing or a curse for the working class. Many of the arguments of the optimists and the pessimists are collected together in two small books: P. A. M. Taylor, ed., *The Industrial Revolution in Britain** (rev. ed., 1970), and C. S. Doty, ed., *The Industrial Revolution** (1969). The impact of industrialization on women is one of the themes of Louise Tilly and Joan Scott in *Women, Work and Family** (1978). The most important (and controversial) book on the impact of industrialization on the working class is E. P. Thompson, *The Making of the English Working Class** (1966).

*Available in paperback.

READING WITH UNDERSTANDING
EXERCISE 5

LEARNING HOW TO IDENTIFY MAIN POINTS
THAT ARE CAUSES OR REASONS

In Exercise 3 we considered cause and effect and underlined a passage dealing with effects or results. This exercise continues in this direction by focusing on causes or reasons.

Exercise

Read the following passage as a whole. Reread it and underline or highlight each cause (or factor) contributing to the Industrial Revolution in England.

Note that there are several causes and that they are rather compressed. (This is because the author is summarizing material presented in previous chapters before going on to discuss other causes or factors—notably technology and the energy problem—in greater detail.) Since several causal points are presented in a short space, this is a very good place to number the points (and key subpoints) in the margin. After you have finished, compare your underlining or highlighting with that in the suggested model on pages E-4 to E-5.

Eighteenth-Century Origins

The Industrial Revolution grew out of the expanding Atlantic economy of the eighteenth century, which served mercantilist England remarkably well. England's colonial empire, augmented by a strong position in Latin America and in the African slave trade, provided a growing market for English manufactured goods. So did England itself. In an age when it was much cheaper to ship goods by water than by land, no part of England was more than twenty miles from navigable water. Beginning in the 1770s, a canal building boom greatly enhanced this natural advantage (see Map 22.1). Nor were there any tariffs within the country to hinder trade, as there were in France before 1789 and in politically fragmented Germany.

Agriculture played a central role in bringing about the Industrial Revolution in England. English farmers were second only to the Dutch in productivity in 1700, and they were continuously adopting new methods of farming as the century went on. The result, especially before 1760, was a period of bountiful crops and low food prices. The ordinary English family did not have to spend almost everything it earned just to buy bread. It could spend more on other items, on manufactured goods—leather shoes or a razor for the man, a bonnet or a shawl for the woman, toy soldiers for the son, and a doll for the daughter. Thus, demand for goods within the country complemented the demand from the colonies.

England had other assets that helped give rise to the Industrial Revolution. Unlike eighteenth-century France, England had an effective central bank and well-developed credit markets. The monarchy and the aristocratic oligarchy, which had jointly ruled the country since 1688, provided stable and predictable government. At the same time the government let the domestic economy operate fairly freely and with few controls, encouraging personal initiative, technical change, and a free market. Finally, England had long had a large class of hired agricultural laborers, whose numbers were further increased by the enclosure movement of the late eighteenth century. These rural wage earners were relatively mobile—compared to village-bound peasants in France and western Germany, for example—and along with cottage workers they formed a potential industrial labor force for capitalist entrepreneurs.

All these factors combined to initiate the Industrial Revolution, which began in the 1780s—after the American war for independence and just before the French Revolution. Thus the great economic and political revolutions that have shaped the modern world occurred almost simultaneously, though they began in different countries. The Industrial Revolution was, however, a longer process. It was not complete in England until 1830 at the earliest, and it had no real impact on continental countries until after the Congress of Vienna ended the era of revolutionary wars in 1815.

Eighteenth-Century Origins

causes

1

a

b

c

2

a

b

c

3

4

5

6

The Industrial Revolution grew out of the expanding Atlantic economy of the eighteenth century, which served mercantilist England remarkably well. England's colonial empire, augmented by a strong position in Latin America and in the African slave trade, provided a growing market for English manufactured goods. So did England itself. In an age when it was much cheaper to ship goods by water than by land, no part of England was more than twenty miles from navigable water. Beginning in the 1770s, a canal building boom greatly enhanced this natural advantage (see Map 22.1). Nor were there any tariffs within the country to hinder trade, as there were in France before 1789 and in politically fragmented Germany.

Agriculture played a central role in bringing about the Industrial Revolution in England. English farmers were second only to the Dutch in productivity in 1700, and they were continuously adopting new methods of farming as the century went on. The result, especially before 1760, was a period of bountiful crops and low food prices. The ordinary English family did not have to spend almost everything it earned just to buy bread. It could spend more on other items, on manufactured goods—leather shoes or a razor for the man, a bonnet or a shawl for the woman, toy soldiers for the son, and a doll for the daughter. Thus, demand for goods within the country complemented the demand from the colonies.

England had other assets that helped give rise to the Industrial Revolution. Unlike eighteenth-century France, England had an effective central bank and well-developed credit markets. The monarchy and the aristocratic oligarchy, which had jointly ruled the country since 1688, provided stable and predictable government. At the same time the government let the domestic economy operate fairly freely and with few controls, encouraging personal initiative, technical change, and a free market. Finally, England had long had a large class of hired agricultural laborers, whose numbers were further increased by the enclosure movement of the late eighteenth century. These rural wage earners were relatively mobile—compared to village-bound peasants in France and western Germany, for example—and

a

along with cottage workers they formed a potential industrial labor force for capitalist entrepreneurs.

All these factors combined to initiate the Industrial Revolution, which began in the 1780s—after the American war for independence and just before the French Revolution. Thus the great economic and political revolutions that have shaped the modern world occurred almost simultaneously, though they began in different countries. The Industrial Revolution was, however, a longer process. It was not complete in England until 1830 at the earliest, and it had no real impact on continental countries until after the Congress of Vienna ended the era of revolutionary wars in 1815.

CHAPTER 23

IDEOLOGIES AND UPHEAVALS,
1815-1850

CHAPTER OBJECTIVES

After reading and studying this chapter you should be able to answer the following questions:

Q-1. How and why did conservatives and radicals view liberalism and nationalism differently?

Q-2. How and why did political revolution break out once again?

Q-3. What ideas did thinkers develop to describe and shape the great political and economic transformation that was taking place?

CHAPTER SYNOPSIS

This chapter examines a number of extremely important ideas: liberalism, nationalism, socialism, and romanticism. Studying these ideas helps us understand the historical process in the nineteenth and twentieth centuries. A key aspect of that process was the bitter and intense struggle between the conservative aristocrats, who wanted to maintain the status quo, and the middle- and working-class liberals and nationalists, who wanted to carry on the destruction of the old regime of Europe that had begun in France in 1789. The symbol of conservatism was Prince Metternich of Austria, Europe's leading diplomat. Metternich was convinced that liberalism and nationalism had to be repressed, or else Europe would break up into warring states. In opposition to Metternich, liberals and nationalists saw their creeds as the way to free humanity from the burden of supporting the aristocracy and from foreign oppression. Metternich's convictions were shared by the other peacemakers at Vienna in 1814, while those of the liberals fanned the fires of revolution, first in

1830 and, more spectacularly, in 1848. Political liberalism, combined with the principles of economic liberalism with its stress on unrestricted economic self-interest as the avenue to human happiness, was extremely attractive to the middle class. Of the major powers, only Britain was transformed by reform and untouched by revolution.

The chapter shows that although many believed nationalism led toward human happiness, it contained in reality the dangerous ideas of national and racial superiority. To make the turbulent intellectual world even more complex, socialism emerged as another, equally powerful set of ideas regarding the creation of a just and happy society. Early socialists were idealistic and utopian, but the socialism of Karl Marx, which later became dominant, claimed to be realistic and scientific. Socialism contributed to the split between the middle and lower classes. This split explains the failure of these classes in the face of the common enemies in the revolutions of 1848. The chapter also discusses romanticism, which was a reaction to the rationalism of the previous century. Romanticism was the central mood of the nineteenth century and the emotional background to its aesthetic landscape.

STUDY OUTLINE

I. The Vienna peace settlement
   A. The Congress of Vienna
      1. By 1814 the conservative monarchs of Europe had defeated French armies and checked the spread of the French Revolution
      2. The victors restored the French boundaries of 1792 and the Bourbon dynasty
      3. They made other changes in the boundaries of Europe and created a new kingdom out of Belgium and Holland
      4. It was believed that the concept of the balance of power would preserve peace in Europe
      5. But the demands of the victors, especially the Prussians and the Russians, for compensation threatened the balance

II. Radical ideas and early socialism
   A. Liberalism—political and economic
      1. Liberalism demanded representative government, equality before the law, and the freedom of speech and assembly
      2. Economic liberalism was known as laissez-faire—the principle that the economy should be left unregulated
         a. Adam Smith argued that a free economy would bring wealth for all—including workers
         b. British businessmen often used the principle of laissez-faire in self-serving ways, backed up by the theories of Malthus, who believed

          that marrying late in life was the best means of population control, and Ricardo, who claimed that because of the pressure of population, wages would always be low

    3. After 1815, political liberalism became increasingly a middle-class doctrine, used to exclude the lower classes from government and business

B. Nationalism

    1. Most liberals believed that the nation was the source of freedom for the people

    2. Nationalists believed that common language and traditions would bring about unity and common loyalties and, therefore, self-government

    3. On the negative side, nationalism generated ideas of racial and cultural superiority

C. French utopian socialism

    1. Early French socialists proposed a system of greater economic equality organized by the government

    2. Saint-Simon and Fourier proposed a planned economy and socialist communities

    3. Blanc believed that the state should promote socialist programs and guarantee employment

    4. Proudhon claimed that the worker was the source of all wealth

D. Marxian socialism

    1. Marx saw history in terms of economic class struggle: the bourgeoisie exploited the working class

    2. He predicted that the future would bring a revolution by workers to overthrow the capitalists

    3. He claimed that labor was the source of all value

    4. His theory of historical evolution came from Hegel—stressing that each idea produces its opposite (antithesis)

III. Romantic movement

A. Romanticism was partly a revolt against classicism and the Enlightenment

    1. Romantics rejected the classical emphasis on order and rationality

    2. Many romantics believed in the supremacy of emotion and the rejection of materialism and modern industry

    3. Romantics stressed a return to nature and the study of history

    4. Reading and writing history was viewed as the way to understand national destiny

B. Romanticism in literature

    1. Romantic literature first developed fully in Britain, as exemplified by Wordsworth, Coleridge, Scott, Byron, Shelley, and Keats

    2. Romantics such as the Frenchwoman George Sand rebelled against social conventions

3. In central Europe romanticism reinforced nationalism

C. Romanticism in art and music
   1. Delacroix and Turner were two of the greatest romantic painters
   2. Romantic composers rejected well-defined structure in their efforts to find maximum range and intensity
   3. Beethoven was the first master of romantic music

IV. Reforms and revolutions

A. National liberation in Greece (1821-1832)
   1. Greek nationalists led by Ypsilanti in 1821 fought for freedom from Turkey
   2. Britain, France, and Russia supported Greek nationalism, and Greece became independent in 1830

B. Liberal reform in Great Britain
   1. The British aristocracy feared liberalism and worked to repress it
   2. The Corn Law, which protected the English landowners, is an example of aristocratic class power and selfishness
   3. Lower-class protest in Britain led to repressive laws (the Six Acts) and violence against the lower class
   4. The growth of the middle class and its desire for reform led to the Reform Bill of 1832, which increased the number of voters significantly
   5. The Chartist demand for universal male suffrage failed, but the Anti-Corn Law League succeeded in getting the Corn Law repealed and free trade established
   6. By 1846, both the Tory and Whig parties were interested in reform

C. The revolution of 1830 in France
   1. Louis XVIII's Constitutional Charter of 1814 protected the people against a return to royal absolutism and aristocratic privilege
   2. Charles X, Louis's successor, tried to re-establish the old order and repudiated the Constitutional Charter
   3. The reaction was an immediate revolution that brought the expulsion of Charles X
   4. The new king, Louis Philippe, accepted the Constitutional Charter but did little more than protect the rich upper middle class

V. The revolutions of 1848

A. A democratic republic was established in France in 1848
   1. King Louis Philippe's regime (since 1830) refused to bring about electoral reform
   2. A revolt in Paris in 1848 led to the establishment of a provisional republic that granted universal male suffrage and other reforms
   3. The revolutionary coalition couldn't agree on a common program as the "liberal" republicans split with the "socialist" republicans

4. National workshops were a compromise between the socialists' demands for work for all and the moderates' determination to provide only temporary relief for the massive unemployment
5. The fear of socialism led to a clash of classes
6. The closing down of the workshops led to a violent uprising (the June Days)
7. Class war led to the election of a strongman, Louis Napoleon, as president in 1848

B. The Austrian Empire in 1848
1. The revolution in France resulted in popular unheaval throughout central Europe, but in the end conservative reaction won
2. Hungarian nationalism resulted in revolution against the Austrian overlords
3. Conflict among the different nationalities (Hungarians against Croats, Serbs and Rumanians; Czechs against Germans) weakened the revolution
4. The alliance of the working and middle classes soon collapsed
5. The conservative aristocrats crushed the revolution
6. The Russian army helped defeat the Hungarians

C. Prussia and the Frankfurt Assembly in 1848
1. Middle-class Prussians wanted to create a unified liberal Germany
2. Inspired by events in France, the working-class people of Prussia demanded and received a liberal constitution
3. Further worker demands for suffrage and socialist reforms caused fear among the aristocracy
4. The Frankfurt National Assembly of 1848 was a middle-class liberal body that began writing a constitution for a unified Germany
5. War with Denmark ended with a rejection of the Frankfurt Assembly and the failure of German liberalism

REVIEW QUESTIONS

Q-1. Discuss how political and economic change might fuse to form the "dual revolution."

Q-2. Describe the treatment of defeated France by the victors in 1814. Why wasn't the treatment harsher?

Q-3. What is meant by "balance of power"? What methods were used by the Great Powers to preserve the balance of power?

Q-4. What were the Hundred Days?

Q-5. Who were the participants and what was the purpose of the Holy Alliance and the congress system?

Q-6. Describe the make-up of the Austrian Empire. How and why were nationalism and liberalism regarded as dangerous to those in power?

Q-7. Describe laissez-faire economic philosophy. Why did the laissez-faire liberals see mercantilism as undesirable?

Q-8. "The ideas of economic liberals like Smith, Malthus, and Ricardo were used by the industrialist middle class for their own interests." Explain.

Q-9. Define nationalism. What were its links to liberalism?

Q-10. What are the goals of socialism? How do the ideas of Saint-Simon, Fourier, Blanc, and Proudhon illustrate socialist thought? Do you agree with them?

Q-11. What was Marx's view of history? What was the role of the proletariat in history?

Q-12. What were the romantics rebelling against?

Q-13. The Enlightenment writers believed that life could be understood through reason, but the romantics of the next century believed life could be understood only through experience, emotion, and feeling. Explain this by making reference to the romantic writers and artists.

Q-14. In what ways was romantic music a radical departure from the past? What was the purpose of romantic music? Why is Beethoven considered a genius?

Q-15. Compare and contrast the political developments in Britain and France between 1814-15 and 1832. Who were the winners and the losers?

Q-16. What were the causes and the outcome of the Greek revolution of 1821-1832?

Q-17. Is there any evidence that between 1815 and 1830 Britain was in a period of the repression of liberalism?

Q-18. What were the goals of the Chartists? The Anti-Corn Law League?

Q-19. "The Reform Bill of 1832 was a middle-class triumph." Explain.

Q-20. Why did Charles X lose his throne?

Q-21. Describe what happened in France in 1848. Why did the French voters turn their backs on the Revolution and elect a strongman as president?

Q-22. Was the national workshop plan a wise compromise for the French socialists?

Q-23. Why did the revolutionary coalition in Hungary in 1848 break down?

Q-24. Why couldn't the middle-class liberals and the urban poor in Austria cooperate in destroying their common enemies?

Q-25. Describe the role of the Archduchess Sophia in the preservation of the Austrian Empire.

Q-26. What were the goals of the Frankfurt Assembly? Why did it fail?

STUDY-REVIEW EXERCISES

Define the following key concepts and terms.

romanticism

conservatism

dual revolution

liberalism

nationalism

radicalism

laissez-faire

iron law of wages

socialism

Marx's theory of historical evolution

classicism

republicanism

Identify each of the following and give its significance.

Quadruple Alliance

Constitutional Charter of 1814 (France)

Napoleon's Hundred Days

Congress of Troppau

congress system

Corn Law

Ten Hours Act of 1847 (Britain)

national workshops

Wealth of Nations

Frankfurt Assembly

Schleswig-Holstein question

Louis Kossuth

Jules Michelet

Johann Herder

Frederick William IV

Alexander Ypsilanti

Chartists

Thomas Malthus

Karl Marx

Louis Philippe

Communist Manifesto

Robert Peel

Explain *what ideas the following romantic figures attempted to convey to their audiences.*

Walter Scott

George Sand

Eugene Delacroix

Ludwig van Beethoven

Explain *the objectives of the following participants at the peace conferences of 1814-15.*

Name of diplomat	*Country*	*Objective*
Metternich		
Castlereagh		
Alexander I		
Talleyrand		
Hardenburg	Prussia	

Explain what the objectives of the revolutionaries in the following countries were and how successful they were. In each case explain why the revolution failed or succeeded.

Country	*Year*	*Revolutionary Goals and Outcome*
Spain	1820-1823	
Two Sicilies	1820-1821	
Greece	1821-1832	
France	1830	
France	1848	
Hungary	1848	
Prussia	1848	

Test your understanding of the chapter by answering the following questions.

1. In the long run, the revolutions in Germany in 1848 resulted in the *victory/ defeat* of German liberalism.

2. The new president of France in 1848 was _____ .

3. The great and moving romantic painter whose masterpiece was *Liberty Leading the People* was _____ .

4. The laissez-faire economists believed that the state *should/should not* regulate the economy.

5. Hungary was a part of the _____ Empire.

6. This German pastor and philosopher argued that every national group has its own

   particular spirit and genius. _____

7. This mid-nineteenth-century Frenchman, author of *Organization of Work*, believed that the right to work was sacred and should be guaranteed by the state.

   _____

8. The revolutions of 1848 in Austria saw *cooperation/competition* between national groups and the eventual *victory/defeat* of the old aristocracy and conservatism.

MULTIPLE-CHOICE QUESTIONS

1. Who of the following was *not* a part of the romantic movement of the nineteenth century?
   a. George Sand
   b. Ludwig van Beethoven
   c. Walter Scott
   d. Alexis de Tocqueville

2. The British Corn Laws were passed to give economic advantage to the
   a. landed aristocracy.
   b. middle class.
   c. urban working class.
   d. agricultural workers.

3. The so-called dual revolution that began in the late eighteenth century refers to
   a. political revolution in France and Russia.
   b. an economic and political revolution.
   c. a joint revolution in improved health care and population increase.

4. Which one of the following is *not true* about the peace settlement worked out at the Congress of Vienna?

    a. It was harsh toward the defeated French and rejected the restoration of the Bourbon monarchy.

    b. France lost a few colonies plus the territories it had conquered in Italy, Germany, and the Low Countries.

    c. Belgium and Holland were united and Prussia received territory on France's eastern border.

5. The problem that almost led to war among the major powers in 1815 was
    a. the refusal of France to participate in the Vienna conference.
    b. the British takeover of the South American trade routes.
    c. Russian and Prussian territorial demands.

6. The major demand of the English Chartists was for
    a. universal male suffrage.
    b. improved prison conditions.
    c. tariff protection for poor farmers.
    d. government-sponsored cooperative workshops.

7. All of the following were members of the Quadruple Alliance *except*
    a. Russia.
    b. Great Britain.
    c. Prussia.
    d. France.

8. Metternich's conservative policies prevailed in
    a. South America.
    b. western Europe.
    c. central Europe.
    d. Great Britain and its colonies.

9. Adam Smith would have been likely to agree that
    a. monopolies are good for a state.
    b. increased competition benefits all classes of society.
    c. increasing workers' wages is harmful in the long run.
    d. population will always grow too fast.

10. All of the following were part of the Vienna peace settlement *except*
    a. harsh treatment of defeated France by the victorious allies.
    b. balance of power politics.
    c. the establishment of a kingdom of Poland under Alexander I.
    d. territory for Prussia on the Rhine.

11. One of the most influential French utopian socialists was
    a. the count de Saint-Simon.
    b. Talleyrand.
    c. Louis Philippe.
    d. Eugène Delacroix.

12. In 1848, great revolutions occurred in all of the following countries *except*
    a. Prussia.
    b. Hungary.
    c. Italy.
    d. Great Britain.

13. With regard to the German area, after the peace settlement of Vienna there
    were
    a. still over three hundred independent German political entities.
    b. thirty-eight indpendent German states, including Austria and Prussia.
    c. only two German states: Austria and Prussia.
    d. approximately one hundred independent German states dominated by
        Austria.

14. All but one of the following were major ideas of liberalism:
    a. representative government
    b. equality before the law
    c. individual freedoms, e.g., freedom of the press, freedom of speech
    d. legally separated classes

15. The writings of Karl Marx are indebted to
    a. French utopian-socialist thinkers.
    b. English classical economists.
    c. Hegel's dialectic of history.
    d. all of the above

16. The first great nationalist rebellion of the 1820s involved the
    a. Germans against the Austrians.
    b. Greeks against the Turks.
    c. Irish against the English.
    d. Greeks against the Russians.

17. The English Corn Law prohibited
    a. the exporting of British grain.
    b. raising the price of British grain above that of continental prices.

    c. the importing of foreign grain unless the price of British grain reached harvest disaster prices.

    d. the domination of the British grain market by the aristocracy.

18. The English Reform Bill of 1832 did not
    a. give the new industrial areas proper representation in Parliament.
    b. relieve the pressure for reform.
    c. gain the House of Commons supremacy over the House of Lords.
    d. establish universal manhood suffrage.

19. Generally the revolutions of 1848 provided
    a. some immediate gains for the liberal forces, only to be crushed later by the combined forces of monarchy, aristocracy, and army.
    b. slow gains at first for the liberals, followed by complete realization of their goals.
    c. immediate and complete success by the liberals.
    d. none of the above

20. All but one of the following was an important nineteenth-century romantic writer:
    a. William Wordsworth
    b. Walter Scott
    c. Victor Hugo
    d. J. M. W. Turner

GEOGRAPHY

Study carefully Map 23.1, Europe in 1815, which is important for understanding the Vienna peace settlement and the entire nineteenth century. Identify the five Great Powers and fix their boundaries in your mind. Also study the boundaries of the reorganized German confederation. What are the two main states in the confederation, and what are some of the smaller ones? Now, refer to Map 21.1 and see how (1) France had lost and (2) Prussia had gained in the Rhineland area. Finally, what two Central European nationalities were politically most fragmented in 1815?

    Now close the text and test your understanding with the outline map. Shade in the five Great Powers and their boundaries, trace the boundary of the German confederation, and name and position (approximately) the capital cities of the five Great Powers.

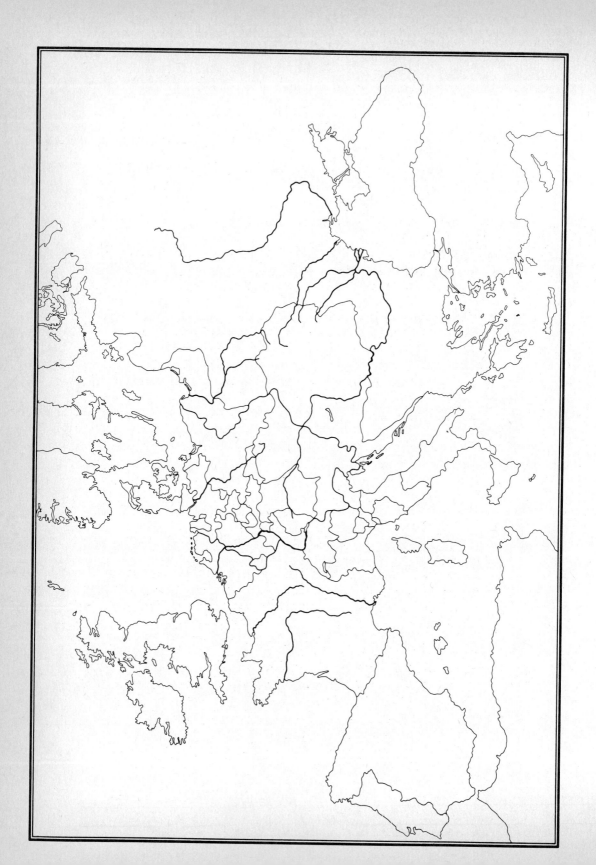

UNDERSTANDING HISTORY THROUGH READING AND THE ARTS

Great novels that accurately portray aspects of the times are Victor Hugo, *Les Mis-erables*,* an exciting story of crime and passion among France's poor; Honoré de Balzac, *Cousin Bette** and *Père Goriot**; Thomas Mann, *Buddenbrooks** (1902), a wonderful historical novel that traces the rise and fall of a prosperous German family over three generations during the nineteenth century; and Charles Dickens, *A Tale of Two Cities*, a portrait of London and Paris during the "dual revolution." One of the best recent historical novels about nineteenth-century life is J. Fowles, *The French Lieutenant's Woman** (1969).

Ludwig van Beethoven was the first great master of romantic music, even though in his early period he was influenced by the classical works of Haydn and Mozart. Beethoven's Symphony No. 9, the Choral Symphony, was greatly influenced by the ideas of the French Revolution—liberty, equality, and fraternity—and the symphony's "Ode to Joy" is based on Schiller's "Ode to Freedom." The score was dedicated to Frederick William III, the king of Prussia.

PROBLEMS FOR FURTHER INVESTIGATION

Was the 1848 revolution in France a modern class struggle in the Marxist sense? Much of the answer depends on whether or not one can show that the working class was of the new proletarian type—that is, modern factory workers rather than traditional artisan craftsmen. Begin your investigation with G. Rude, *The Crowd in History: A Study of Popular Disturbances in France and England, 1730-1848** (1964), Chapters 9 and 11, and then for the other side of the argument see Charles Tilly, "The People of June, 1848," in R. Price, ed., *Revolution and Reaction* (1977).

Did the British aristocrats give power to the middle class (in the Reform Bill of 1832) because they were afraid that it was the only alternative to violent revolution? This and other questions of interpretation of the famous bill are considered

---

*Available in paperback.

by seventeen different historians in W. H. Maehl, Jr., ed., *The Reform Bill of 1832** (1967).

Those interested in the subject of romanticism should see J. B. Halsted, ed., *Romanticism: Definition, Explanation, and Evaluation** (1965), and a good starting point for an investigation of nationalism in H. Kohn, *Nationalism: Its Meaning and History** (1955).

*Available in paperback.

CHAPTER 24

LIFE IN URBAN SOCIETY

CHAPTER OBJECTIVES

After reading and studying this chapter you should be able to answer the following questions:

Q-1. What did the emerging urban-industrial society mean for its members? Did the quality of life improve?

Q-2. What impact did the city have on family life, sexuality, marriage, and child-rearing?

Q-3. What changes in thought and culture inspired and reflected the new urban civilization?

CHAPTER SYNOPSIS

This chapter looks at the exciting and complex world of towns and cities, which expanded greatly because of the Industrial Revolution and which came to dominate life in the later nineteenth century. The chapter shows that although the urban environment had long been crowded and unhealthy, the rapid growth of urban population made such problems worse. However, by the 1840s, urban problems were attacked and partly solved both in Great Britain and in the continental countries. For example, throughout Europe a movement for better public health brought about sewer and water systems and gradually cleaned up the worst filth. Likewise, there were revolutionary breakthroughs in preventive medicine in the 1860s and after as Pasteur and his followers discovered how germs spread disease and how disease could be controlled. Urban planning and public transportation helped people move to better, less crowded housing. Thus, by the late nineteenth century the quality of life in cities had improved dramatically for ordinary people and the working classes.

However, enormous social and economic differences between upper and lower classes continued to exist as urban and industrial growth created new classes, class conflict, and a more complex social hierarchy. The chapter illustrates these differences by describing the different classes and some of the fascinating details of their distinctive lifestyles. During this period family life, sexual practices, and the role of women changed dramatically. In general, family life became more stable and affectionate in the later nineteenth century, but economic activities became rigidly separated according to sex. The results of these developments were both good and bad for women and young people.

Major intellectual developments in the urban society included a major expansion of scientific knowledge and the rise of realism as the dominant artistic mood. Scientific thought scored theoretical triumphs, which resulted in practical improvements, a growing faith in progress, and great prestige for scientists and their methods. Influential social thinkers such as Comte and Marx sought to determine society's unalterable scientific laws, while Social Darwinists applied Darwin's theory of natural selection to human affairs. The trend toward secular thinking strengthened. Literary realism, fascinated by scientific laws, ordinary people, and urban problems, fully reflected the spirit of the age.

STUDY OUTLINE

I. Taming the city
    A. Industry and the growth of cities
        1. Deplorable urban conditions of congestion, filth, and disease existed before the Industrial Revolution
        2. The Industrial Revolution and population growth made urban reform necessary
        3. Housing was crowded and poor and living conditions unhealthy
            a. A lack of transportation, which necessitated the crowding, and the slowness of government enforcement of sanitary codes contributed to the problem
            b. The legacy of rural housing also contributed to the problem
    B. The public health movement
        1. The reformer Chadwick was influenced by Bentham's ideas of the greatest good for the greatest number
            a. He believed that cleaning the city would curtail disease
            b. He proposed the installation of running water and sewers
        2. New sanitation methods and public health laws were adopted all over Europe
    C. The bacterial revolution
        1. The prevailing theory of disease was that it was caused by bad odors

      2. Pasteur's theory that germs caused disease was a major break-through, and its application meant disease could be controlled through vaccines

      3. Lister developed the concept of sterilization of wounds

  D. Urban planning and public transportation

      1. Better urban planning contributed to improved living conditions

      2. After 1850, Paris was transformed by the urban planning of Hauss-mann; it became a model city

      3. Electric streetcars revolutionized urban life and enabled the cities to expand

II. Social groups

  A. Social structure

      1. The standard of living for the average person improved substantially

      2. But differences in wealth continued to be enormous; society remained stratified in a number of classes

  B. The middle classes were diverse

      1. The upper middle class was composed of successful business families who were attracted to the aristocratic lifestyle

      2. The middle middle-class group contained merchants, lawyers, and doc-tors—people who were well off but not wealthy

      3. Next came the lower middle class: shopkeepers, small businessmen, white-collar workers

      4. Experts, such as engineers, chemists, accountants, and managers, were also considered members of the middle class

      5. The middle-class lifestyle included large meals, dinner parties, servants, an interest in fashionable dressing, and a good education for their chil-dren

      6. Their code of expected behavior stressed hard work, self-discipline, reli-gion, and restraint from vices

  C. The working class

      1. The vast majority of people belonged to the working class, yet the class had varying lifestyles and little unity

      2. The most highly skilled workers constituted a "labor aristocracy"

        a. They developed a lifestyle of stern morality

        b. They considered themselves the leaders of the working class

      3. Next came the semiskilled and unskilled urban workers

        a. Domestic servants constituted one of the largest subgroups of the unskilled workers

        b. Women employed in the "sweated industries" were another large group

        c. Drinking was a favorite leisure activity of the working class; other pastimes included sports and the music halls

       4. In Europe, church attendance by the working-class declined, while in the United States working-class churches thrived

III. Changes in family life

    A. Premarital sex and marriage

        1. "Romantic love" had triumphed by 1850—and premarital sex and illegitimacy had increased compared to the eighteenth century

        2. After 1850, illegitimacy decreased, indicating the growing morality and stability of the working class

        3. Economic factors remained more important in middle-class marriages than in working-class marriages

    B. Prostitution

        1. Men commonly turned to prostitutes because marriages were so often made later in life, especially in the middle and upper classes

        2. Brutal sexist behavior was a part of life

    C. Kinship ties

        1. Marriage and family ties were often strong

        2. Kinship networks were an important source of mutual support and welfare

    D. Women and the family

        1. The preindustrial pattern of women working disappeared except for working-class women

        2. Women became full-time mothers and homemakers, not wage earners

        3. Women were excluded from good jobs, but they wielded power in the family

        4. The home increased in emotional importance in all social classes; it symbolized shelter from the harsh working world

        5. Strong emotional bonds between mothers and children and between wives and husbands developed

    E. Child-rearing

        1. There was more breast-feeding and less abandonment of babies

        2. The birthrate declined, so each child became more important and could receive more advantages

        3. Many children were too controlled by parents, however, and suffered the effects of excessive parental concern

        4. Relations between fathers and children were often tense; fathers tended to be very demanding

        5. In studying family dynamics, Freud developed his theory of the Oedipal complex: that sons compete with their fathers for their mothers' love

        6. Working-class youths probably had more avenues of escape from family tensions than middle-class youths

IV. Scientific and intellectual developments

    A. The triumph of science

    1. Theoretical discoveries resulted increasingly in practical benefits, as in chemistry and electricity
    2. Scientific achievements strengthened faith in progress and gave science unrivaled prestige
  B. Social science and evolution
    1. Many thinkers, such as Auguste Comte, tried to study society "scientifically" and find general social laws
    2. Theories of dynamic development and evolution fascinated the nineteenth century
      a. Charles Darwin theorized that all life had evolved gradually through an unending "struggle for survival"
      b. Social Darwinists, such as Herbert Spencer, applied Darwin's ideas to human affairs
  C. Realism in literature
    1. Realism replaced romanticism as the dominant artistic trend after 1850
    2. Realists gloried in everyday life, taboo subjects, and urban problems
    3. French novelists, notably Balzac, Flaubert, and Zola, led the way
    4. Mary Ann Evans (George Eliot), Hardy, Tolstoy, and Dreiser were also great realists

REVIEW QUESTIONS

Q-1. To what extent was industrialization responsible for the deplorable conditions of the cities in the early nineteenth century?

Q-2. Who was Edwin Chadwick? What role did he play in the health movement?

Q-3. What was the miasmatic theory of disease? How did it retard progress?

Q-4. What contributions did Pasteur, Koch, and Lister make to life in urban Europe? Give examples.

Q-5. What were the reasons for the rebuilding of Paris? Who was responsible for this change?

Q-6. Why was the electric streetcar so important in improving urban life?

Q-7. Marx claimed that as a result of industrialization there was an increasing polarization of society into rich and poor. Do the facts warrant such a conclusion?

Q-8. Describe the differences and similarities between groups within the middle class. What separated and what united them?

Q-9. What were the goals of the middle class?

Q-10. Describe the "labor aristocracy." What were the interests of its members? How did they differ from the rest of the working class?

Q-11. What were the interests, motives, and lifestyle of the working class? How were they changing by the late nineteenth century?

Q-12. Why was there a decline in illegitimacy after 1850?

Q-13. Why did middle-class men marry late? What effect did this have on their sexual behavior?

Q-14. How common was prostitution in the nineteenth century? What sort of evidence on the subject exists?

Q-15. Did kinship ties disappear in the new urban environment? Explain.

Q-16. What was the social and economic position of women in the nineteenth century? Were they better off than in preindustrial society?

Q-17. What kind of changes occurred in child care and the attitudes toward children in the nineteenth century?

Q-18. What was the nineteenth-century view of masturbation?

Q-19. Overall, did family life improve in the nineteenth century? Explain.

Q-20. In what practical ways did breakthroughs in scientific inquiry transform life for the general population of the nineteenth century?

Q-21. What impact did science have on the study of society—that is, "social science"?

Q-22. Explain the new evolutionary views of biological development and how these views influenced religious and social thought.

Q-23. What was the realist movement in literature about? Who were the major writers of this movement, and how did they differ from previous writers?

STUDY-REVIEW EXERCISES

Define the following key concepts and terms.

antiseptic principle

Darwin's theory of biological evolution

sweated industries

labor aristocracy

literary realist movement

miasmatic theory

middle-class morality

Comte's positivism

<u>*Study*</u> *Figures 29.2 and 29.4 in the text. What important characteristics of nineteenth-century society do they reveal?*

<u>*Explain*</u> *how each of the following people contributed to the improvement of nineteenth-century life.*

Edwin Chadwick

Louis Pasteur

Robert Koch

Jean Baptiste Lamarck

Charles Darwin

Sigmund Freud

Gustave Flaubert

Emile Zola

Auguste Comte

Joseph Lister

Baron Haussmann

Gustave Droz

<u>*Test*</u> *your understanding of the chapter by answering the following questions.*

1. The birthrate *increased/decreased* in the last half of the nineteenth century.
2. He advocated the principle of "the greatest good for the greatest number."

3. Lister believed that infection could be controlled by the application of his

   "_____ principle."

4. Electric streetcars first came to the city in about the year _____ .

5. Overall, treatment of children and infants *improved/deteriorated* in the nineteenth century.

6. Generally speaking, the European aristocracy experienced *no change/a decrease* in relative income in the nineteenth century.

7. The highly skilled upper 15 percent of the working class was known as the

   _____ .

8. The status and income of schoolteachers and nurses *rose/fell* during the nineteenth century.

9. "It is to the _____ that the vast body of the working people look for recreation and entertainment."

10. By 1850, working-class young people tended to marry for *love/economic reasons*.

11. Kinship ties tended to *grow stronger/grow weaker* as a result of urban society.

12. Sex roles for men and women in the nineteenth century tended to become *more/less* rigid.

13. Women's economic power in the nineteenth century *increased/decreased* as compared to that of the eighteenth century.

MULTIPLE-CHOICE QUESTIONS

1. As compared to preindustrial society, the relative distribution of wealth among the three classes in industrial society
   a. probably did not change.
   b. shifted in favor of the working class.
   c. shifted significantly in favor of the middle class.

2. Which class was most opposed to drinking?
   a. Aristocracy
   b. Middle class
   c. Working class

3. Comte's "stages of knowledge" theory held that the third and final stage of all intellectual activity was the

a. scientific.
b. theological, or fictitious.
c. metaphysical, or abstract.

4. The new movement in writing, as found in the works of Zola, Flaubert, and Hardy and which pursued the typical and commonplace and claimed that human action was a result of heredity and environment, was called
a. romanticism.
b. secularism.
c. realism.

5. Which of the following factors was *not* a reason for the deplorable conditions of English cities up to the 1850s?
a. People's acceptance of dirt
b. The abundance of urban land
c. The absence of urban transportation facilities
d. The rapid growth of urban population

6. The development of urban society between 1850 and 1900 brought
a. a decrease in wages.
b. a drop in the average standard of living.
c. less of a gap between the income of rich and poor.
d. more diversity of occupation in the middle and lower classes.

7. By 1900, people of the lower class
a. were divided into well-defined subclasses.
b. had generally similar lifestyles.
c. were united against the rich.
d. hated to go to music halls.

8. One change the nineteenth century brought to women was
a. less distinction between the duties of husband and wife.
b. a rise in factory employment after marriage.
c. more equal employment opportunities.
d. increased control over money and family decisions.

9. The birthrate declined in the later nineteenth century for all of the following reasons *except* the
a. desire to give more individual care and attention to children.
b. desire to give more educational opportunities to children.
c. acceptance of birth-control practices by the Catholic church.
d. declining value of children as an economic asset.

10. After 1850, ordinary women
    a. were more likely to marry for money.
    b. were more likely to breast-feed their babies.
    c. hardly ever got pregnant before marriage.
    d. generally cut themselves off from parents and relatives after they got married.

11. White-collar workers generally
    a. grew in importance in the nineteenth century.
    b. were uninterested in moving up in society.
    c. kept many servants.
    d. felt a common tie with manual workers.

12. The country in which the problems of urban congestion and deplorable conditions were felt first and most acutely was
    a. France.
    b. Germany.
    c. Great Britain.
    d. Ireland.

13. Sigmund Freud's most revolutionary idea was that
    a. unconscious psychological energy was sexual energy.
    b. masturbation was a source of psychological disturbance.
    c. spontaneous affection was damaging.
    d. family life had little to do with mental illness.

14. Comte's social philosophy of positivism was based on the idea that the laws of human relations were discoverable through
    a. God.
    b. political action.
    c. social science.
    d. Marxism.

15. The realist writers held to all but one of the following principles in their writing:
    a. The romantic search for the sublime
    b. An emphasis on strict scientific objectivity
    c. A general criticism of middle-class values and life
    d. A focus on everyday life, particularly of that of the working classes

16. The transformation of Paris in the 1850s was a result of
    a. new streets and boulevards.
    b. improved sewer and water systems.

    c. comprehensive urban planning.
    d. all of the above

17. After the Industrial Revolution, the gap between the rich and poor
    a. decreased.
    b. increased.
    c. stayed about the same as previously.
    d. none of the above

18. The typical nineteenth-century *middle-class* social occasion was
    a. a trip to the music hall.
    b. gambling.
    c. a dinner party.
    d. a relaxing evening at the local pub.

19. By the late nineteenth century, indulging in heavy drinking and practicing cruel sports, such as cockfighting,
    a. were on the increase because of more leisure time.
    b. were both in decline.
    c. fluctuated from year to year.
    d. resulted in the prohibition of such activities.

20. After 1850, the illegitimacy rate in Europe
    a. increased.
    b. decreased.
    c. remained about the same.
    d. fluctuated depending upon economic conditions.

21. Evidence suggests that prostitution increased in the nineteenth century in consequence to
    a. the growth of a stern puritanical morality.
    b. middle-class men delaying marriage.
    c. sexual freedom enjoyed by middle-class men.
    d. all of the above

22. It is possible that kinship ties within nineteenth-century working-class homes
    a. hardly existed.
    b. were greater than often believed.
    c. did not exist after marriage.
    d. existed *only* in crisis situations.

23. The division of labor by sex in the last half of the nineteenth century tended to
    a. increase.
    b. decrease.
    c. not change from the earlier period.
    d. decrease only for middle-class women.

24. Late-nineteenth-century roles of father and mother tended to become
    a. more alike.
    b. more rigid.
    c. more democratic, with the father showing more affection.
    d. none of the above

UNDERSTANDING HISTORY THROUGH READING AND THE ARTS

The best way to learn about life for the common folk is to read historical novels. The life of a family in early twentieth-century Scotland (Ayrshire) is told in W. McIlvanney's *Docherty* (1975); the London underworld of crime is mixed with upper-class life in M. Crichton's exciting *The Great Train Robbery** (1975); and life in a slum is the subject of Robert Robert's autobiography, *The Classic Slum** (1973). Charles Dickens' *Hard Times** has become a classic statement about life in the new industrial society, as has E. Gaskill's *Mary Barton**. Another interesting fictional account of hardship and survival in the nineteenth century is C. Kingsley, *Alton Locke**.

Victorian social and moral codes were expressed in painting. These highly popular works of the time (they have since fallen out of fashion) are known as modern-life or "narrative" paintings, and are interestingly described (and shown) in C. Wood, *Victorian Panorama: Paintings of Victorian Life* (1977), and J. Hadfield, *Every Picture Tells a Story: Images of Victorian Life* (1985). Impressionist painting is very popular today but a new light on how it related to social change of the time is sketched out in T. Clark, *The Painting of Modern Life: Paris in the Art of Manet and His Followers* (1985). The student interested in architecture and the city should begin with the general work by M. Girouard, *Cities and People* (1985), and socialism and art was a subject taken up by the influential Englishman William Morris—who is the subject of A. Briggs, *William Morris, Selected Writings and Designs* (1957).

The tragedy of industrialial-urban life for the lower classes is woven into Puccini's highly popular and romantic opera *La Bohème*, which takes place in Paris. Many recordings of his opera are available.

*Available in paperback.

PROBLEMS FOR FURTHER INVESTIGATION

What was life like for members of the nineteenth-century working class? Historians are just now beginning to understand how they lived. One of the problems, however, is that the working people wrote little about themselves. Some autobiographical and biographical material that exists for the British working classes is H. Mayhew, *London Labour and London Poor** (reprint, 3 vols., 1969); E. Yeo, *The Unknown Mayhew** (1972); J. Burnett, ed., *Annals of Labour* (1974); P. Thompson, *The Edwardians* (1975); and J. Saville and J. Bellamy, eds., *Dictionary of Labour Biography* (4 vols., 1973).

*Available in paperback.

CHAPTER 25

THE AGE OF NATIONALISM,
1850-1914

CHAPTER OBJECTIVES

After reading and studying this chapter you should be able to answer the following questions:

Q-1. How did "nation building" transform the major states of nineteenth-century Europe?

Q-2. Why did nationalism become a universal faith in Europe between 1850 and 1914?

Q-3. How did it evolve so that it gained the support of the broad masses of society?

CHAPTER SYNOPSIS

The theme of this chapter is the triumph of nationalism after the unsuccessful nationalist revolutions of 1848. Between 1850 and 1914, strong nation-states developed, which won the enthusiastic support of all the social classes, caused a shift in the balance of international political power, and pulled the masses away from the socialist doctrine of class war.

Napoleon III of France played a pioneering role in this triumph of nationalism. His mild dictatorship, which came into being illegally and which lasted from 1852 to 1870, showed how the national state and its programs could appeal to rich and poor, conservative and radical. In this way, the national state became a way of coping with the challenge of revolutionary political and economic change. In Italy, Count Cavour, the moderate nationalist leader of the kingdom of Sardinia, managed to unify most of Italy in 1860 into a single political state that was far from radical in social and economic matters. Shortly thereafter, in 1862, Otto von Bismarck became chief minister of Prussia. A master of power politics, Bismarck skillfully fought three wars to unify the states of Germany into a single nation under Prussian leadership. In doing so, Bismarck strengthened German nationalism and gave it to a conservative and antiliberal thrust. Nationalism was also important in Russia. There it led to major reforms after the Crimean War: in 1861 the serfs were freed, and the government encouraged the development of railroads and modern industry. Frustrated nationalism was an important factor in the Russian revolution of 1905, after defeat in a war with Japan.

Nationalism continued to grow in strength in the emerging urban society of the late nineteenth century. This was because national governments and politicians responded effectively to many of the political demands and social needs of the people. Throughout most of Europe socialists and socialist political parties looked increasingly toward unions and parliaments for continued gradual improvement. They only paid lip service to the idea of radical, violent revolution and class war. The growing moderation of European socialists reflected the great appeal of nationalism for the masses. Only in multinational states, most notably the Austro-Hungarian Empire, did the growth of competing nationalisms promote fragmentation as opposed to unity.

STUDY OUTLINE

  I. Napoleon III and the French tradition of authoritarian rule
      A. The Second Republic and Louis Napoleon
          1. The reasons for Napoleon's election include middle-class and peasant fears of socialism and a disgust with class politics
          2. Many people wanted a strong national leader who would serve all the people and help them economically
          3. Napoleon cooperated with the conservative National Assembly, but it refused to change the constitution so he could run for another term
          4. Therefore, he seized power in a coup d'état in 1851 and dismissed the assembly; these actions were approved by the voters
      B. Napoleon III's Second Empire
          1. Napoleon III's greatest success was improving the economy of France
          2. His political system allowed only limited opposition
          3. His dilemma was to reconcile a strong state with democracy
 II. Nation building in Italy and Germany
      A. Italy to 1850: a battleground for great powers
          1. "Italy" was divided; much of it was under the control of Austria and the pope
          2. Between 1815 and 1848, the goal of national unity began to appeal to Italians

   3. Sardinia was the logical leader in the nationalist movement
   4. Pope Pius IX opposed nationalism and other modern ideas
B. Cavour and Garibaldi
   1. Count Cavour, the liberal minister of Sardinia, built Sardinia into a liberal and economically sound state
      a. He was a moderate nationalist who sought unity only for the northern and perhaps central areas of Italy
      b. He worked to consolidate Sardinia as a liberal state capable of leading northern Italy
   2. Cavour used France to engineer a war with Austria to further his plans for unification
   3. Central Italy was united with Sardinia in 1860
   4. Garibaldi "liberated" southern Italy and Sicily, and Italy was further unified
   5. Except for Rome and Venice, Italy was politically united by 1860
      a. But there were strong class divisions
      b. There were also strong cultural divisions between the northern and southern areas
C. Bismarck takes command
   1. Bismarck's "blood and iron" policy was centered on nationalism and war as a means of increasing Prussia's power
   2. Competition between Prussia and Austria caused a stalemate in Germany
   3. The Zollverein encouraged the move toward a non-Austrian Germany
   4. The Prussians, William I and Bismarck, supported militarism rather than liberalism to strengthen Germany and defeat Austria
D. The Austro-Prussian War of 1866—the first step toward unification
   1. Denmark's attempted annexation of Schleswig-Holstein led to the war with Austria
   2. Bismarck isolated Austria from France and Russia
   3. Prussian victory meant Austria had to give up its role in Germany
E. The taming of Parliament
   1. The middle class preferred national unity to liberal institutions
   2. Bismarck outmaneuvered the liberals in the parliament, and the middle class ended up supporting monarchial authority
F. The Franco-Prussian War (1870-71)
   1. Bismarck used war with France to bring southern Germany into the union
   2. As a result of military success, semi-authoritarian nationalism in Germany won out over liberalism

III. The modernization of Russia
   A. The "Great Reforms"
      1. Serfdom was still the basic social institution of agrarian nineteenth-century Russia
      2. The Crimean War (1853-1856) speeded up the modernization of Russia
         a. Russia's defeat showed how badly the country had fallen behind the industrializing West
         b. The war also created the need for reforms because its hardships led to the threat of peasant uprisings
      3. Serfdom was abolished in 1861, and other reforms were undertaken
         a. Local assemblies (zemstvos) were established
         b. The legal system was reformed
   B. The industrialization of Russia (1860-1900)
      1. Railroad construction stimulated the economy and inspired nationalism and imperialism
      2. The assassination of Alexander III (1881) brought political reform to an end
      3. Economic reform was carried out by Sergei Witte, the minister of finance from 1892 to 1903
         a. More railroads were built
         b. Protective tariffs were raised
         c. Foreign ideas and money were used to build factories
   C. The revolution of 1905
      1. Defeat at the hands of Japan brought political upheaval at home
      2. Popular revolution forced Nicholas II to issue the October Manifesto, which granted full civil liberties and promised some form of representative government
      3. Partially modernized Russia became a conservative constitutional monarchy, dominated by the bureaucracy and the properties
IV. The responsive national state (1871-1914)
   A. Characteristics of the new national state
      1. Ordinary people felt increasing loyalty to their governments
      2. By 1914, universal male suffrage was the rule, and women were beginning to demand the right to vote too
   B. The German Empire
      1. The German Empire was a union of twenty-five German states in 1871 governed by a chancellor (Bismarck) and a parliament (the Reichstag)
      2. Bismarck and the liberals attacked the Catholic church (the *Kulturkampf*) in an effort to maintain the superiority of state over church, but abandoned the attack in 1878
      3. Worldwide agricultural depression after 1873 resulted in the policy of economic protectionism in Germany

4. Bismarck outlawed socialist parties
5. Bismarck gave Germany an impressive system of social-welfare legislation, partly to weaken socialism's appeal to the workers
6. King William II dismissed Bismarck to try to win the support of the workers, but he couldn't stem the rising tide of socialism
7. The Social Democratic Party became the largest party in the parliament, but it was strongly nationalistic, not revolutionary

C. Republican France (the Third Republic)
  1. The defeat of France in 1871 led to revolution in Paris (the Commune)
  2. The Paris Commune of 1871 was brutally defeated
  3. A new Third Republic was established and led by skilled men such as Gambetta and Ferry
  4. The Third Republic passed considerable reforms, including legalizing trade unions and creating state schools, and it built a colonial empire
  5. The Dreyfus affair (1898-99) weakened France and caused anti-Catholic reaction

D. Great Britain and Ireland
  1. The reform bills of 1867 and 1884 further extended the franchise in Britain
  2. Others, like Mill, looked to safeguarding the individual
  3. Led by David Lloyd George, the Liberal party ushered in social-welfare legislation between 1906 and 1914
  4. The issue of home rule divided Ireland into the northern Protestant Ulsterites, who opposed it, and the southern Catholic nationalists, who favored it

E. The Austro-Hungarian Empire
  1. After 1866, the empire was divided in two and the nationalistic Magyars ruled Hungary
  2. Austria-Hungary suffered from competing nationalisms, which pitted ethnic groups against one another and weakened the state
  3. Anti-Semitism grew rapidly, especially in Vienna

V. Marxism and the socialist movement
A. The Socialist International
  1. A rapid growth of socialist parties occurred throughout Europe after 1871
  2. Socialists united to form an international socialist movement
B. Unions and revisionism
  1. There was a general rise in the standard of living for workers in the late nineteenth century, so they became less revolutionary
  2. Unions were gradually legalized in Europe, and they were another factor in the trend toward moderation

3. Revisionist socialists believed in working within capitalism (through labor unions, for example) and no longer saw the future in terms of capitalist-worker warfare
4. In the late nineteenth century, the socialist movements within each nation became different from one another and thereby more and more nationalistic

REVIEW QUESTIONS

Q-1. How did "nation building" transform the major states of nineteenth-century Europe?

Q-2. Why did nationalism become a universal faith in Europe between 1850 and 1914?

Q-3. How did it evolve so that it gained the support of the broad masses of society?

Q-4. Why did the voters of France elect Louis Napoleon president in 1848? Why did they elect him emperor a few years later?

Q-5. What were some of the benefits Napoleon bestowed on his subjects?

Q-6. Did Napoleon allow any political opposition to exist? Explain his political system and why it eventually broke down.

Q-7. Italy before 1860 was merely a "geographical expression." Explain.

Q-8. What were the three basic approaches to Italian unification? Which one prevailed?

Q-9. What was the nature and significance of Garibaldi's liberation of Sicily and Naples in 1860? Why was Cavour so nervous about Garibaldi?

Q-10. What were the causes and results of the Austro-Prussian War?

Q-11. What was the significance of the Zollverein in German history?

Q-12. Why did the Prussian liberals make an about-face and support their old enemy Bismarck after 1866?

Q-13. Describe the status of the Russian serf in the early nineteenth century. How beneficial was the reform of 1861 to the serf?

Q-14. Why was the Crimean War a turning point in Russian history?

Q-15. Describe the economic nationalism of the Russian minister of finance, Sergei Witte.

Q-16. Russia used the West to catch up with the West. Explain by citing examples.

Q-17. Compare and contrast the consequences of the Crimean and Russo-Japanese wars.

Q-18. What does it mean to say that "Russia was partially modernized on the eve of World War One"?

Q-19. Was the new Germany a democracy? Where did power reside in the Germany of 1871?

Q-20. What was Bismarck's relationship (after 1871) with (a) the Catholic church, (b) the liberals, and (c) the socialists?

Q-21. What were the German social-welfare laws? What were their origins?

Q-22. Describe the fortunes and misfortunes of the German socialists (Social Democratic Party) from about 1878 to 1912.

Q-23. Discuss the causes and the outcome of the Dreyfus affair in France in 1898-99.

Q-24. What were the major political developments and issues in Britain and Ireland? Was the Irish problem solvable?

Q-25. In what ways were ethnic rivalries and growing anti-Semitism related in Austro-Hungary?

Q-26. How does one account for the rapid growth of socialist parties in Europe in the last quarter of the nineteenth century?

Q-27. What was the purpose of the socialist internationals? To what degree did they represent working-class unity?

Q-28. What were the general arguments of the revisionist and gradualist socialists? Were they true Marxists?

STUDY-REVIEW EXERCISES

Identify each of the following people and give his or her significance.

Benjamin Disraeli

Emmeline Pankhurst

Jules Ferry

Sergei Witte

Alexander II

Camillo Benso di Cavour

Edward Bernstein

Pius IX

William Gladstone

Giuseppe Garibaldi

William II

John Stuart Mill

Explain what the following events were, who participated in them, and why they were important.

The "People's Budget" (Britain)

Napoleon III's coup d'état

May Day

assassination of Tsar Alexander II

establishment of the Zollverein (1834)

establishment of the Austro-Hungarian monarchy

Treaty of Villafranca

Paris Commune of 1871

Ulster revolt of December 1913

Explain the outcome and significance of each of the following wars.

	Year	Outcome and Significance
Danish War		
Austro-Prussian War		
Franco-Prussian War		
Crimean War		
Russo-Japanese War		

Test your understanding of the chapter by answering the following questions.

1. In 1851, the French voters *approved/disapproved* of Louis Napoleon's seizure of power.
2. Increasingly, the main opposition to Napoleon III came from the *middle class/ working class/upper class*.
3. The Russian *victory/defeat* in the Crimean War of 1853-1856 contributed to *freedom/serfdom* for the Russian peasants after 1861.
4. After 1848, the pope *supported/opposed* Italian unification.
5. After 1873, the price of wheat on the world market *rose/fell* rather dramatically.
6. The minority Irish Ulsterites were *Catholic/Protestant* and *for/against* home rule.
7. Bismarck used war with *Austria/France/Russia* in order to bring the south Germans into a united Germany.

MULTIPLE-CHOICE QUESTIONS

1. The most industrialized, socialized, and unionized continental country by 1914 was
    a. France.
    b. Germany.
    c. Italy.
    d. Belgium.

2. The Russian zemstvo was a(n)
    a. industrial workers' council.
    b. local government assembly.
    c. terrorist group.
    d. village priest.

3. The *Kulturkampf* in Germany was an attack on
    a. liberals.
    b. socialists.
    c. the Catholic church.
    d. Prussian culture.

4. The first modern social security laws were passed in the 1880s in
    a. Britain.
    b. France.
    c. Russia.
    d. Germany.

5. The general tendency of unions toward the end of the century was
   a. to move closer to Marxism.
   b. to move toward evolutionary socialism.
   c. to reject socialism altogether.
   d. increasingly to favor revolution.

6. After 1850, the disciples of nationalism in Italy looked for leadership from
   a. Prussia.
   b. the papacy.
   c. Sardinia-Piedmont.
   d. the Kingdom of the Two Sicilies.

7. Cavour's program for the unification of northern Italy included all of the following *except*
   a. improved transportation.
   b. increased power for the Catholic church.
   c. civil liberties.
   d. war and secret diplomacy.

8. Russian social and political reforms in the 1860s could best be described as
   a. revolutionary.
   b. totally ineffective.
   c. halfway measures.
   d. extremely effective.

9. Witte's plans for the economic development of Russia included
   a. lowering protective tariffs.
   b. taking Russia off the gold standard.
   c. encouraging foreign investment.
   d. bringing Russian Marxists into the government.

10. Bismarck's *Kulturkampf* was directed against
    a. German liberals.
    b. the Catholic church.
    c. the aristocracy.
    d. the Russians.

11. Those who fought for conviction in the Dreyfus case of 1898 in France included all *except*
    a. Catholics.
    b. the army.
    c. radical republicans.
    d. anti-Semites.

12. Among those opposing home rule in Ireland were
    a. Catholics.
    b. Ulsterites.
    c. Irish peasants.
    d. William Gladstone.

13. After 1870, Marxian socialists
    a. accepted the revisionist theories of Eduard Bernstein.
    b. failed to grow in number.
    c. formed a second international organization.
    d. refused to participate in national elections.

14. Which of the following is *not* true with regard to German unification?
    a. It was completed in 1871 with a war with France.
    b. The chief architect of the movement was Otto von Bismarck.
    c. The unification process was directed by the German state of Austria.
    d. Unification did not include liberal and democratic ideas and methods.

15. After 1871, the European balance of power
    a. shifted in favor of Russia.
    b. broke down because of British naval supremacy.
    c. shifted in favor of Germany.
    d. all of the above

16. After 1873, European agriculture was
    a. in a state of depression.
    b. inefficient compared with North America's.
    c. experiencing a glut in the world grain market.
    d. all of the above

17. The Third French Republic
    a. brutally crushed the Commune of 1871.
    b. passed considerable reforms.
    c. legalized trade unions.
    d. all of the above

18. The Russian defeat in the Crimean War of 1853-56 hastened
    a. the modernization of Russia.
    b. legal and local political reform.
    c. the abolition of serfdom.
    d. all of the above

19. The German Zollverein was
    a. a trade union.
    b. a customs union.
    c. an "all-German" parliament.
    d. none of the above

20. Bismarck's policy toward the Social Democrats was one of
    a. limited support.
    b. political alliance to defeat the military party.
    c. total repression.
    d. none of the above

UNDERSTANDING HISTORY THROUGH READING AND THE ARTS

The nineteenth century saw the publication of a good number of books based on the idea that humanity could transform itself and build a new world ruled by justice and equality. One of the most popular of these utopian works in Europe was the American author Edward Bellamy's *Looking Backward*,* which was first published in 1888. Life and revolutionary activity among rural workers is told in the fascinating *Autobiography of Joseph Areh*, J. O'Leary, ed. (1966). One of the most interesting women of the nineteenth century was Queen Victoria, whose life is dealt with in the lively biography *Queen Victoria** (1964) by E. Longford.

In music the mood of the last half of the nineteenth century was romantically nationalistic. Brahms wrote *Song of Triumph* to celebrate the German victory over France in 1870, while Smetana, the first great Czech nationalist composer, glorified the folk history of the Czech people in his *My Country*. In opera Moussorgsky wrote *Boris Godunov* (1874), a historical drama about Russia during the time of Ivan the Terrible. The popularity of German heroic music-drama continued to grow, and it drew added inspiration from Wagner's *The Ring of the Nibelung* (four parts, 1869-1876), a monumental national epic of Germany based on Nordic mythology. All of these works are available on a number of recordings.

PROBLEMS FOR FURTHER INVESTIGATION

Who was Napoleon III and what were his motives—a police state or a unified and prosperous France? Begin your investigation with the problem series book *Napoleon III—Man of Destiny*,* B. D. Gooch, ed. (1963).

*Available in paperback.

The problems of interpreting the Italian unification movement are discussed by a number of historians in C. F. Delzell, *The Unification of Italy** (1963).

Those interested in the political activities of British workers will want to start with H. Pelling, *The Origins of the Labour Party* (1954), and for the interesting story of the politicization of the German working class, from Marx to the present, begin with H. Grebing, *The History of the German Labour Movement* (1969).

How did the Franco-German War change the course of history? French-German relations and French history took a tragic turn in 1870 with the siege of Paris and then the grim civil war that followed. This is the subject of A. Horne, *The Fall of Paris: The Siege and the Commune of 1870-1** (1965, 1981).

What were the goals and interests of women in the nineteenth-century women's rights movement? Begin with T. Lloyd, *Suffragettes International: The World Wide Campaign for Women's Rights** (1971), M. Thomis and J. Grimmett, *Women in Protest, 1800-1850** (1983), and O. Banks, *Faces of Feminism* (1981). Further, in an era in which most women were confined to either the kitchen or drawing room, three Victorian women (Josephine Butler, Octavia Hill, and Florence Nightingale) became important makers of social policy. This is the subject of N. Boyd, *Three Victorian Women Who Changed Their World* (1982).

*Available in paperback.

CHAPTER 26

THE WEST AND THE WORLD

CHAPTER OBJECTIVES

After reading and studying this chapter you should be able to answer the following questions:

Q-1. What was the "new imperialism" and how and why did it occur?
Q-2. What were its consequences for Europe and the new colonial peoples?

CHAPTER SYNOPSIS

We live in a world today in which the consequences of nineteenth-century Western imperialism are still being felt. In the nineteenth century, Western civilization reached the high point of its longstanding global expansion. Western expansion in this period took many forms. There was, first of all, economic expansion. Europeans invested large sums of money abroad, building railroads and ports, mines and plantations, factories and public utilities. Trade between nations grew greatly, and a world economy developed. European economic penetration was very often peaceful, but Europeans (and Americans) were also quite willing to force isolationist nations such as China and Japan to throw open their doors to Westerners. Second, millions of Europeans migrated abroad. The pressure of poverty and overpopulation in rural areas encouraged this migration, but once in the United States and Australia, European settlers passed laws to prevent similar mass migration from Asia.

A third aspect of Western expansion was that European states established vast political empires, mainly in Africa but also in Asia. This was called the "new imperialism," and it occurred primarily between 1880 and 1900, when European governments scrambled frantically for territory. White people came, therefore, to rule millions of black and brown people in Africa and Asia. The causes of the new imperialism are still hotly debated. Competition for trade, superior military force, European power politics, and a racist belief in European superiority were among the most important. Some Europeans bitterly criticized imperialism as a betrayal of Western ideals of freedom and equality.

Western imperialism produced various reactions in Africa and Asia. The first response was simply to try to drive the foreigners away. The general failure of this violent response then led large masses to accept European rule, which did bring some improvements. A third response was that of Western-educated natives, who were repelled by Western racism and attracted by Western ideals of national independence and economic progress. Thus, imperialism and reactions to it spread Western civilization to non-Western lands.

STUDY OUTLINE

I. Building a world economy
    A. Trade and communications in the nineteenth century
        1. The Industrial Revolution caused an enormous growth in world trade, with Britain playing a key role
        2. The railroad, the steamship, refrigeration, and other technological innovations revolutionized trade patterns
        3. The Suez and Panama canals fostered intercontinental trade
        4. Most trade was among European nations, the United States, and Canada
    B. The growth of foreign investment
        1. Beginning about 1840, Europeans continuously invested large amounts of capital abroad and in other European countries
        2. This investment resulted in cheap raw materials and an increased demand for European manufactured goods
    C. The opening of China and Japan
        1. European trade with China increased, but not without a struggle
            a. China had never been interested in European goods
            b. British merchants and the Chinese clashed over the sale of opium and the opening of Chinese ports to Europeans
            c. The opium war in 1842 led to the British acquisition of Hong Kong and the opening of four cities to trade
            d. A second war in 1856-1860 resulted in more gains for Europeans
        2. Japan also was unwilling to trade with the West or to have diplomatic relations with it
            a. Japan wanted to maintain its long-standing isolation
            b. An American fleet under Perry "opened" Japan in 1853 with threats of naval bombardment

    D. The Western penetration of Egypt
       1. Mohammed Ali built a modern state in Turkish-held Egypt that attracted European traders
       2. Ismail continued the modernization of Egypt but also drew the country deeply into debt
       3. To prevent Egypt from going bankrupt, Britain intervened politically
       4. Foreign financial control provoked a violent nationalistic reaction in Egypt that led to British occupation of the country

II. The great migration from Europe and Asia
    A. The pressure of population
       1. The population of Europe more than doubled between 1800 and 1900
       2. This population growth was the impetus behind emigration
       3. Migration patterns varied from country to country depending largely on economic opportunities at home and abroad
       4. Only about half the migrants came to the United States
    B. European migration
       1. Most European migrants were peasants lacking adequate land holdings or craftsmen threatened by industrialization
       2. Most were young and unmarried
       3. Many returned home after some time abroad
       4. Many were spurred on by the desire for freedom
    C. Asian migration
       1. Many Asians became plantation laborers
       2. Asian migration led to racist reactions in the West

III. Western imperialism (1880-1914)
    A. The new imperialism
       1. European nations scrambled for political as well as economic control over foreign nations
       2. This scramble led to new tensions between European states and wars with non-European powers
    B. The scramble for Africa
       1. Prior to 1880, European penetration of Africa was limited
       2. British occupation of Egypt and Belgian penetration into the Congo started the race for colonial possessions
       3. The Berlin conference (1884-85) laid ground rules for this new imperialism
          a. European claims to African territory had to be based on military occupation
          b. No single European power could claim the whole continent
       4. Germany entered the race for colonies and cooperated with France against Britain

      5. The British massacred Muslim tribesmen at Omdurman (1898) in their drive to conquer the Sudan and nearly went to war with the French at Fashoda

  C. Imperialism in Asia

      1. The Dutch extended their control in the East Indies while the French took Indochina

      2. Russia and the United States penetrated Asia

  D. The causes of the new imperialism

      1. Economic motives—especially trade opportunities—were important, but in the end general economic benefits were limited

      2. Political and diplomatic factors encouraged imperialism

        a. Colonies were believed to be crucial for national security, military power, and international prestige

        b. Colonies were also needed to provide naval bases

      3. Nationalism and racism contributed to imperialism

      4. Humanitarians, including missionaries, as well as military men often encouraged imperial growth

      5. Europeans saw themselves as giving a superior civilization to the world

  E. The critics of imperialism

      1. The British journalist J. A. Hobson set forth the argument that imperialism was the result of capitalism and only special-interest groups benefited from colonial possessions

      2. Others were critical for humanitarian or liberal reasons

IV. Responses to imperialism

  A. Imperialism threatened traditional society

      1. Traditionalists wanted to drive Western culture out and preserve the old culture and society

      2. Modernizers believed it was necessary to adopt Western practices

      3. Anti-imperialist leaders found inspiration in Western liberalism and nationalism

  B. The British Empire in India

      1. The last traditionalist response in India was the Great Rebellion of 1858

      2. After 1858, India was ruled by a white elite that considered itself superior to the Indians

      3. An Indian elite was educated to aid the British in administration

      4. Imperialism brought many benefits, including unity and peace

      5. But nationalistic sentiments grew among the Western-educated Indian elite

  C. The example of Japan

      1. The Meiji Restoration (1867) was a reaction to American intrusion, the unequal treaties, and humiliation of the shogun

     2. The Meiji leaders were modernizers, and they brought liberal and economic reforms

     3. Japan looked increasingly toward the German empire and rejected democracy in favor of authoritarianism in the 1890s

     4. Japan became an imperial power in the Far East

  D. Toward revolution in China

     1. The traditionalist Manchu rulers staged a comeback after the opium wars

     2. The Chinese defeat by Japan in 1894-95 led to imperialist penetration and unrest

     3. Modernizers hoped to take over and strengthen China

     4. Boxer traditionalists caused violence and a harsh European reaction

     5. Revolutionary modernizers overthrew the Manchu dynasty in 1912

REVIEW QUESTIONS

Q-1. Describe the enormous increase in world trade after 1800. What were the reasons for this growth?

Q-2. Discuss the opium wars (1839-1842, 1856-1860) by describing the motives of both the British merchants and the Chinese government.

Q-3. Trace the flow of European capital in the nineteenth century and note its effects.

Q-4. Khedive Ismail once said, "My country is no longer in Africa, we now form part of Europe." What did he mean?

Q-5. Explain the British-Egyptian conflict of 1882. What were the causes and the results?

Q-6. What were some of the differences in migration patterns among the various European states?

Q-7. Where did the European migrants go?

Q-8. Why did the migrants leave? Why did so many return?

Q-9. Why was migration from Italy so heavy? Who were the migrants and where did they go?

Q-10. What distinguished the "new imperialism" from earlier forms of European expansion in the nineteenth century?

Q-11. Why was Leopold II of Belgium interested in Africa?

Q-12. What was meant by "effective occupation"? Did it cause or curtail further imperialism?

Q-13. In 1898, a British army faced a French army at Fashoda in north-central Africa. How did each power get to such a location, and how was the confrontation solved?

Q-14. What do you believe was the chief cause of European imperialist expansion? Was it an inevitable result of capitalism, as some have argued?

Q-15. What impact did Christianity have on both imperialism and the contrast between imperialists and natives?

Q-16. What was the purpose of the Great Rebellion in India in 1857-1858?

Q-17. What were the advantages and disadvantages of British rule for the Indians?

Q-18. What was the Meiji Restoration in Japan? Why was it a turning point in Japanese history?

Q-19. How well did the Japanese copy the Europeans? What European ideas were most attractive to them?

Q-20. Does the Manchu dynasty in the period 1860-1912 represent a traditionalist or modernist response to Europe and imperialism?

Q-21. In the light of Chinese history and Chinese-European relations in the nineteenth century, what do you consider to be the causes of the Chinese Revolution of 1911-1912?

STUDY-REVIEW EXERCISES

Define the following key concepts and terms.

"new imperialism"

European foreign investment

traditionalist response to imperialism

modernist response to imperialism

Social Darwinism

racism

nationalism

Identify each of the following and give its significance.

Manchu dynasty

"Pale of [Jewish] Settlement"

International Association for the Exploration and Civilization of Central Africa

Egyptian Nationalist Party

Suez Canal

Omdurman

British opium trade

Pierre de Brazza

Mohammed Ali

Leopold II

Matthew Perry

Boers

Emile Aguinaldo

Dowager Empress Tzu Hsi

John Hobson

Explain what the following events were, who participated in them, and why they were important.

Japanese "opening" of Korea in 1876

Berlin conference of 1884-85

Fashoda crisis of 1898

Great Trek of the Boers

Alexandria riots of 1882

Treaty of Nanking, 1842

Clermont experiment of 1807

Meiji Restoration of 1867

Sino-Japanese War (1894-95)

the opium wars

Test your understanding of this chapter by filling in the blank line with the letter of the correct answer.

_____ 1. He took the Sudan for the British with his victory at Omdurman.

_____ 2. His attempt to modernize Egypt resulted in bankruptcy and foreign intervention.

_____ 3. He was a journalist, explorer, and employee of Leopold II.

_____ 4. He was a British paternalistic reformer in Egypt.

_____ 5. He argued that the strongest nations tend to be the best.

_____ 6. He "opened" Japan to the West in 1853.

_____ 7. He was a Chinese revolutionary and republican.

_____ 8. Under her leadership China was able to strengthen itself and maintain its traditional culture.

a. Sun Yat-sen
b. Evelyn Baring
c. Lord Kitchner
d. Walter Bagehot
e. Khedive Ismail
f. Commodore Perry
g. Empress Dowager Tzu Hsi
h. H. M. Stanley
i. Rudyard Kipling

MULTIPLE-CHOICE QUESTIONS

1. The Treaty of Nanking of 1842 ended a war between Great Britain and China that had started over
   a. Chinese expulsion of British diplomats from Canton.
   b. disagreement over shipping rights in Chinese ports.
   c. opium smuggled into China from British India.
   d. the British annexation of Manchuria.

2. The great migration of the nineteenth century was caused by
   a. population pressure.
   b. lack of employment in Europe.
   c. desire for political and social rights.
   d. all of the above.

3. The most persuasive Western argument against European imperialism was that
   a. it was not economically profitable.
   b. European control of nonwhites was immoral and hypocritical.
   c. not enough investment was made in colonies.
   d. it was unworthy of great nations.

4. Western influence on Japan resulted in
   a. a Westernized country that began to practice its own form of imperialism.
   b. a country subject to Britain in the same way that India was.
   c. a country subject to the United States in the same way that India was subject to Britain.
   d. no effect at all.

5. After the opium wars China
   a. began to industrialize rapidly.
   b. recovered for a number of years under the Empress Dowager.
   c. defeated Japan in the Sino-Japanese War of 1894-95.
   d. established a communist dictatorship to crush the Boxer Rebellion.

6. After 1840, world trade
   a. grew slowly as prices increased.
   b. grew rapidly as prices decreased.
   c. remained about the same as during the early decades of the century.
   d. declined because of the rise of protective barriers.

7. Which of the following did not facilitate the growth of world trade after 1840?
   a. The British policy of free trade
   b. Reduction of transportation costs
   c. The opening of the Suez and Panama canals
   d. The rise in price of raw materials and food

8. Which of the following characterizes the traditional attitude of Chinese society toward European society?
   a. Great interest in European products
   b. A desire to open trade ports to European capitalists
   c. A need for Europe as a source of capital and market for Chinese tea
   d. Considerable disinterest in Europe

9. The war between Britain and China, which ended in 1842, was caused by
   a. Chinese penetration into southeast Asia.
   b. British merchants' demand to sell opium to the Chinese.
   c. the Chinese naval blockade of the Japanese coast.
   d. all of the above

10. Japan was "opened" by the United States as a result of
    a. a military display of force.
    b. long and arduous negotiations.
    c. a willingness on the part of Japan.
    d. the opium wars.

11. Throughout the nineteenth century, European population and emigration tended to
    a. increase.
    b. decrease slightly.
    c. remain about the same.
    d. decrease significantly.

12. As a percentage of the total population, the area that was most affected by the entrance of Europeans into its land was
    a. the United States.
    b. Argentina.
    c. Russia.
    d. Peru.

13. For the most part, the people who left Europe to settle elsewhere were
    a. the poorest and least skilled of society.
    b. middle-class adventurers in search of new fortunes.
    c. small landowners and village craftsmen.
    d. none of the above

14. The return of the migrant to his or her native land was
    a. rare.
    b. not uncommon.
    c. common only among the Irish.
    d. common only among those migrating to Argentina.

15. In the nineteenth century, two out of three migrants to Argentina and Brazil came from
    a. Italy.
    b. Africa.

    c. Ireland.

    d. northern Europe.

16. The groups of east European migrants *least* likely to return to Europe were
    a. Poles.
    b. Jews.
    c. Germans.
    d. migrants from the Balkan lands.

17. The great European scramble for possession of Africa occurred
    a. prior to 1850.
    b. after 1900.
    c. between 1880 and 1900.
    d. around 1850.

18. The victor of the Fashoda incident in Africa was
    a. Britain.
    b. France.
    c. Germany.
    d. Belgium.

19. By the late 1870s the British were increasingly interested in acquiring colonies because of
    a. the increased belief that colonies were necessary to support naval supremacy.
    b. the rise of Germany and America as industrial powers.
    c. the fear of "protectionism" on the part of other European powers and the United States.
    d. all of the above

20. The radical English economist J. S. Hobson argued in his book, *Imperialism*, that the motive for colonial imperialism was
    a. economic.
    b. political.
    c. military.
    d. overpopulation.

GEOGRAPHY

1. On the map of Africa, locate and label each of the following colonies and indicate to which European nation it belonged.

Union of South Africa	Madagascar	Algeria	French Equatorial Africa
Belgian Congo	Orange Free State	Libya	Nigeria
German East Africa	Transvaal	Egypt	
British East Africa	Gold Coast	Morocco	

2. Explain why and how Britain and France acquired so much African territory.

3. Locate Fashoda. What happened here and where else may the British and the French come into conflict?

4. Use earlier history to help explain why little Portugal got so much African territory.

5. On the map of Asia, locate and label the following places and indicate which western nation exercised control or domination.

French Indochina	Philippine Islands	Port Arthur	Korea
India	Canton	Macao	Manchuria
Suez Canal	Dutch East Indies	Hong Kong	Formosa
Vladivostok			

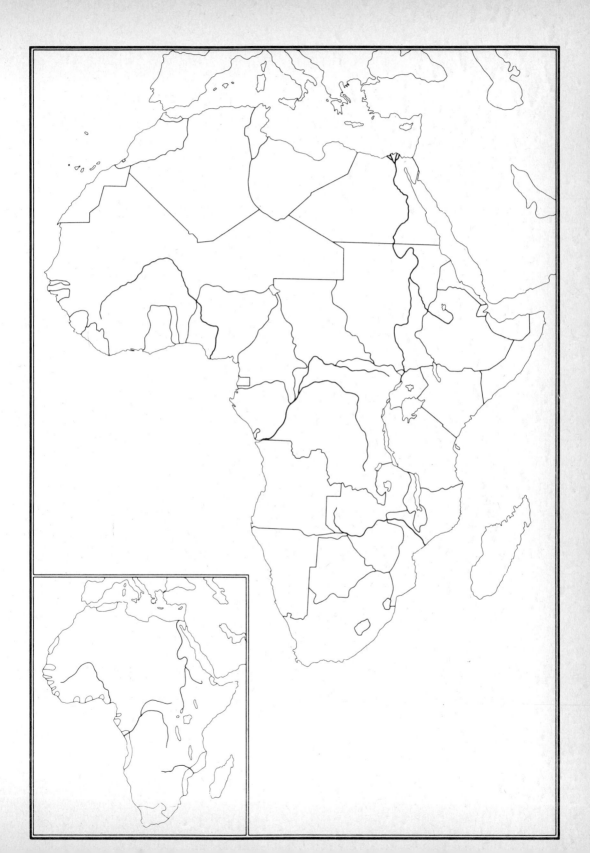

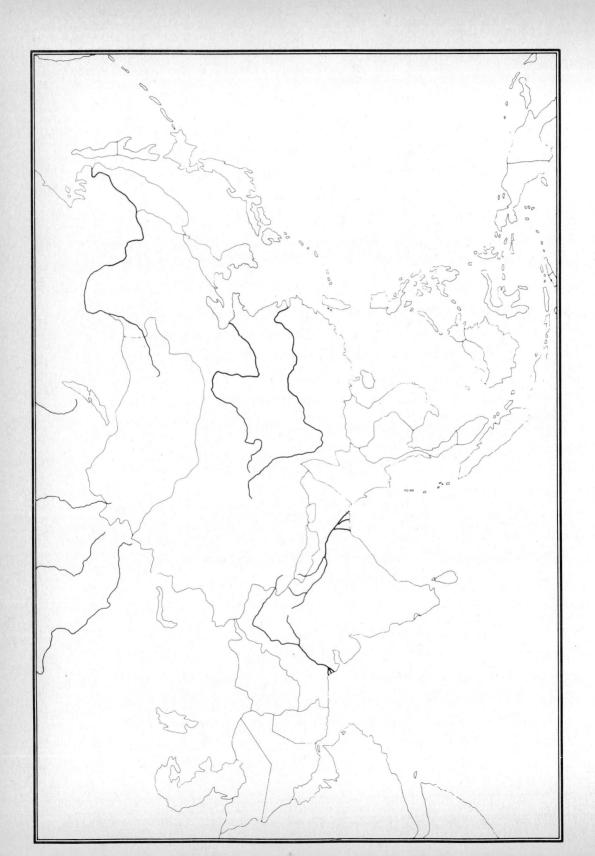

6. Why were Russian and Japanese imperialists likely to collide in Korea?

7. What were the economic and political motives of the British on Asia? What was the importance of the Suez Canal to the British military or to British merchants?

UNDERSTANDING HISTORY THROUGH READING AND THE ARTS

A striking and fascinating study of one of the greatest of the imperialist-militarists is P. Magnus, *Kitchner: Portrait of an Imperialist** (1959, 1968). Imperialist adventure, as found in works such as R. Kipling, *Kim* and *In Black and White*, and J. Conrad, *Lord Jim*, has become part of the classical literature of our time.

One woman's life in Africa is the subject of the award winning film *Out of Africa* (1984) and can be found in I. Dinesen, *Letters from Africa, 1914-1931** (1981, translated by A. Born).

Few operas have enjoyed the popularity of Giacomo Puccini's *Madame Butterfly* (1904). This Italian tragic grand opera is set in Japan and centers on the marriage of an American naval lieutenant and a Japanese woman.

PROBLEMS FOR FURTHER INVESTIGATION

What were the causes of imperialism and what made the system of "empire" work? Was empire a system that developed its own internal logic and reason for being? The various causes for the changed nature of imperialism in the 1880s are discussed in H. M. Wright, ed., *The "New Imperialism"** (1961). Imperialism in Africa is analyzed by a number of historians in R. F. Betts, ed., *The "Scramble" for Africa** (1966), and a good general description of the greatest imperialist nation, Great Britain, is to be had in B. Porter, *The Lion's Share, A Short History of British Imperialism, 1850-1970* (1975)*.

*Available in paperback.

CHAPTER 27

THE GREAT BREAK: WAR AND
REVOLUTION

CHAPTER OBJECTIVES

After reading and studying this chapter you should be able to answer the following questions:

Q-1. What were the causes of the First World War?
Q-2. How and why did the war have such enormous and destructive consequences?
Q-3. What impact did the war have on the ways in which people lived and thought?

CHAPTER SYNOPSIS

The First World War had enormous and destructive consequences. Western civilization would never be the same again—as the war caused not only death and destruction, but a variety of revolutions as well. The First World War was long and destructive, opening a new era in European history. This chapter shows how and why this was so. Beginning with the system of alliances that had formed two hostile military blocs by 1914, the author shows how nationalism and fears of nationalism touched off a world war in 1914. Contrary to expectations, the First World War became a ghastly military stalemate. The stalemate forced each government to make a total war effort, which demanded great sacrifices and major social changes. Economic life was strictly controlled, women entered defense plants, and nationalistic propaganda strengthened genuine popular support for the war. By 1916, however, there was growing discontent and war weariness in all countries.

Russia broke first under the enormous strains of total war. In March 1917, a moderate patriotic revolution established a Russian republic. In November 1917, Lenin and the Bolsheviks took power in a socialist revolution. Lenin was a dedicated revolutionary who had reinterpreted Marxism in a radical way before 1914, and he took Russia out of the war and established a harsh dictatorship. This dictatorship allowed the Bolshevik government to survive and to defeat many different foes in a bloody civil war. Revolution also occurred in Germany and Austria. Germany established a republic, and Austria-Hungary broke into pieces. In 1919, the world of 1914 lay in ruins, due to the impact of total war and radical revolution. Nor did the peace settlement of Versailles bring stability, since the defeated Germans hated the peace treaty and the victorious Americans rejected it.

STUDY OUTLINE

I. The First World War (1914-1918)
    A. The Bismarckian system of alliances
        1. Germany was the powerful European country after 1871
        2. Bismarck sought to guarantee European peace through alliances
        3. The Three Emperors' League (Austria, Russia, and Germany) was created (1873) to maintain the status quo
        4. Because of tensions with France, Italy joined Germany and Austria to form the Triple Alliance (1882)
        5. In 1887, the Russian-German Reinsurance Treaty promised neutrality by each state if the other was attacked
    B. The rival blocs
        1. William II's termination of the German-Russian Reinsurance Treaty led to a new Russian-French alliance
        2. Under William II, the British-German "natural alliance" deteriorated into a rivalry
            a. The Boer War, German envy of British imperialism, and economic and military rivalry drove the British and the Germans apart
            b. Then Britain turned to France and formed the Anglo-French Entente of 1904, which further alienated Germany
        3. As a result, Germany became increasingly distrustful, and other European countries began to see Germany as a threat
    C. The outbreak of war (August 1914)
        1. Nationalism in the Balkans threatened the Ottoman Empire and European peace
        2. Independence was acquired by Serbia, Rumania, and part of Bulgaria in 1878
        3. Austria's annexation of Bosnia in 1908 greatly angered Serbia, which was forced to turn southward in its nationalistic desire to expand, and so began the first Balkan War (1912)

    4. The Balkan wars of 1912-13 were a victory for Balkan nationalism
    5. The assassination of the Austrian archduke Francis Ferdinand (1914) resulted in a Balkan war between Serbia and Austria
    6. Germany gave Austria full support in her foreign policy
    7. Military considerations dictated policy, and an all-European war resulted

  D. Reflections on the origins of the war
    1. With German support, Austria was the immediate cause
    2. Germany's failure to keep Bismarck's system of alliances was fateful
    3. Nationalism contributed to war fever
    4. All the European leaders underestimated the consequences of war

  E. The first battle of the Marne (September 1914)
    1. The original Schlieffen plan—a German invasion of France through Belgium—had to be altered when British troops landed to help the Belgians
    2. The battle of the Marne turned the war into a long stalemate

  F. Stalemate and slaughter
    1. Trench warfare meant much horrible death but no end to the war
    2. The war's horrors caused a profound disillusionment with society and mankind

  G. The widening war
    1. Despite huge Austrian losses, Austria and Germany defeated Russia and Serbia on the eastern front (1914-15)
    2. Italy and Bulgaria entered the war (1915)
    3. With Arab help Britain defeated the Ottoman Empire (1918)
    4. The United States entered the war in 1917 because of German submarine warfare

II. The home front
  A. Mobilizing for total war
    1. Most people saw the war in nationalistic terms
    2. Total war meant that economic planning was necessary
    3. This control of economic and social life ultimately strengthened socialist ideas
    4. In Germany, food and raw materials were rationed and universal draft was initiated

  B. The social impact
    1. Labor shortages brought about benefits for organized labor
    2. The role of women changed dramatically as many women entered the labor force
      a. Some European women gained the right to vote after the war
      b. Women displayed a growing spirit of independence
    3. War brought about greater social equality

C. Growing political tensions
    1. Wartime propaganda was widespread
    2. By 1916, people were growing weary of war; morale had declined
    3. Demands for social reform and national self-determination re-emerged

III. The Russian Revolution (1917)
  A. The fall of imperial Russia
    1. War losses and mistakes pointed to the incompetence of the tsar and the Russian government
    2. Tsar Nicholas II's poor leadership contributed to military defeat
    3. The Duma sought a more responsive and democratic government
    4. The influence of Rasputin on the royal family further weakened the government and created a national scandal
    5. Food shortages led to revolution in March 1917
      a. A provisional government was proclaimed by the parliament (Duma)
      b. The tsar abdicated

  B. The provisional government (March 1917)
    1. After the March Revolution, Russia became the freest country in the world
    2. Yet the new revolutionary government, led by Kerensky, wanted to postpone land reform, fearing it would further weaken the peasant army; the continuation of the war was Kerensky's primary concern
    3. The provisional government had to share power with the Petrograd Soviet (council) of Workers' and Soldiers' Deputies
      a. The Petrograd Soviet's Army Order No. 1 placed military authority in the hands of ordinary soldiers
      b. Army discipline broke down completely, and massive desertions began
    4. Liberty was rapidly turning into anarchy

  C. Lenin and the Bolshevik Revolution
    1. Lenin believed that revolution was necessary to destroy capitalism
    2. He also believed that Marxist revolution could occur in Russia if led by an intellectual elite
    3. Russian Marxists became divided over Lenin's theories
      a. Lenin's Bolsheviks demanded a small, disciplined, elitist party
      b. The Mensheviks wanted a democratic party with mass membership
    4. Lenin led an attack against the provisional government in July 1917, but it failed and he went into hiding
    5. Kerensky's power was weakened by an attack on the provisional government by his commander in chief, Kornilov, and he lost favor with the army

  D. Trotsky and the seizure of power

1. A radical Marxist and supporter of Lenin, Trotsky centered his power in the Petrograd Soviet
2. Trotsky engineered a Soviet overthrow of the provisional government (November 1917)

E. Dictatorship and civil war
1. Lenin gave approval to the peasants' seizure of land and the urban workers' takeover of the factories
2. Lenin arranged for an end of the war with Germany, but at a high price: the sacrifice of all of Russia's western territories (the Treaty of Brest-Litovsk, 1918)
3. Opposition to the Bolsheviks led to civil war (1918-1921)
   a. The officers of the old army (the Whites) organized the opposition to the Bolsheviks (the Reds)
   b. The Whites came from many social groups and wanted self-rule, not Bolshevik dictatorship
4. The Bolshevik victory in the civil war was due to a number of factors: unity, a better army, a well-defined political program, mobilization of the home front, an effective secret police force, and an appeal to nationalism in the face of foreign aid to the Whites
5. World War I brought on the Russian Revolution, which signaled the rise of world communism

IV. The Versailles peace settlement (1918-19)
A. The end of the war
1. By early 1917, the German populace was weary of war, and the German army was decisively defeated in the second battle of the Marne
2. The Allies were strengthened by American intervention.
3. The German military arranged for a new liberal German government to accept defeat, but it tried to bargain for an advantageous settlement
4. German soldiers and workers began to demonstrate for peace, and Germany surrendered (1918)

B. Revolution in Austria-Hungary and Germany
1. Revolution in Austria-Hungary led to the breakup of the Austro-Hungarian Empire into new national states
2. Revolution in Germany led to a socialist government
3. Moderate German socialists attacked the radical socialists who then founded the German Communist Party

C. The Treaty of Versailles
1. President Wilson was obsessed with creating a League of Nations to avert future wars
2. Clemenceau of France and Lloyd George of England were more interested in permanently weakening Germany and making it pay for the war

   3. The conflicting desires of the Allies led to a deadlock and finally a compromise
      a. France gave up its demand for a protective buffer state in return for a defensive alliance with Britain and the United States
      b. The League of Nations was created
   4. Germany lost her colonies and territory in Europe—largely Alsace-Lorraine, Danzig, and eastern land to Poland.
   5. Germany had to admit responsibility for the war and thus pay enormous damages
   6. Austria-Hungary and Turkey were the big losers in the separate peace treaties; the principle of self-determination still applied only to Europeans, and thus Western imperialism lived on
D. American rejection of the Versailles treaty
   1. World peace rested on
      a. The success in upholding the principle of national self-determination
      b. The success of the new democratic German government
      c. American support of the Western alliance—including the League of Nations, which the United States refused to join
   2. President Wilson refused to accept any modifications to the treaty, so it was never ratified, and the Senate also refused to ratify the defensive alliance with France
E. World War I had revolutionary consequences
   1. The war was a result of nationalism
   2. The war swept away monarchs and multinational empires, and national self-determination triumphed
   3. The war brought on the Russian Revolution
   4. It ushered in a new age that saw the increased presence of government in everyday life, more economic planning, and greater social equality

REVIEW QUESTIONS

Q-1. Discuss the motives and interests of each of the Great Powers between 1871 and 1914.

Q-2. What was the purpose of the German-Russian Reinsurance Treaty? Why did it end in 1890 and with what results?

Q-3. What were the reasons for Britain and Germany's so-called love-hate relationship?

Q-4. Why was the Moroccan crisis of 1905 a turning point in European diplomacy?

Q-5. What impact did the Congress of Berlin (1878) have on the Balkan area? Who was bound to be the loser in the Balkans?

Q-6. Describe the origins and causes of the "third Balkan war" in 1914.

Q-7. Which of the major powers do you believe most responsible and least responsible for the war? Explain.

Q-8. What impact did the war have on the economy and the people at home? How cooperative was the population?

Q-9. Did the war have any effect on the power of organized labor? On women in society?

Q-10. "The war tended to have an equalizing effect on society." Explain.

Q-11. What evidence is there that the strain of war was beginning to take its toll on the home front in Russia, Austria, France, and Germany by 1916?

Q-12. What were the reasons for the Russian Revolution in March 1917? Was revolution inevitable?

Q-13. What were the soviets? What role did they play in the Bolshevik Revolution?

Q-14. What was it about Lenin's character that made him a successful revolutionary? Why would his ideas be popular with peasants and urban workers?

Q-15. Why did Kerensky and the provisional government fail?

Q-16. What were the reasons for the Bolshevik victory in the civil war?

Q-17. Were there one, two, or many Russian revolutions in 1917? Explain.

Q-18. What happened to the Austro-Hungarian and Turkish empires after 1918?

Q-19. What were the goals of Wilson, Lloyd George, and Clemenceau at the Versailles peace conference?

Q-20. The Treaty of Versailles is often seen as a major reason for World War II. Do you agree? Why?

Q-21. Compare and contrast the Versailles settlement of 1919 with the Vienna settlement of 1815. What similarities do you see? What were the most striking differences?

STUDY-REVIEW EXERCISES

Explain who or what each of the following was and what role each played in the Russian Revolution.

Petrograd Soviet

Leon Trotsky

Petrograd bread riots (1917)

Congress of the Soviets

Kiev mutiny (1918)

Alexander Kerensky

Vladimir Lenin

Army Order No. 1

Constituent Assembly

White opposition

Treaty of Brest-Litovsk (1918)

Number the following events in Russian history in chronological order.

1. _____ Marx writes the *Communist Manifesto*

2. _____ Lenin's return from Switzerland

3. _____ The establishment of the provisional government

4. _____ The outbreak of war between Russia and Germany

5. _____ The Kornilov plot

6. _____ The abolishment of the Constituent Assembly

7. _____ The overthrow of Kerensky and the provisional government

8. _____ American, British, and Russian invasion of Archangel and Vladivostok

Define the following key concepts and terms.

Schlieffen Plan

"total war"

totalitarian

"blank check" policy

the western front

Bolsheviks

"war communism"

principle of national self-determination

war reparations

Identify each of the following and give its significance.

Lawrence of Arabia

Reinsurance Treaty

Algerciras Conference of 1906

Anglo-French Entente of 1904

Third Balkan War (1914)

Lusitania

Admiral Tirpitz

(German) Auxiliary Service Law of 1916

David Lloyd George

Rasputin

Francis Ferdinand

Georges Clemenceau

Duma

Test your understanding of the chapter by answering the following questions.

1. Germany violated this country's neutrality in 1914. _____

2. He was exiled to Siberia for socialist agitation. _____

3. Called "the tiger," he wanted to punish Germany. _____

4. He was the Bolshevik war commissar. _____

5. This Russian was called "our Friend Grigori." _____
6. The name of the important German war plan designed for a two-front war.

   _____

7. The date of the assassination of Archduke Francis Ferdinand. _____
8. The president of the revolutionary provisional government.

   _____

9. Russian workers' councils were called _____ .

10. He aroused the Arab princes to revolt in 1917. _____
11. The name of the treaty between the Germans and the Russian Bolshevik govern-

    ment in 1918. _____

12. The German chancellor fired by William II. _____

13. A Serbian revolutionary group. _____

14. The first country to mobilize for European war in 1914. _____
15. This country received control over Iraq and Palestine in 1919.

    _____

16. The Russian parliament that Nicholas adjourned in 1914.

    _____

MULTIPLE-CHOICE QUESTIONS

1. The Bismarckian system of alliances was meant to
   a. expand Germany's borders.
   b. help German allies expand their borders.
   c. restrain Russia and Austria-Hungary and isolate France.
   d. encourage relations with France.

2. Which group of events is in chronological order?
   a. The Three Emperors' League, the Alliance of the Three Emperors, the Russian-German Reinsurance Treaty
   b. The Russian-German Reinsurance Treaty, the Alliance of the Three Emperors, the Three Emperors' League
   c. The Alliance of the Three Emperors, the Russian-German Reinsurance Treaty, the Three Emperors' League
   d. The Russian-German Reinsurance Treaty, the Three Emperors' League, the Alliance of the Three Emperors

3. Which of the following was *not* a factor in the strained German-British relations before the First World War?
   a. The Boer War
   b. The Anglo-French Entente
   c. The German naval buildup
   d. The Anglo-American Agreement

4. The Schlieffen Plan called for Germany to knock out
   a. England by marching through France.
   b. Russia by marching through Poland.
   c. France by marching through Belgium.
   d. Belgium by marching through France.

5. Which of the following is *not* usually considered a cause of the First World War?
   a. British appeasement of the Germans
   b. Nationalism
   c. German aggressiveness
   d. Unawareness of political conditions on the part of governing classes

6. Which of the following was *not* a consequence of the First World War?
   a. The strengthening of socialism
   b. The exclusion of labor leaders from government
   c. Better jobs for women
   d. A lessening gap between rich and poor

7. Which of the following was *not* a central idea of Lenin?
   a. Revolution can occur in a backward country
   b. Revolution is determined more by human leadership than by intangible historical laws
   c. The necessity for a strictly controlled worker's party
   d. The continuation of the war against Germany

8. The end of the war in 1918 brought revolution to which of the following countries?
   a. France and Britain
   b. Germany and Italy
   c. Germany and Austria-Hungary
   d. France and Italy

9. Which was *not* an issue at the peace conference at Versailles after the war?
   a. A league of nations
   b. A defensive alliance in favor of France with the United States and Britain
   c. The re-establishment of Russian borders
   d. The cost of German reparations

10. The phrase that best describes Bismarck's attitude toward German expansion after 1871 is
    a. German control of all Europe.
    b. the annexation of Austria-Hungary to Germany.
    c. no territorial ambitions.
    d. a great German navy and German colonies.

11. The young Emperor William II of Germany made the fateful decision to reverse Bismarck's foreign policy by refusing to renew the treaty between Germany and
    a. Austria.
    b. Britain.
    c. France.
    d. Russia.

12. As a result of the Moroccan crisis, European powers viewed which of the following countries as a threat to peace and stability?
    a. France
    b. Germany
    c. Britain
    d. Japan

13. The countries with the most at stake in the Balkans and most fearful of nationalism were
    a. Germany and Austria.
    b. France and Turkey.
    c. Turkey and Austria.
    d. Russia and Germany.

14. The first country to mobilize in 1914 for general warfare was
    a. France.
    b. Germany.
    c. Russia.
    d. Britain.

15. The chief feature of the war on the western front was
    a. inconclusive battles fought in ceaseless trench warfare.
    b. the invasion of Germany by French and British troops.
    c. a series of German victories at the German-French border.
    d. a propaganda war with little actual fighting.

16. The major impact of World War I on economic thought was the
    a. promotion of government planning and involvement in the economy.
    b. strengthening of capitalism based on laissez-faire principles.
    c. reaffirmation of imperialism.
    d. proof that civilian populations were unimportant to the war economy.

17. For women in European society, the First World War brought about
    a. overall economic and political improvement.
    b. some economic gains but no political gains.
    c. a setback in the struggle for women's rights.
    d. a deterioration of their economic position.

18. The Petrograd Soviet's "Army Order No. 1" resulted in
    a. a renewed and effective war effort.
    b. a complete breakdown of army discipline.
    c. increased authority of the Russian military elite.
    d. large numbers of new recruits.

19. Lenin's appeal to the people of Russia centered on the cry
    a. "All land to the peasants."
    b. "All power to the Soviets."
    c. "Stop the war now."
    d. none of the above

20. As a result of the Treaty of Brest-Litovsk, Russia
    a. acquired considerable territory.
    b. re-entered the war on the German side.
    c. agreed to spread the revolution to western Europe.
    d. lost one-third of its population.

21. Which of the following was *not* included in the Treaty of Versailles?
    a. A clause was inserted that placed blame for the war on Germany and her allies.
    b. German colonies were taken away.
    c. German territory was given to Poland.
    d. Germany was allowed to keep Alsace-Lorraine but had to give up the city of Danzig.

22. The most anti-German of the major power representatives at the Versailles treaty conference in 1919 was
    a. Clemenceau of France.
    b. Lloyd George of Britain.
    c. Wilson of the United States.
    d. Orlando of Italy.

GEOGRAPHY

1. Study Maps 27.1 and 27.2. Referring to the text when necessary, answer the following questions.

    a. Using Map 27.2, describe the ethnic make-up of the Balkans.

    b. Locate the extent of Ottoman (Turkish) control in the Balkans in 1878 and in 1914. Describe how and why it lost territory.

c. What were the territorial ambitions of Serbia and Austria-Hungary in the Balkans?

2. Study Map 27.3. Referring to the text when necessary, answer the following questions.

   a. What was the western front and where did it exist? Compare it with the eastern front.

   b. Locate the following important battles of the First World War: Gallipoli, Passchendaele, Tannenburg, and Verdun. In each case, who fought, what was the outcome, and what was the significance?

3. Study Map 27.4 to understand some of the changes brought by the First World War. Answer the following questions.

   a. Locate the Polish corridor, Alsace and Lorraine, the three new Baltic states, and Galicia. What happened to each of these areas because of the First World War, and what was the significance?

   b. Locate the demilitarized zone along the Rhine. How did this strengthen the French military position?

c. Locate the territorial losses experienced by the three great empires—Germany, Austria, and Russia. How did the losses reflect the principle of self-determination?

UNDERSTANDING HISTORY THROUGH READING AND THE ARTS

Few books have captured the tragedy of World War I as well as Erich Remarque's novel *All Quiet on the Western Front**, while A. Horne's *The Price of Glory: Verdun 1916* (1979) recounts the horror of the western-front battle that cost 700,000 lives.

The war, the hemophiliac child, Rasputin, and the murder of the royal family by the Bolsheviks are all brought together in an interesting book about Russia in the era of the revolution, *Nicholas and Alexandra** (1971) by R. Massie. Lenin's impact on history is best covered in L. Fischer, *The Life of Lenin** (1964, 1965), and in C. Hill, *Lenin and the Russian Revolution* (1947, 1971)*, while the standard work on Leon Trotsky is a three-volume work (1954-63) by I. Deutscher. Bismarck's important foreign policy is covered in W. Medlicott and D. Coveney, eds., *Bismarck and Europe* (1972).

PROBLEMS FOR FURTHER INVESTIGATION

Was Germany responsible for the Great War? This has been one of the most-debated subjects in political-diplomatic history in recent years. One of the chief revisionists is A. J. P. Taylor, *The Struggle for Mastery in Europe, 1848-1919* (1954), while a recent anti-German argument has come from E. Fischer, *The German War Aims in World War I* (1967). The debate is discussed in D. E. Lee, *The Outbreak of the First World War** (1970).

The problem of interpreting the revolution in Russia, current interpretations, and key themes are examined in a short but valuable book, *The Russian Revolution and Bolshevik Victory: Why and How?** by A. E. Adams (1960).

*Available in paperback.

READING WITH UNDERSTANDING
EXERCISE 6

LEARNING HOW TO MAKE HISTORICAL COMPARISONS

An important part of studying history is learning how to *compare* two (or more) related historical developments. Such comparisons not only demonstrate a basic understanding of the two objects being compared, but also permit the student-historian to draw distinctions that indicate real insight.

For these reasons, "compare-and-contrast" questions have long been favorites of history professors, and they often appear on essay exams. Even when they do not, they are an excellent study device for synthesizing historical information and testing your understanding. Therefore, as the introductory essay suggests, *try to anticipate* what compare-and-contrast questions your instructor might ask. Then work up your own study outlines that summarize the points your essay answer would discuss and develop. The preparation of study outlines of course is also a useful preparation for essay questions that do not require you to compare and contrast.

Exercise

Read the brief passage below. Reread it and underline or highlight it for main points. Now study the passage in terms of "compare and contrast." Prepare a brief outline (solely on the basis of this material) that will allow you to compare and contrast the Russian and German revolutions (of 1917-1919). After you have finished, compare your outline with the model on page F-3. Remember: the model provides a *good* answer, not the *only* answer.

The German Revolution of November 1918 resembled the Russian Revolution of March 1917. In both cases a genuine popular uprising toppled an authoritarian monarchy and established a liberal provisional republic. In both countries liberals and moderate socialists took control of the central government, while workers' and soldiers' councils formed a "countergovernment." In Germany, however, the moderate socialists won and the Lenin-like radical revolutionaries in the councils lost. In communist terms, the liberal, republican revolution in Germany in 1918 was only "half" a revolution: a "bourgeois" political revolution without a communist second installment. It was Russia without Lenin's Bolshevik triumph.

There were several reasons for the German outcome. The great majority of Marxian socialist leaders in the Social Democratic party were, as before the war, really pink and not red. They wanted to establish real political democracy and civil liberties, and they favored the gradual elimination of capitalism. They were also German nationalists, appalled by the prospect of civil war and revolutionary terror. Moreover, there was much less popular support among workers and soldiers for the extreme radicals than in Russia. Nor did the German peasantry, which already had most of the land, at least in western Germany, provide the elemental force that has driven all great modern revolutions, from the French to the Chinese.

Of crucial importance also was the fact that the moderate German Social Democrats, unlike Kerensky and company, accepted defeat and ended the war the day they took power. This act ended the decline in morale among soldiers and prevented the regular army with its conservative officer corps from disintegrating. When radicals headed by Karl Liebknecht and Rosa Luxemburg and their supporters in the councils tried to seize control of the government in Berlin in January, the moderate socialists called on the army to crush the uprising. Liebknecht and Luxemburg were arrested and then brutally murdered by army leaders. Finally, even if the moderate socialists had taken the Leninist path, it is very unlikely they would have succeeded. Civil war in Germany would certainly have followed, and the Allies, who were already occupying western Germany according to the terms of the armistice, would have marched on to Berlin and ruled Germany directly. Historians have often been unduly hard on Germany's moderate socialists.

Comparison of Russian and German Revolutions (1917-1918)

Similarities

1. Both countries had genuine
   liberal revolutions.
   a. Russia—March 1917
   b. Germany—November 1918

2. In both countries moderate
   socialists took control.

Differences

1. Russia had a second, radical
   (Bolshevik) revolution; Germany
   did not.

2. In Germany workers and peasants
   gave radicals less support than in
   Russia.

3. In Germany the moderate Socialists stopped the war immediately
   and therefore the German army,
   unlike the Russian army, remained
   intact to put down radical uprisings.

CHAPTER 28

THE AGE OF ANXIETY

CHAPTER OBJECTIVES

After reading and studying this chapter you should be able to answer the following questions:

Q-1. How were the postwar feelings of crisis and anxiety reflected in Western thought, art, and culture?

Q-2. How did political leaders try to maintain peace and prosperity between 1919 and 1939?

CHAPTER SYNOPSIS

Because war and revolution had shattered so many traditional ideas, beliefs, and institutions, many people of the postwar era found themselves living in an age of anxiety and continuous crisis. The first half of this chapter deals with major changes in ideas and in culture that were connected to this age of anxiety. Some of these changes began before 1900, but they became widespread only after the great upheaval of World War I affected millions of ordinary people and opened an era of uncertainty and searching. People generally became less optimistic and had less faith in rational thinking. Radically new theories in physics associated with Albert Einstein and Werner Heisenberg took form, while Sigmund Freud's psychology gave a new and disturbing interpretation of human behavior. Philosophy and literature developed in new ways, and Christianity took on renewed meaning for thinking people. There was also great searching and experimentation in architecture, painting, and music, all of which went in new directions. Much painting became abstract, as did some music. Movies and radio programs, which offered entertainment and escape, gained enormous popularity among the general public. In short, there were revolutionary changes in thought, art, and popular culture.

The second half of this chapter discusses efforts to re-establish real peace and political stability in the troubled era after 1918. The author believes Germany was the key area. In 1923, hostility between France and Germany led to an undeclared war when French armies occupied Germany's industrial heartland. This crisis was resolved, though, and followed by a period of cautious hope in international politics between 1924 and 1929. The stock market crash in the United States in 1929, however, brought renewed economic and political crisis to the Western world. Attempts to meet this crisis in the United States, Sweden, Britain, and France were only partly successful. Thus, economic and political difficulties accompanied and reinforced the revolution in thought and culture. It was a hard time in Western society.

STUDY OUTLINE

I. Uncertainty in modern thought
    A. The effects of World War I
        1. Many people rejected the long-accepted beliefs in progress and the power of the rational mind to understand a logical universe and an orderly society
            a. Even before the war, Nietzsche believed that Western civilization had lost its creativity by neglecting emotion
            b. Bergson and Sorel pointed out the limits of rational and scientific thinking
            c. Valéry wrote about the crisis of the cruelly injured mind
        2. Throughout the 1920s and 1930s there arose a growing pessimism
    B. The new physics
        1. The challenge to Newtonian physics by scientists such as Planck and Einstein undermined belief in constant natural laws
        2. The 1920s was the "heroic age of physics"
            a. Rutherford split the atom
            b. Subatomic particles were identified, notably the neutron
        3. The new physics described a universe that lacked absolute objective reality and direct relevance to human experience
    C. Freudian psychology
        1. According to Freud, human behavior is basically irrational
            a. The key to understanding the mind is the irrational unconscious (the id)
            b. Behavior is a compromise between the needs of the id (which is driven by sexual and instinctual desires) and the controls of the ego

(which tries to determine what a person can do) and the superego (moral values that tell what a person should do)

    2. Instinctual drives can easily overwhelm the control mechanisms; yet rigid repression can cripple people with guilt and neuroses

D. The intellectual crisis in philosophy: logical empiricism and existentialism

    1. In English-speaking countries, the main development in philosophy was logical empiricism, while on the Continent the primary development was existentialism

        a. Logical empiricism, as defined by Wittgenstein, claimed that philosophy was nothing more than the logical clarification of thought; it could not answer the great issues of the ages

        b. Existentialism, exemplified by Sartre and Camus, was the search for human and moral values in an uncertain world

    2. Unlike logical empiricism, existentialism offered a positive answer to profound moral issues and contemporary crises

E. The revival of Christianity

    1. A revitalization of fundamental Christianity took place after the First World War

    2. Christian Protestant theologians, who had previously sought to harmonize religious belief with scientific findings, stressed a return to faith and traditional doctrines, as in the writings of Kierkegaard and Barth

    3. Christian Catholic theologians, such as Marcel, found new hope in religion

F. Twentieth-century literature

    1. The postwar moods of pessimism, relativism, and alienation influenced novelists

    2. Literature focused on the irrationality of the human mind

    3. Writers such as Proust embraced psychological relativity—the attempt to understand oneself by looking at one's past—and the stream-of-consciousness technique (Woolf, Faulkner, Joyce)

    4. Much literature, such as that of Spengler, Kafka, and Orwell, was anti-utopian; that is, it predicted a future of doom

II. Modern art and music

A. Architecture and design

    1. The new idea of functionalism, or usefulness, revolutionized architecture with its emphasis on efficiency and clean lines instead of ornamentation

    2. The Chicago school of architects, led initially by Sullivan, pioneered in the building of skyscrapers

        b. Frank Lloyd Wright then used the same ideas to design truly modern houses

    3. The German Bauhaus school under Gropius became the major proponent of functional and industrial forms

    4. Le Corbusier stressed town planning while van der Rohe took European functionalism to Chicago

B. Modern painting

    1. French impressionism yielded to nonrepresentational expressionism, which sought to portray the worlds of emotion and imagination, as in the works of van Gogh, Gauguin, Cézanne, and Matisse

    2. Cubism (founded by Picasso) and abstract painting emerged from expressionism

    3. Surrealism became prominent in the 1920s and 1930s

C. Modern music

    1. The concept of expressionism also affected music, as in the work of Stravinsky

    2. Some composers, led by Schönberg, abandoned traditional harmony and tonality

D. Movies and radio

    1. The general public embraced movies and radio enthusiastically

    2. The movie factories and Charlie Chaplin created a new medium and a new culture

    3. Moviegoing became a form of escapism

    4. Radios and film were used for propaganda as well as entertainment

III. The search for peace and political stability

A. Germany and the Western powers

    1. Germany was the key to lasting peace, and the Germans hated the Treaty of Versailles

    2. France believed that an economically weak Germany was necessary for peace in Europe

    3. Britain needed a prosperous Germany in order to maintain the British economy

        a. J. M. Keynes, an economist, argued that the Versailles treaty crippled the European economy and needed revision

        b. His attack on the treaty contributed to guilt feelings about Germany in Britain

        c. As a result, France and Britain drifted apart

    4. When Germany refused to continue its heavy reparation payments, French and Belgian armies occupied the Ruhr (1923)

B. The occupation of the Ruhr

    1. Since Germany would not pay gold, France wanted to collect reparations in coal, steel, and machinery

    2. The Germans stopped work in the factories and France could not collect reparations, but the French occupation affected the German economy drastically

        a. Inflation skyrocketed

        b. Resentment and political unrest among the Germans grew

    3. Germany agreed to revised reparations payments and France withdrew its troops, but many Germans were left financially ruined and humiliated

C. Hope in foreign affairs (1924-1929)

    1. The Dawes and Young plans provided a solution to the reparations problem; the United States loaned money to Germany so it could pay France and Britain so they could pay the United States

    2. The treaties of Locarno eased European disputes

        a. Germany and France accepted their common border

        b. Britain agreed to fight if either country invaded the other

    3. The Kellogg-Briand Pact (1928) condemned war

D. Hope in democratic government

    1. Although republican democracy appeared to have the support of most Germans, Germany split into extreme right and left groups: the unrepentant nationalists and the Communists

    2. In France, the democratically elected government rested in the hands of the middle-class-oriented moderates, while the Communists battled for the support of the workers

    3. Northern France was rebuilt, and Paris became the world's cultural center

    4. Britain's major problem was unemployment, and the government's efforts to ease it led the country gradually toward socialism

IV. The Great Depression (1929-1939)

A. The economic crisis

    1. The depression began with the American stock market crash (October 1929)

    2. Financial crisis led to a decline in production in Europe and the United States and an unwise turn to protective tariffs

    3. The absence of international leadership and poor national policies added to the depression

B. Mass unemployment

    1. As production decreased, workers lost their jobs and had no money to buy goods, which cut production even more

    2. Mass unemployment also caused great social and psychological problems

C. The New Deal in the United States

    1. Roosevelt's goal was to preserve capitalism through reform

    2. Government intervention in and regulation of the economy first took place through the National Recovery Administration (NRA), whose task it was to fix prices and wages for everyone's benefit

      3. The NRA was declared unconstitutional (1935), and Roosevelt decided to attack the problem of unemployment directly by using the federal government to employ as many people as possible

          a. The Work Projects Administration was set up (1935) and employed millions of people

          b. It was very popular and helped check the threat of social revolution

      4. Other social measures, such as social security and government support for labor unions, also eased the hardships of the depression

      5. Although the New Deal helped, it failed to pull the United States out of the depression

          a. Some believe Roosevelt should have nationalized industry so national economic planning could have worked

          b. Many economists argued that the public works projects were not extensive enough

  D. The Scandinavian response to depression

      1. Backed by a strong tradition of community cooperation, socialist parties were firmly established in Sweden and Norway by the 1920s

      2. Deficit spending to finance public works and create jobs was used to check unemployment and revive the economy after 1929

      3. Scandinavia's welfare socialism offered an appealing middle way between capitalism and communism or fascism in the 1930s

  E. Recovery and reform in Britain and France

      1. Britain's concentration on its national market aided its economic recovery

      2. Government instability in France prevented recovery and needed reform

          a. The Socalists, led by Blum, became the strongest party in France and attempted New Deal-type reforms

          b. France was drawn to the brink of civil war, and Blum was forced to resign (1937), leaving the country to drift aimlessly

REVIEW QUESTIONS

Q-1. Define "quanta" and its implications for the definition of matter and energy.

Q-2. Define and discuss the relationship among the id, ego, and superego.

Q-3. Freud's view that human beings are basically irrational coincides with the picture of the universe drawn by modern physics. Discuss this relationship between psychology and science.

Q-4. Discuss the meaning of Sartre's statement that "man is condemned to be free." How is this thought connected to the existential belief that man must seek to define himself?

Q-5. What impact did the loss of faith in reason and progress have on twentieth-century Christian thought?

Q-6. French impressionism has been defined as "superrealism." Explain.

Q-7. Compare and contrast Gauguin's and Le Corbusier's concepts of art.

Q-8. How do impressionism and expressionism reflect the rationality and irrationality of the nineteenth and twentieth centuries, respectively?

Q-9. What influence did Freud have on twentieth-century painting?

Q-10. Discuss the attitudes of Britain, France, and Germany with regard to the Treaty of Versailles.

Q-11. The most serious international crisis of the 1920s occurred in the German Ruhr in January 1923. What was the crisis and what were its consequences?

Q-12. Describe the part played by the United States in the economic and political settlements of the mid-1920s in Europe.

Q-13. What problems faced the British governments of the 1920s and with what ideas did the Labour Party approach these problems?

Q-14. Discuss the origins, interests, and goals of the Labor and Liberal parties in Britain.

Q-15. What were the causes of the Great Depression?

Q-16. Trace the cause and effect of the recall of public and private loans to European countries.

Q-17. What was the NRA and why did it not work well?

Q-18. The New Deal ultimately failed to halt mass unemployment. Why? Why is it said that the WPA helped prevent social revolution in the United States?

Q-19. Why was the Scandinavian response to the economic crisis the most successful one in the Western democracies?

STUDY-REVIEW EXERCISES

Explain who the following people were and note how their work contributed to and reflected the uncertainty and anxiety in modern thought.

Friedrich Nietzsche

Georges Sorel

Henri Bergson

Max Planck

Sigmund Freud

Ludwig Wittgenstein

Jean-Paul Sartre

James Joyce

Oswald Spengler

George Orwell

Define the following philosophic and artistic schools and movements by describing their basic aims and characteristics and naming some participants and works.

modern existentialism

functionalism in architecture

Chicago school of architecture

expressionism in painting

cubism

dadaism

surrealism

expressionism in music

atonality

logical empiricism

Identify each of the following and give its significance.

Ramsay MacDonald

Treaty of Versailles

"Little Entente" of 1921

Ruhr crisis of 1923

Locarno meetings of 1925

Munich beer hall "revolution" of 1923

principle of uncertainty

French Popular Front

National Recovery Administration

BBC

Raymond Poincare

John Maynard Keynes

Guglielmo Marconi

Leni Riefenstahl

Test your understanding of the chapter by answering the following questions.

1. In January 1923, the German Ruhr was occupied by _____

    and _____ .

2. Most modern (postimpressionist) artistic movements *were/were not* concerned
    with the visible world of fact.

3. The Dawes Plan provided that _____ would get

    loans from the United States to pay reparations to _____

    and _____ so that they could repay their

    loans to _____ .

4. Modern painting grew out of a revolt against the _____ school of painting.

5. After 1914, people tended to *strengthen/discard* their belief in progress.

6. The works of modern physics tended to *confirm/challenge* the dependable laws of Newton.

7. The British economist who criticized the Versailles treaty and advocated a "counter-cyclical policy" to deal with depressed economies was

_____ .

MULTIPLE-CHOICE QUESTIONS

1. The country most interested in strict implementation of the Treaty of Versailles was
   a. France.
   b. Britain.
   c. the United States.
   d. Italy.

2. Which of the following did *not* occur during the early years of the Great Depression?
   a. Most countries went off the gold standard.
   b. Most countries raised tariffs.
   c. Americans recalled loans.
   d. Most governments increased their budgets and spending.

3. Which of the following countries was the most effective in dealing with the depression?
   a. France
   b. Britain
   c. Sweden
   d. The United States

4. Existentialists believed that
   a. the world was perfectible.
   b. only God was certain in this lost world.
   c. human beings can conquer life's absurdity.
   d. no human action can bring meaning to life.

5. The trend in literature in the postwar period was
    a. toward a new faith in God and mankind.
    b. the glorification of the state.
    c. the new belief in a world of growing desolation.
    d. utopian dreams of the future.

6. The German philosopher Friedrich Nietzsche believed that Western civilization
    a. had lost its creativity by neglecting emotion.
    b. should be rebuilt around Christian morality.
    c. needed to increase political democracy.
    d. should place more stress on social equality.

7. The modern or "international" style in architecture emphasized all but which one of the following?
    a. Practical and functional construction
    b. Town planning
    c. Massive exterior ornamentation
    d. The merger of fine and applied arts

8. According to the British economist J. M. Keynes, the key to lasting peace and prosperity in Europe after World War I was
    a. a powerful France and Russia.
    b. the growth of the British Empire.
    c. the enforcement of the Treaty of Versailles.
    d. a prosperous and strong Germany.

9. Which one of the following was *not* a cause of the Great Depression?
    a. Financial panic in the United States
    b. The absence of world financial leadership
    c. Unemployment
    d. The reduction of national spending

10. The British Labour Party leader and prime minister in 1924 and 1929 was
    a. MacDonald.
    b. Blum.
    c. Sartre.
    d. Keynes.

11. The "spirit of Locarno" after 1924 was a general European feeling that
     a. the communist overthrow of European governments was inevitable.
     b. Germany must be forced to pay her original reparation debts.
     c. European peace and security were possible.
     d. Hitler would bring about the recovery of Germany.

12. The decade following World War I was generally a period of
     a. uncertainty and dissatisfaction with established ideas.
     b. increasing belief in the goodness and perfectability of humanity.
     c. emphasis on the idea that a new science and technology would build a
         more democratic and liberal world.
     d. religious revival based on the human nature of Christ, and the basic good-
         ness of human beings.

13. The philosophy of logical empiricism held that
     a. great philosophical issues can never be decided.
     b. humanity must accept all truths as being absolute.
     c. humanity is basically sinful.
     d. there is no God.

14. The writings of Virginia Woolf, Marcel Proust, James Joyce, and William Faulk-
     ner all reflect the postwar concern with
     a. the reconstruction of society.
     b. an attempt to discover the reasons for the loss of faith in God.
     c. the conflict between materialism and spiritualism.
     d. the complexity and irrationality of the human mind.

15. Modern painting grew out of a revolt against
     a. classicism.
     b. capitalism.
     c. French impressionism.
     d. German romanticism.

16. The movement in painting that attacked all accepted standards of art and be-
     havior and delighted in outrageous conduct was
     a. the Bauhaus movement.
     b. brutalism.
     c. dada.
     d. cubism.

17. The great maker of Nazi propaganda films in Germany was
    a. Sergei Eisenstein.
    b. Mack Sennet.
    c. Alban Berg.
    d. none of the above

18. For the people of Britain, the greatest problem of the 1920s was
    a. increased class tension.
    b. the Irish problem.
    c. the rise of socialist dictatorship.
    d. unemployment.

19. The antifascist movement in France in 1936-1937, led by Leon Blum, was known as the
    a. Radical Alliance.
    b. Communist Coalition.
    c. Popular Front.
    d. New Deal Republic.

20. In January 1923 the German Ruhr was occupied by
    a. Russia.
    b. France.
    c. Britain.
    d. Austria.

UNDERSTANDING HISTORY THROUGH READING AND THE ARTS

The message of existentialist philosophy is movingly told in Albert Camus's *The Myth of Sisyphus*,* and the Paris Gertrude Stein claimed was "where the twentieth century was" is the subject of Ernest Hemingway's *A Moveable Feast** and of Janet Flanner's *Paris Was Yesterday* (1972)*. The text bibliography lists a number of excellent books, including several on life during the depression. George Orwell's *Animal Farm** and *1984** are classics for good reason, and his book *Road to Wigan Pier** is a view of British working class life in the era of the Great Depression.

Functionalism in architecture (including the Chicago school) is treated in N. Pevsner, *Pioneers of Modern Design** (1960). The international style and the man who made Chicago the most important architectural center in America are the subjects of P. Blacke, *Mies van de Rohe: Architecture and Structure** (1964), and more

*Available in paperback.

recently, *Mies van der Rohe, A Critical Biography* (1985) by F. Schulze. An excellent review of Le Corbusier's buildings and his writings is found in S. von Moos, *Le Corbusier** (1985), and the aims and achievements of the German Bauhaus movement is examined in two books by G. Naylor: *The Bauhaus** (1968) and *The Bauhaus Reassessed** (1985).

One of the most chilling examples of the use of film for the ideological transformation of a country is Leni Riefenstahl's documentary *The Triumph of the Will* (1984), showing the 1934 Nazi party rally at Nuremburg. It reveals a great deal about what Nazis wanted to believe about themselves and their leader, Adolf Hitler. It is available on video film.

PROBLEMS FOR FURTHER INVESTIGATION

Those interested in the complexities of interwar economic history will find B. W. E. Alford, *Depression and Recovery? British Economic Growth, 1918-1939** (1972), a short and readable discussion of a number of interpretations on the nature of the British economy. The Versailles treaty is dealt with in the Problems in European History book *The Versailles Settlement** (1960), edited by I. J. Lederer.

The dramatic changes in domestic life, sport, amusement, politics, sex, and other aspects of life in the twenty-one-year period between the two great wars make a stimulating subject for student research. Begin your investigation with R. Graves and A. Hodge, *The Long Week End, A Social History of Great Britain, 1918-1939** (1940, 1963).

*Available in paperback.

CHAPTER 29

DICTATORSHIPS AND THE
SECOND WORLD WAR

CHAPTER OBJECTIVES

After reading and studying this chapter you should be able to answer the following questions:

Q-1. What are the characteristics of the twentieth-century totalitarian state?
Q-2. How did the totalitarian state affect ordinary people?
Q-3. How did it lead to war?

CHAPTER SYNOPSIS

The anxiety and crisis that followed the First World War contributed to the rise of powerful dictatorships in parts of Europe. Some of these dictatorships were old-fashioned and conservative, but there were new totalitarian dictatorships as well, notably in Soviet Russia and Nazi Germany. This chapter examines the different kinds of dictatorship in a general way and then looks at Stalin's Russia and Hitler's Germany in detail.

In Soviet Russia, Lenin relaxed rigid state controls in 1921 after the civil war in order to revive the economy successfully. After defeating Trotsky in a struggle for power, Stalin established a harsh totalitarian dictatorship, which demanded great sacrifices from the people. But Soviet Russia built up its industry while peasants lost their land and a radically new socialist society came into being. Mussolini's government in Italy was much less radical and totalitarian.

This chapter concludes with Adolf Hitler and the totalitarian government of the Nazis in Germany. The roots of Nazism are found in racism, extreme nationalism, and violent irrationality, all of which drove Hitler relentlessly. Hitler was also a master politician and this helped him gain power legally. His government was popular, especially because it appeared to solve the economic problems of the Great Depression. Hitler also had the support of the German masses because of his success in foreign affairs. He used bullying and fears of communism in Britain and France to rearm and expand, until finally war broke out over Poland in 1939. By 1942, Hitler and the Nazis had temporarily conquered a great empire and were putting their anti-Jewish racism into operation.

STUDY OUTLINE

I. Authoritarianism and totalitarianism in Europe after the First World War
   A. Conservative authoritarianism
      1. Conservative authoritarianism had deep roots in European history and led to an antidemocratic form of government that believed in avoiding change but was limited in its power and objectives
      2. Conservative authoritarianism revived after the First World War in eastern Europe, Spain, and Portugal
      3. The new authoritarian governments were more concerned with maintaining the status quo than with forcing society into rapid change
   B. Modern totalitarianism
      1. Modern totalitarianism emerged from World War I and the Russian civil war when individual liberties were subordinated to the military effort
      2. Nothing was outside of the control of the all-important state: it was a dictatorship that sought to control the political, economic, social, intellectual, and cultural components of its subjects' lives
      3. Unlike old-fashioned authoritarianism, which was based on elites, modern totalitarianism was based on the masses
      4. Totalitarian regimes believed in mobilizing society toward some great goal
   C. Totalitarianism of the left and right
      1. In Stalinist Russia, the leftists prevailed, and private property was taken over by the state
      2. In Nazi Germany, private property was maintained
II. Stalin's Russia
   A. From Lenin to Stalin
      1. By 1921, the economy of Russia had been destroyed
      2. Lenin's New Economic Policy (NEP) restored some capitalistic incentive
         a. Peasants bought and sold goods on the free market
         b. Agricultural production grew and industrial production surpassed the prewar level

      3. Economic recovery and Lenin's death brought a struggle for power between Stalin and Trotsky, which Stalin won

         a. Stalin met the ethnic demands for independence within the multinational Soviet state by granting minority groups limited freedoms

         b. Stalin's theory of "socialism in one country," or Russia's building its own socialist society, was more attractive to many Communists than Trotsky's theory of "permanent revolution," or the overthrow of other European states

      4. By 1927, Stalin had crushed all opposition and was ready to launch an economic-social revolution

B. The five-year plans

      1. The first five-year plan to increase industrial and agricultural production was extremely ambitious, but Stalin wanted to erase the NEP, spur the economy, and catch up with the West

      2. Stalin waged a preventive war against the better-off peasants, the kulaks, to bring them and their land under state control

         a. Collectivization of the kulaks' land resulted in disaster for agriculture

         b. But it was a political victory for Stalin and the Communist party, as the peasants were eliminated as a potential threat

      3. The five-year plans brought about a spectacular growth of heavy industry, especially with the aid of government control of the workers and foreign technological experts

      4. Massive investment in heavy industry, however, meant low standards of living for workers

C. Life in Stalinist society

      1. The Communists wanted to create a new kind of society and human personality

      2. Stalin's reign of terror and mass purges eliminated any opposition

      3. Propaganda and indoctrination were common features of life, and even art and literature became highly political

      4. Life was hard, but people were often inspired by socialist ideals and did gain some social benefits and the possibility of personal advancement through education

D. Women in Soviet Russia

      1. Women were given much greater opportunities in industry and education

      2. Medicine and other professions were opened to them

      3. Most women had to work to help support their families in addition to caring for the home and the children

III. Mussolini's Italy
    A. Mussolini and the Fascist seizure of power
        1. The First World War and postwar problems ended the move toward democracy in Italy
        2. By 1922, most Italians were opposed to liberal, parliamentary government
        3. Mussolini's Fascists opposed the "socialist threat" with physical force (the Black Shirts)
        4. Mussolini marched on Rome in 1922 and forced the king to name him head of the government
    B. The regime in action
        1. Mussolini's Fascists manipulated elections and killed the Socialist leader Matteotti
        2. Between 1924 and 1926 Mussolini built a one-party Fascist dictatorship—but never really totalitarian
            a. Much of the old power structure remained—particularly the capitalists
            b. The Catholic Church supported the Fascists
            c. Women were repressed but Jews were not persecuted until late in the Second World War
IV. Hitler's Germany
    A. The roots of Nazism
        1. Hitler became a fanatical nationalist while in Vienna, where he absorbed anti-Semitic and racist ideas
        2. He believed that Jews and Marxists lost the First World War for Germany
        3. By 1921, he had converted the tiny extremist German Workers' group into the Nazi party
            a. The party grew rapidly
            b. Hitler and the party attempted to overthrow the Weimar government, but he was defeated and sent to jail (1923)
    B. Hitler's road to power (1923-1933)
        1. The trial after Hitler's attempted coup brought him much publicity, but the Nazi party remained small until 1929
        2. Written in jail, his autobiography, *Mein Kampf*, was an outline of his desire to achieve German racial supremacy and domination of Europe, under the leadership of a dictator (fuhrer)
        3. The depression made the Nazi party a major party that was especially attractive to the lower middle class and to young people
        4. By 1932, the Nazi party was the largest in the Reichstag
        5. The Weimar government's orthodox policies intensified the economic collapse and convinced the middle class that its leaders were incompetent; hence, they welcomed Hitler's attacks on the republican system

      6. The Communists refused to ally with the socialists to block Hitler

      7. Hitler was a skilled politician, a master of propaganda and mass psychology who generated enormous emotional support with his speeches

      8. Hitler was appointed chancellor in 1933

C. The Nazi state and society

      1. The Enabling Act of March 1933 gave Hitler absolute dictatorial power

      2. Nazis took over every aspect of German life—political, social, economic, cultural, and intellectual

      3. Hitler took over total control of the military

      4. The Gestapo, or secret police, used terror and purges to strengthen Hitler's hold on power

      5. Hitler set out to eliminate the Jews

        a. The Nuremberg Laws deprived Jews of their citizenship

        b. Jews were constant victims of violence and outrages

D. Hitler's popularity

      1. Hitler promised and delivered economic recovery through public works projects and military spending

      2. Hitler reduced Germany's traditional class distinctions

      3. He appealed to Germans for nationalistic reasons

      4. Communists, trade unionists, and some Christians opposed Hitler; many who opposed him were executed

V. Nazi expansion and the Second World War

A. Aggression and appeasement (1933-1939)

      1. Hitler's main goal was territorial expansion for the superior German race

      2. In violation of the Treaty of Versailles, he occupied the demilitarized Rhineland

      3. The British policy of appeasement led to their approval of Hitler's aggression

      4. Mussolini attacked Ethiopia and joined Germany in supporting the Fascists in Spain

      5. Germany, Italy, and Japan formed an alliance

      6. Hitler annexed Austria and demanded part of Czechoslovakia in 1938

      7. Chamberlain flew to Munich to appease Hitler and agree to his territorial demands

      8. Hitler accelerated his aggression and occupied all of Czechoslovakia

      9. Hitler and Stalin signed a secret pact that divided eastern Europe into German and Russian zones

     10. Germany attacked Poland, and Britain and France declared war on Germany (1939)

B. Hitler's empire (1939-1942)

      1. The key to Hitler's military success was speed and force

2. He crushed Poland quickly and then France; by July 1940 the Nazis ruled nearly all of Europe except Britain
3. He bombed British cities in an attempt to break British morale but did not succeed
4. In 1941 Hitler's forces invaded Russia and conquered the Ukraine and got as far as Leningrad and Moscow
5. After Japan attacked Pearl Harbor (1941) Hitler also declared war on the United States
6. Hitler was determined to rid Europe of Slavs and Jews, and millions died in forced-labor or concentration camps

REVIEW QUESTIONS

Q-1. Evaluate the rise of conservative authoritarianism in Poland, Hungary, Yugoslavia, and Portugal. How do you explain this development?

Q-2. What are the characteristics of modern totalitarianism? How does it differ from conservative authoritarianism?

Q-3. What was the purpose of Lenin's New Economic Policy?

Q-4. How successful was Stalin's program of five-year plans for the industrialization of Soviet Russia? What were its strengths and weaknesses?

Q-5. How does one explain that despite a falling standard of living, many Russians in the 1920s and 1930s willingly worked harder and were happy?

Q-6. Generally, did women gain or lose status and power in the new Stalinist Russian state?

Q-7. What were the circumstances under which Mussolini rose to power in Italy? What were his goals and tactics?

Q-8. Many Germans in the 1920s and 1930s viewed Hitler as a reformer. What were his ideas about the problems and the future of Germany?

Q-9. Evaluate the impact of the Great Depression on German political life.

Q-10. Discuss the role of mass propaganda and psychology in Hitler's rise to power.

Q-11. Why did Hitler acquire such a mass appeal? Did he improve German life?

Q-12. Describe the Munich Conference of 1938 and Chamberlain's policy of appeasement. Why were so many British willing to appease Hitler? What was the result of the Munich Conference?

Q-13. Describe Hitler's foreign and military policy up to 1938. Was there enough evidence of aggression to convince the world that Hitler was dangerous?

Q-14. What was the "final solution of the Jewish question"?

Q-15. Describe German-Soviet relations between 1939 and 1941. Was war between the two inevitable?

STUDY-REVIEW EXERCISES

Define the following key concepts and terms.

Hitler's final solution policy

modern totalitarianism

"socialism in one country"

appeasement

fascism

anti-Semitism

Identify the following people and give their significance.

Béla Kun

Weimar Republic

National Socialist German Workers' Party

Benito Mussolini

Oliveira Salazar

Leon Trotsky

General Paul Hindenburg

King Alexander of Yugoslavia

Neville Chamberlain

Russian kulaks

Nazi Storm Troopers (the SA)

Joseph Goebbels

German Social Democrats

Explain *what the following events were, who participated in them, and why they were important.*

Stalin's collectivization program

Lenin's New Economic Policy (1921)

Mussolini's march on Rome (1922)

Hitler's Munich plot (1923)

Great Depression in Germany (1929-1933)

Nuremberg Laws (1935)

Munich Conference (1938)

Russio-German ("Nazi-Soviet") nonaggression pact (1939)

Stalin's five-year plans

Test your understanding of the chapter by answering the following questions.

1. Unlike his rival Trotsky, Stalin *favored/opposed* the policy of "socialism in one country."
2. In Germany, the Communists *agreed/refused* to cooperate with the Social Democrats in opposition to Hitler.
3. Stalin's forced collectivization of peasant farms was a political *victory/failure* while it was an economic *success/disaster*.
4. Hitler's Nazi party ruled a modern totalitarian state of the *right/left*.
5. Totalitarian states of the right usually *do/do not* advocate state takeover of private property.
6. He was an antisocialist and the leader of the Italian Black Shirts.

7. Lenin's New Economic Policy *was/was not* a return to capitalism.
8. He was legally appointed chancellor of Germany in 1933.

---

9. The standard of living of the average Russian worker in the 1930s *improved/declined* as a result of Stalin's five-year plans.
10. The foreign policy of Prime Minister Chamberlain tended to be *pro-German/anti-German*.
11. Mussolini's Italy *did/did not* have all the characteristics of a modern totalitarian state.

MULTIPLE-CHOICE QUESTIONS

1. The German Nuremburg laws related to
    a. antidepression programs.
    b. the Versailles treaty.
    c. the elimination of the Fascists.
    d. Jewish citizenship.

2. The Vichy government of 1940 was established in
    a. Poland.
    b. Germany.
    c. Czechoslovakia.
    d. France.

3. Which of the following was *not* a modern totalitarian state in the 1930s?
    a. Germany
    b. Italy
    c. Russia
    d. France

4. The two countries in which modern totalitarianism reached its most complete form in the 1930s were
    a. Russia and Germany.
    b. Italy and France.
    c. Germany and Italy.
    d. Russia and Italy.

5. Before the modern totalitarian state, the traditional form of antidemocratic government in Europe was

   a. conservative authoritarianism.

   b. absolutism.

   c. republicanism.

   d. none of the above

6. The modern totalitarian state is
   a. lethargic in its approach.
   b. built on elite groups.
   c. concerned only with survival.
   d. characterized by rapid and profound changes.

7. Lenin's New Economic Policy of 1921
   a. nationalized industries.
   b. called for the collectivization of agriculture.
   c. restored limited economic freedom.
   d. set five-year goals.

8. Before Lenin died, he named what man as his successor?
   a. Stalin
   b. Trotsky
   c. No one
   d. Dzhugashvili

9. Stalin became Lenin's successor because he
   a. was chosen by Lenin.
   b. was able to work outside the party.
   c. successfully related Russian realities to Marxist teachings.
   d. devised a system whereby minorities enjoyed total freedom.

10. Stalin's plans for rapid industrialization were based on
   a. importing coal from Japan.
   b. factories staffed exclusively by party members.
   c. depriving peasants in order to feed workers.
   d. a huge domestic market for consumer goods.

11. Under Stalin, women's greatest real benefits were
   a. sexual liberation and abortion.
   b. easy divorce and day-care centers.
   c. work freedom and accessible education.
   d. easier work than in the past and freedom from family worries.

12. Most Germans reacted to Hitler's purge of Jews with
    a. hostility and anger.
    b. protests and demonstrations.
    c. apathy and indifference.
    d. joy and celebration.

13. Which of the following was *not* found in Stalinist society?
    a. Police terrorism
    b. The scorning of religion
    c. The politicization of art and literature
    d. Large-scale discrimination against women in the job market

14. For Italian women, the fascist regime of Mussolini meant
    a. no improvement and a probable decline in status.
    b. considerable gains, especially in finding new careers in industry.
    c. more birth control and better-paying jobs.
    d. greater political participation and legal rights.

15. The people within German society whom Hitler appealed to most were
    a. industrial workers.
    b. the poor.
    c. Social Democrats.
    d. the middle class.

16. Which of the following opposed Hitler?
    a. Communists
    b. Social Democrats
    c. Some Catholic and Protestant clergy
    d. All of the above

17. Conservative authoritarianism differed from modern totalitarianism in that it
    a. did not result in dictatorships.
    b. allowed popular participation in government.
    c. was more concerned with maintaining the status quo than with rapid change or war.
    d. did not persecute liberals or socialists.

18. Which of the following countries did *not* experience a revival of conservative authoritarianism in the 1920s and 1930s?

  a. Hungary
  b. Russia
  c. Yugoslavia
  d. Poland

19. In essence, the totalitarian state was
  a. a radical break with liberalism.
  b. an extension of the dictatorial state.
  c. a dynamic society moving toward some goal.
  d. all of the above

20. One major reason for British appeasement of Hitler was that
  a. he was seen as a way to block German capitalist expansion.
  b. he was seen as the bulwark against communism.
  c. the British government was prosocialist.
  d. none of the above

GEOGRAPHY

1. Using Map 29.1 as a guide, show on the outline map the area of Germany in 1933.
2. Show the step-by-step growth of Nazi Germany through September 1939 by shading in each area taken and giving the date of acquisition. Do you consider the remilitarization an important step in the growth of Nazi Germany? Why was Czechoslovakia dismembered in two stages?

3. Locate on the outline map and label the following places. Why was each significant?

Ruhr	Poland	Austria	Rhine River
East Prussia	Czechoslovakia	Sudetenland	Munich
Rhineland	Danzig		

4. In the space below, explain (a) what happened to Poland as a result of the German-Soviet agreement of 1939, and (b) what were Hitler's intentions (and actions) with regard to Russia between 1939 and 1941.

UNDERSTANDING HISTORY THROUGH READING AND THE ARTS

There has been a burst of literature on Hitler and Nazi Germany in recent years.
Two of the most readable books are A. Speer, *Inside the Third Reich** (1971) and
L. S. Davidowicz, *The War Against the Jews, 1933-1945** (1975). Speer was an
architect who became Hitler's chief war planner and one of the persons closest to
Hitler. His picture of Hitler is revealing in many ways. Davidowicz writes about the
German "final solution." It's a horrible story but one that needs to be told to every
generation. The relationship between anti-Semitism and German Fascism is further
examined in Y. Bauer, *A History of the Holocaust* (1982),* and the motives of a
concentration camp commandant are evaluated in G. Sereny, *Into That Darkness**
(1974, 1982). The least known of the Nazi atrocities is dealt with in F. Rector, *The
Nazi Extermination of Homosexuals* (1981).

A large number of first-rank films have been made about Europe in the 1930s.
The Shop on Main Street (1966) is a drama of a man living under Nazi occupation in
Czechoslovakia who is sent to take over a button shop from an old Jewish woman.
Similarly moving is *The Diary of Anne Frank* (1959), which is about a Jewish family
hiding in an attic in Amsterdam in World War II. John Gielgud and Irene Worth nar-
rate a French documentary about the Spanish Civil War entitled *To Die in Madrid*
(1965). The film *Night and Fog*, by Renais, is a chilling documentary of the Nazi
concentration camps.

PROBLEMS FOR FURTHER INVESTIGATION

The period considered in this chapter is constantly undergoing reinterpretation, and
new material appears each year. Helpful is A. Funk et al., *A Select Bibliography on
Books on the Second World War** (1975). This is a bibliography of books published
from 1966 to 1975.

*Available in paperback.

Those interested in examining the tangle of views on the life and motives of Hitler should begin with R. G. L. Waite, ed., *Hitler and Nazi Germany* (1965), and A. Bullock, *Hitler: A Study in Tyranny* (revised, 1962), and for Hitler's impact on German society, D. G. Williamson, *The Third Reich* (1984). About the Italian dictator, the student should read D. M. Smith, *Mussolini* (1982). A highly scholarly account of Hitler's appeal to the German people is R. Hamilton, *Who Voted for Hitler* (1982)*. The problem of the origins of the Second World War is the subject of W. L. Kleine-Ahlbrandt, ed., *Appeasement of the Dictators* (1970).

Stalin's contribution to history has been the subject of much debate. The best overall summary of this debate is M. McCauley, *Stalin and Stalinism** (1983), while the chilling horrors of one aspect of Stalin's reign is dealt with (including photographs) in I. Deutscher and D. King, *The Great Purges* (1985). And a good short discussion of the origins and motives of the political extremes of the decades between the two world wars is D. Smith, *Left and Right in Twentieth-Century Europe** (1970).

*Available in paperback.

CHAPTER 30

THE RECOVERY OF EUROPE AND
THE AMERICAS

CHAPTER OBJECTIVES

After reading and studying this chapter you should be able to answer the following questions:

Q-1. What were the strengths and the weaknesses of the Grand Alliance and how did it defeat Germany?
Q-2. How did Europe recover from the Second World War?
Q-3. What were the causes of the cold war?
Q-4. How did "economic nationalism" transform Latin America?

CHAPTER SYNOPSIS

This chapter discusses the main political and economic trends in the Western world since the dark days of the Second World War. It shows how Europe, especially western Europe, recovered from the destruction of 1945, how the cold war split the Continent into communist and non-communist blocs, how European empires came to an end as the peoples of Africa and Asia achieved national independence, and how North and South America also revived and evolved in the postwar era.

The author examines why the Grand Alliance of Britain, the Soviet Union, and the United States failed to hold together after it succeeded in defeating Nazi Germany. Military decisions, ideological differences, and disputes over eastern Europe were key factors in the origins of the cold war. By 1950, the Iron Curtain was in place and western and eastern Europe were going their separate ways. Battered western Europe rebuilt quickly and successfully, helped by new leaders and attitudes, American aid, and the creation of the Common Market. Developments in east European countries closely followed those in Soviet Russia. Stalin reimposed a harsh dictatorship after the war, which Khrushchev relaxed and which Brezhnev tightened once again. An anti-communist popular revolt in Hungary failed, while material conditions in communist countries gradually improved and communist governments remained firmly in control.

European empires in Asia and Africa went out of business after the Second World War. India led the way to national independence right after the war, and other British, French, and Dutch territories followed. Most countries gained independence peacefully, but there were bitter colonial wars in Vietnam and Algeria. Western influence lives on in Asia and Africa, since most of the newly independent countries have retained Western nationalism and either communism or democracy as guiding ideas.

STUDY OUTLINE

I.   Allied victory and the cold war (1942-1950)
A.   The Grand Alliance
1.   The twenty-six allied nations were led by Britain, the United States, and the Soviet Union
2.   America's war policy was to defeat Germany before Japan
3.   The Allies put military decisions, such as the Allied invasion of Germany, above political questions, such as the political makeup of postwar Europe
4.   At Casablanca (1943) it was decided that the unconditional surrender of Japan and Germany would be necessary
5.   Allied strength was enormous, and it was aided by the resistance groups, many of which were communist
a.   America's strength lay in its industry and national unity
b.   Britain drew on its empire and on the United States for resources and also effectively mobilized its own economy
c.   Russia drew on its large industrial capacity and the heroic determination of its people
B.   The tide of battle
1.   The Germans were turned back at Stalingrad at the end of 1942
2.   American victories in the Pacific in 1942 put Japan on the defensive
3.   British-American victories in North Africa in 1942 gave the Allies a springboard for the Italian campaign
4.   Italy surrendered in 1943, but fighting continued as the Germans seized Rome and northern Italy
5.   The Allies pushed into Germany from the east and the west; Germany surrendered in May 1945, and Hitler committed suicide
6.   The United States dropped two atomic bombs on Japan, and it too surrendered

C. The origins of the cold war
   1. American-British invasion via France meant that Soviet Russia alone would occupy Eastern Europe
   2. At the Yalta Conference the Allies decided to divide Germany into occupation zones
   3. The British and the Americans wanted free elections in eastern Europe, but the Russians wanted pro-Russian, pro-communist governments
   4. In general, Soviet control over eastern Europe could not be prevented by the United States after 1945
D. West versus East
   1. Truman cut off aid to Russia because of Stalin's insistence on having communist governments in eastern Europe
   2. By 1947, many Americans believed that Stalin was trying to export communist revolution throughout Europe
   3. The Marshall Plan was established to help European recovery; the Truman Doctrine was meant to ward off communist subversion
   4. The Soviet blockade of Berlin led to a successful allied airlift
   5. In 1949, the United States formed an anti-Soviet military alliance of Western governments, the North Atlantic Treaty Organization (NATO); in return, Stalin united his satellites in the Warsaw Pact
   6. In 1949, Communists won in China
   7. In 1950, when Communist north Korea invaded the south, American-led UN troops intervened
   8. The Western attempt to check Stalin probably came too late and may have encouraged Russian aggression
II. The western European renaissance
   A. The postwar challenge
      1. The war left Europe physically devastated and in a state of economic and moral crisis
      2. New leaders and new parties, especially the Catholic Christian Democrats, emerged in Italy, France, and Germany and provided effective leadership and needed reforms
      3. In many countries, such as Britain, France, and Italy, socialists and communists emerged from the war with considerable power and a strong desire for social reform
      4. The Marshall Plan aided in economic recovery and led to the Organization for European Economic Cooperation (OEEC), while NATO led to military protection
   B. Economic "miracles"
      1. Led by West Germany, a European economic miracle was underway by 1963

    2. A free-market economy—with a social welfare net—brought rapid growth to Germany

    3. A mixed state and private economy brought rapid growth to France

    4. Old skills, new markets, and the Common Market stimulated economic development in western Europe

C. Toward European unity

    1. Democratic republics were re-established in France, West Germany, and Italy

    2. The Christian Democrats were committed to a unified Europe, but economic unity proved to be more realistic than political unity

    3. The six-nation Coal and Steel Community marked the beginning of a movement toward European unity and led to further technical and economic cooperation

    4. The Treaty of Rome (1957) created the European Economic Community (EEC, or Common Market), whose immediate goal was to create a free-trade area and reduce tariffs

    5. But regenerated hopes for political union in Europe were frustrated by a resurgence of nationalism in the 1960s

        a. De Gaulle, a romantic nationalist, wanted France to lead the Common Market

        b. He withdrew from NATO and vetoed British attempts to join the Common Market

D. Decolonization of Asia and Africa

    1. The causes of imperial decline

        a. Nationalism brought demands for political self-determination in old colonial areas, especially after the First World War

        b. The Second World War reduced European power and destroyed the Western sense of moral superiority

    2. Nationalism in India and China

        a. Gandhi led the Indian nationalist movement, and India won limited self-government in 1937

        b. Britain granted independence after the Second World War by creating a Hindu state of India and a Muslim state of Pakistan

        c. After a bitter civil war, the Communists forced the nationalists out of China to the island of Taiwan in 1949

        d. Mao Tse-tung began building a Communist society along Soviet lines, with five-year plans concentrating on heavy industry

    3. Arab nationalism and African independence

        a. Arab nationalism challenged imperial power and the new Jewish nation

        b. A Jewish state was created out of part of British-controlled Palestine (1948) and was attacked by the Arab countries, who were defeated

    c. Palestinian refugees refused to accept defeat; meanwhile a successful nationalist revolution took place in Egypt

    d. Arab nationalists in Algeria fought for and won independence from France in 1962

    e. In most of the rest of Africa, independence was achieved without war, although many new African countries remained dependent on France and the Common Market

III. Soviet Eastern Europe

  A. Stalin's last years

    1. The national unity of the war period ended in rigid dictatorship again

    2. Stalin began a new series of purges and enforced cultural conformity

      a. Soviet citizens living outside Russia were forced to return, and nearly a million of them plus other Russians died in labor camps

      b. Culture, art, and the Jewish religion were attacked

    3. Five-year plans were reintroduced

    4. Stalin's system was exported to eastern Europe

      a. Only Tito in Yugoslavia was able to build an east European communist state free from Stalinist control

      b. Tito's success led Stalin to purge the Communist parties of eastern Europe in an attempt to increase their obedience to him

  B. Reform and de-Stalinization

    1. Khrushchev and fellow reformers won the leadership of Russia over the conservatives, who wanted to make as few changes as possible in the Stalinist system

    2. Krushchev denounced Stalin and began a policy of liberalization

      a. The Soviet standard of living was improved and greater intellectual freedom was allowed

      b. Khrushchev pushed for "peaceful coexistence" with the West and a relaxation of cold war tensions

    3. This de-Stalinization caused revolution in eastern Europe

      a. Poland won greater autonomy

      b. Hungary expelled Soviet troops and declared its neutrality but was invaded by Russia and defeated

  C. The fall of Khrushchev

    1. Re-Stalinization began with Khrushchev's fall (1964)

      a. Khrushchev was opposed by conservatives in foreign policy

      b. He was successful in Berlin but lost to the U.S. over Cuba

      c. Brezhnev stressed the ties with the Stalinist era and launched an arms buildup

IV. The western hemisphere

  A. Postwar prosperity in the United States

      1. Conversion to a peacetime economy went smoothly and a generation experienced ever-greater prosperity

      2. Until the 1960s, domestic politics consisted largely of consolidating the New Deal and maintaining the status quo

B. The civil-rights revolution

      1. School segregation was declared unconstitutional by the Supreme Court in 1954

      2. Blacks used militant nonviolence and growing political power to gain reforms in the 1960s, while the United States became more of a welfare state

C. Economic nationalism in Latin America

      1. Beginning with the Great Depression, more popularly based governments encouraged the development of local manufacturing to reduce their dependence on raw-materials production and foreign markets

      2. In Mexico the revolution of 1910 opened a new era of economic nationalism, social reform, and industrialization

         a. President Cardenas nationalized American oil companies

         b. The Mexican state successfully promoted industrialization from the early 1940s to the late 1960s

      3. Under the strongman Vargas, Brazil also embraced economic nationalism and moderate social reform

D. The Cuban revolution

      1. Cuba was relatively rich but suffered from dictatorship, corruption, and a tradition of American intervention

      2. The magnetic Fidel Castro led a successful revolution, which had major consequences

         a. Castro repelled an American-supported invasion by Cuban exiles, thereby winning great prestige

         b. He established a typical communist dictatorship

         c. The Cuban revolution brought the cold war to Latin America

E. The new authoritarianism

      1. Democratic government has been in retreat in Latin America since the Cuban revolution

      2. In Brazil and Argentina the military has generally ruled since 1964, with the support of conservatives and most of the middle class

      3. In Chile the army overturned a leftist government and imposed a harsh dictatorship

      4. The new authoritarians oppose communism, but they are also determined modernizers, committed to national independence and industrialization

REVIEW QUESTIONS

Q-1. What were the strengths and weaknesses of the Grand Alliance? Can you identify any sources of future problems?

Q-2. If the Americans and the British did not open the western front against Germany until June 1944, on what fronts was the war against Hitler carried on?

Q-3. One of the controversies over World War II military strategy is whether the bombing of cities and civilians helped to defeat the enemy. What is the answer?

Q-4. Why was the Teheran Conference important in shaping the map of postwar Europe? What were the alternatives?

Q-5. Describe the dispute between the United States and Russia at the end of the war. How and why did it escalate into a cold war?

Q-6. What are the sources of the Soviet Union's paranoia about Germany and vice versa? What do they tell us about the cold war?

Q-7. How did Europe accomplish economic recovery after the war? What factors contributed to its growth?

Q-8. Which approach toward European unity was most successful, the political or the economic? Why?

Q-9. Describe the steps taken toward European economic unity. What impact does this unity have on the European and world economy?

Q-10. Was nationalism completely dead in postwar Europe? Who was Charles de Gaulle and what was his ambition?

Q-11. What impact did the second World War have on thinking about imperialism and European empires?

Q-12. Compare and contrast the development of nationalism in India and China.

Q-13. "Postwar domestic politics in the United States consisted largely of making modest adjustments to the status quo." Why was this so?

Q-14. What were the milestones in the civil-rights revolution?

Q-15. What are some of the key components of economic nationalism? How and why did it arise in Latin America?

Q-16. Compare and contrast Mexico under Cardenas with Brazil under Vargas.

Q-17. What were the causes and the consequences of the Cuban revolution?

Q-18. What is meant by "the new authoritarianism in Latin America?" Are military governments in Latin America reacting to fears of social reform of communist revolution?

Q-19. Evaluate Soviet foreign policy toward eastern Europe by discussing Poland and Hungary in 1956.

Q-20. Evaluate Stalin's postwar policy and actions. Why were many Russian nationalists disappointed in them? How would you judge Stalin's place in Soviet history?

Q-21. Describe the circumstances surrounding Khrushchev's famous Twentieth Party Congress speech in 1956. What were the results of his policy?

Q-22. What were the reasons for Khrushchev's fall from power and the beginning of the re-Stalinization of Russia in 1964?

Q-23. Describe life in the Soviet Union after 1964. What are the positive and negative features of the Soviet state in the Brezhnev era?

STUDY-REVIEW EXERCISES

Define the following key concepts and terms.

economic nationalism

cold war

mixed economy

Truman Doctrine

Great Leap Forward

de-Stalinization

decolonization

Identify each of the following and give its significance.

battle of Stalingrad

NATO

European Coal and Steel Community

British Labour party

Hiroshima and Nagasaki

Indian Congress Party

Kuomintang

Atlantic Charter

Alliance for Progress

Marshall Plan

Warsaw Pact

Common Market

Taft-Hartley Act

Identify the following people and explain their importance.

Josip Tito

Ho Chi Minh

Mahatma Gandhi

Nikita Khrushchev

Lazaro Cardenas

Clement Atlee

Salvador Allende

Mao Tse-tung

Charles de Gaulle

Fidel Castro

Winston Churchill

Leonid Brezhnev

Chiang Kai-shek

Anwar Sadat

Getulio Vargas

Yevgeny Yevtushenko

Explain what the following events were, who participated in them, and why they were important.

Normandy invasion (June 6, 1944)

Schuman Plan (1950)

Twentieth Party Congress of the Soviets (1956)

election of the Nagy regime in Hungary (1956)

election of the Allende government (1970)

Chinese civil war (1945-1949)

partition of Palestine (1948)

Bay of Pigs invasion (1961)

Explain what happened at the following wartime conferences of the Big Three and what impact each one had on the postwar world.

Conference and Date

Casablanca (January 1943)

Teheran (November 1943)

Yalta (February 1945)

Potsdam (July 1945)

Test your understanding of the chapter by answering the following questions.

1. The successor to Sun Yat-sen and the leader of the revolutionary Kuomintang

   in China was _____.

2. The American aid program that led to the establishment of the Organization for European Economic Co-operation was known as the

   _____.

3. The post-World War II Soviet bloc's military alliance is known as the

   _____.

4. The resurgence of traditional nationalism in France was led, from 1958 to 1969,

   by President _____.

MULTIPLE-CHOICE QUESTIONS

1. French economic recovery following World War II centered on
   a. free-market capitalism alone.
   b. socialism.
   c. a mixed state and private economy.
   d. trade unionism.

2. Stalin's successor, Khrushchev,
   a. denounced Stalinist policies and Stalin himself.
   b. carried on the Stalinist traditions.
   c. opposed reconciliation with the West.
   d. placed restrictions on cultural freedom.

3. Most of the actual fighting against Germany in World War II was done by
   a. Russia.
   b. Britain.
   c. the United States.
   d. France.

4. The only eastern European communist leader to build an independent communist state free from Stalinist control was
   a. Nagy.
   b. Tito.
   c. Dubček.
   d. Schumann.

5. In Italy, the leading political party in the immediate postwar elections were the
   a. Communists.
   b. Catholic Center.
   c. Socialists.
   d. Christian Democrats.

6. American-Soviet conflict in the post-World War II era first centered on the problem of the future of
   a. France.
   b. East Germany.
   c. Yugoslavia.
   d. Poland.

7. All but which one of the following had embraced military authoritarian government by the 1970s?
   a. Chile
   b. Mexico
   c. Brazil
   d. Argentina

8. Which one of the following was *not* a policy of Stalin after the Second World
   War?
   a. Belief in the war against capitalism
   b. Political conformity but cultural freedom
   c. Rigid control of east European states
   d. The revival of forced labor camps

9. Prior to June 1944, most of the fighting on land against Hitler's Germany was
   carried out by
   a. France.
   b. Britain.
   c. Russia.
   d. the United States.

10. During and after World War Two, American leaders were most concerned that after the war the east European countries would
    a. become American allies.
    b. be friendly toward Russia.
    c. have freely elected governments.
    d. reject German fascism.

11. The Frenchman who came to symbolize the resurgence of European nationalism was
    a. Jean Monnet.
    b. Charles de Gaulle.
    c. Robert Schuman.
    d. André Malraux.

12. Since the Second World War, Communist participation in west European governments has
    a. decreased.
    b. disappeared entirely.
    c. been outlawed in most countries.
    d. increased.

13. The only east European Communist country able to remain free of Stalin's control was
    a. Poland.
    b. Yugoslavia.
    c. East Germany.
    d. the Ukraine.

14. The country that blocked British entry into the Common Market and that withdrew forces from NATO was
    a. Belgium.
    b. West Germany.
    c. Italy.
    d. France.

15. Under Stalin, top priority in production in the Soviet Union was given to
    a. consumer goods.
    b. military goods.
    c. aid for rebuilding East Germany.
    d. building new housing.

16. The turning point of the Second World War on the eastern front was fought at
    a. Leningrad.
    b. Brest-Litovsk.
    c. Stalingrad.
    d. El Alemain.

17. The allied nations of the Second World War included each of the following except
    a. the Soviet Union.
    b. the United States.
    c. Austria.
    d. Britain.

18. The battle of Dien Bien Phu in 1954 marked the end of French control of
    a. Indochina.
    b. Algeria.
    c. South Sudan.
    d. Teheran.

19. The de-Stalinization program in the Soviet Union led to revolts in
    a. Italy and Turkey.
    b. Poland and Hungary.
    c. Volgograd and Leningrad.
    d. all of the above

20. Which of the following was a feature of the views of the government of France (the Fifth Republic) under Charles de Gaulle?
    a. anti-British
    b. anti-American
    c. anti-NATO and a reluctant participant in the Common Market.
    d. all of the above

GEOGRAPHY

1. Show on the outline map the location of the so-called Iron Curtain that has divided Europe since the Second World War.
2. Shade in the territory lost by Germany after the Second World War. Should East Germany be considered "lost" territory?
3. Shade in the territory gained by the Soviet Union after the Second World War. Did Poland gain anything in return for its losses to the Soviet Union?

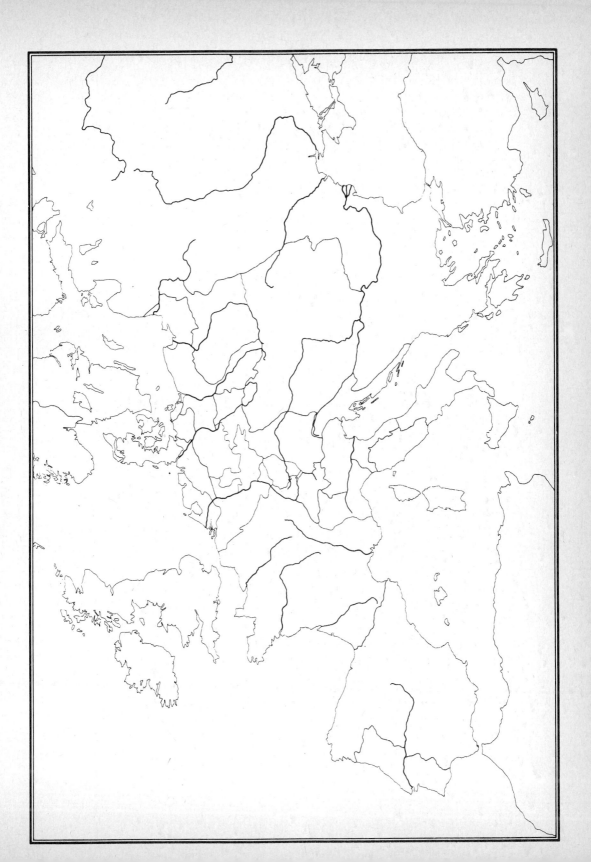

4. Locate on the map and label the original members of the Common Market. Label the countries that have joined in later years. How does the subsequent expansion illustrate the success of the Common Market?

5. Locate on the map and label the following places.

Berlin	Brussels	Paris	London
Warsaw	Rome	Belgrade	Moscow
Bonn	Prague		

What do all of these cities have in common?

UNDERSTANDING HISTORY THROUGH READING AND THE ARTS

Alexander Solzhenitsyn's *One Day in the Life of Ivan Denisovich** is a powerful and moving story of one human being in a postwar prison camp in Stalinist Russia. One of the best books on the cold war is L. Halle, *The Cold War as History* (1967).

What do today's Germans think of Hitler? This is the subject of D. Lang's interesting article "Reporter in Germany: A Backward Look," *The New Yorker* (October 3, 1978): 47-107.

The release from Nazi occupation gave an enormous boost to popular song throughout Europe. Nowhere were songwriters and young artists as inspired as in France, and no one was as loved by the French people as Edith Piaf. Piaf was a nightclub singer who sang *chansons réalistes*—songs about the joys, frustrations, and sorrows of the people of the streets. She made her first recording in 1936. Her first recording after the war, *Les Trois Cloches*, was described as "the folklore of the future." She died in 1963 after a full and sometimes tragic life. Many recordings of her performances are available.

PROBLEMS FOR FURTHER INVESTIGATION

Those interested in the military history of the Second World War and the postwar era will want to begin with P. Paret, *Makers of Modern Strategy, from Machavelli*

*Available in paperback.

to the Nuclear Age* (1986). The origins of the cold war, according to its earliest interpreters, were rooted in the conflict between communist aggression and American benevolence. Preoccupied with the task of defeating the Axis powers, the United States misjudged the intentions of the Soviet Union and, unknowingly, opened the door to communist expansion. American policy makers then adopted policies designed to "contain" Russian aggression. For example, see G. F. Kennan, *American Diplomacy, 1900-1950* (1951).

Then the turbulent sixties, which were characterized by a reappraisal of American truths, led some historians to re-examine the origins of the cold war. Revisionists such as W. A. Williams, *The Tragedy of American Diplomacy** (1959), and W. Lafeber, *America, Russia and the Cold War, 1945-1975** (1976), emphasized American economic expansion as a major reason for the confrontation between East and West. Armed with a monopoly of atomic weapons, the United States threatened Soviet security and thereby forced communist leaders to forge eastern Europe into a protective buffer under Soviet hegemony. For a good brief survey of cold war literature see the pamphlet by B. Tierney, et al., *The Cold War—Who Is to Blame?** (1967).

*Available in paperback.

CHAPTER 31

LIFE IN THE POSTWAR ERA

CHAPTER OBJECTIVES

After reading and studying this chapter you should be able to answer the following questions:

Q-1. How has everyday life changed in the postwar era and why?
Q-2. What have these changes meant to people?

CHAPTER SYNOPSIS

This chapter focuses on three of the most important areas of change in today's Western world: science, class structure, and the family.

Examining first science and technology, the author shows how the Second World War speeded up scientific achievement and gave rise to very large scientific projects involving great numbers of researchers and large government grants. This development has led to major changes in the lives of scientists and technicians, who have great influence in modern society. A second trend has been toward a more flexible and democratic class structure, where white-collar professionals and highly trained specialists provide the model for a new middle class. Reforms in education and expanded social security have strengthened the move toward social democracy. Although discontent like that which brought a student revolution in France in 1968 has not been eliminated, changes in education and new opportunities for men and women of talent resulted in a more fluid and less antagonistic class structure. The family and the role of women also underwent well-publicized changes. The divorce rate went up while the marriage rate and birth rates fell. Married women were having fewer children and were ever more likely to work outside the home for wages.

This trend reflects and encourages a growing spirit of independence among women. Women and the family are experienced a truly revolutionary transformation.

STUDY OUTLINE

I. Science and technology
  A. The union of science and technology
    1. Generally, science and technology were joined together only occasionally until the 1930s
    2. The Second World War focus on military problems brought them together
    3. The results have been both good and bad
      a. New industries were created, and rapid economic growth was achieved after 1945
      b. The environment was adversely affected
  B. The stimulus of the Second World War
    1. With the Second World War pure science lost its independence as leading scientists worked for their governments to help fight the war
    2. The war led to major technological breakthroughs, such as radar, improved jet engines, computers, and the atomic bomb
  C. The rise of Big Science
    1. Big Science could attack difficult problems by combining theoretical work with engineering techniques
    2. It needed a great deal of money, which it received from government and large corporations
    3. Russia pioneered in the development of a manned space program
    4. European countries undertook financing of Big Science in order to stop the "brain drain" to the United States
  D. The life of scientists and technologists
    1. There were many scientists and much specialized knowledge
    2. Specialization made teamwork, bureaucracy, and managers necessary
    3. Competition among scientists was often fierce
II. Toward a new society
  A. The changing class structure in Europe
    1. After 1945 the traditional class distinctions became less clear-cut, and society became more democratic
    2. Educational and employment opportunities made the middle class more open
      a. Talent and expertise became more important to success than inherited property or family connections
      b. The middle class grew greatly as entry became easier

3. The rural working class shrank in size due to the mass exodus from the country

B. Social security reforms and rising affluence
   1. Social security reforms reduced class tensions
   2. These reforms promoted greater social and economic equality
   3. Lower food costs allowed for greater consumption of other goods
   4. Leisure and recreation, especially travel, became big business

C. Renewed discontent and the student revolt
   1. Many of the younger generation claimed that increasing materialism was harmful and that postwar society was repressive and flawed
   2. The number of people entering European universities increased in the 1950s and 1960s
      a. Overcrowding resulted and a new "youth culture" emerged
      b. Many students believed they were not getting the kind of education they needed
   3. With help from workers, student revolts over these issues occurred in the late 1960s and early 1970s
   4. The student rebellion reflected a disillusionment with materialism, technological society, and the Vietnam War

III. Women and the family

A. Women's emancipation
   1. Women became better educated and more independent
   2. The changing position of women in society altered the modern family

B. Marriage and motherhood
   1. Since the Second World War, the trend has been toward earlier marriage and greater birth control within marriage
   2. The birthrate in Western countries declined
   3. Motherhood came to occupy a smaller portion of a woman's life than it used to
      a. The average woman's life expectancy increased from fifty years to seventy-five years between 1900 and 1970
      b. At the same time, most women were having their children when they were in their twenties
   4. The age-old link between sexual intercourse and motherhood was severed by the development and use of birth control methods

C. Women at work
   1. Women entered the labor market as full-time wage earners
   2. Rising employment contributed to the growth of the women's liberation movement and the declining birthrate
   3. Women came to understand that interruption of their careers to care for small children led to lower wages

4. The emotional aspects of marriage became more important, but the divorce rate kept moving up
5. The divorce rate rose dramatically—partly because of increased female independence

REVIEW QUESTIONS

Q-1. Why did science become Big Science in the postwar era? What is the purpose of Big Science?

Q-2. Why did the birth rate in Europe and the United States fall in the 1952-1979 era? (see Figure 31.2 in the text)

Q-3. Cite the evidence supporting the claim that the standard of living improved in North America and Europe. Has the *quality* of life improved as well?

Q-4. For the first time in history science and technology have been effectively joined on a massive scale. Explain why this happened and what the implications are.

Q-5. How has the rise of Big Science altered the lives of modern scientists?

Q-6. Some historians have argued that wars have actually promoted progress by speeding up technical change, while others have dismissed this idea. Analyze and discuss this in relation to the Second World War.

Q-7. What changes have taken place in the European class structure since the war? Does greater or less mobility exist? Has the distribution of income remained the same?

Q-8. What were the reasons and outcome of the European student rebellions of the late 1960s?

Q-9. What changes in lifestyle for women have occurred in the past thirty or so years? Have these changes been beneficial to both men and women? Explain.

Q-10. What has happened to the fertility period of women to cause a greater need for birth control?

Q-11. How successful has modern science been in making a healthier society? Has the progress of medicine been oversold?

Q-12. What are the seven habits that have been shown to be related to good health?

STUDY-REVIEW EXERCISES

Define each of the following key concepts and terms.

Big Science

scientific specialization

"brain drain"

the managerial class

social welfare reforms

women's emancipation/women's liberation movement

the "consumer society"

the anti-nuclear movement of the 1980s

Explain each of the following and give its significance.

development of radar

microwave transmission

large-scale entry of women into the labor force

the post-Second World War explosion in university education

student protest of the 1960s

changes in women's fertility

the population decline in Europe and America

the decline of the European peasant class

Test your understanding of the chapter by answering the following questions.

1. Since 1945, the number of agricultural workers in western Europe has *increased/ decreased*.
2. In the past twenty years, European society has witnessed a fairly significant *rise/ fall* in the birthrate.
3. Since the Second World War, the percentage of women who are full-time wage earners has *increased/decreased* sharply.
4. The average European family today spends *more/less* of its income on food, as compared to a family living in the late nineteenth century.

5. Welfare-state reforms in Britain since the Second World War have resulted in *greater/lesser* economic equality in that country.
6. Sweden, where the rate of marriage has *risen/declined*, typifies the changing marriage patterns in Europe since 1945.
7. The trend since the 1940s has been *an increase/a decrease* in the cooperation between pure science and technology.
8. Since 1945, European society has moved toward a *more/less* rigid class structure.
9. It appears that the increase in economic independence among women has had *little/significant* effect on divorce and birth rates.
10. The trend in Europe and the United States since 1945 has been toward *greater/fewer* scientific bureaucracies.

MULTIPLE-CHOICE QUESTIONS

1. The close and lasting cooperation of pure science and applied technology began
   a. during the depression.
   b. about 1900.
   c. during World War II.
   d. during World War I.

2. In Eastern Europe today, most women
   a. seldom work out of the home.
   b. work until marriage.
   c. are usually employed until retirement.
   d. quit the work force after pregnancy.

3. The major cause for the increase of human life expectancy in twentieth-century Europe has been
   a. the sanitary revolution.
   b. more and better food.
   c. less war.
   d. the reduction of infant mortality.

4. Which of the following is *not* a present trend in European marriage and family practices?
   a. Later marriage
   b. Marriage for romantic reasons
   c. A decline in the birthrate
   d. Less emphasis on motherhood

5. Which of the following is *not* true about the European job market since World
    War II?
    a.   A decline in farm labor
    b.   Little or no increase in industrial labor
    c.   A decrease in white-collar and service jobs
    d.   A decrease in small businesses

6. Big Science is characterized by all but which one of the following?
    a.   Considerable emphasis on weapons production
    b.   A dramatic increase in private individual research
    c.   A reliance on government research grants
    d.   The union of science and technology

7. The welfare-state reforms of Europe have resulted in
    a.   little if any redistribution of national income.
    b.   slight redistribution of national income.
    c.   considerable redistribution of national income.
    d.   no changes in the standard of living.

8. As a result of Big Science, the control scientists have over their experimenta-
    tion has
    a.   increased.
    b.   decreased.

9. Since about 1950 the number of European married women who work outside
    the home has considerably
    a.   increased.
    b.   decreased.

10. Since the Second World War, women have
    a.   become more independent.
    b.   married earlier.
    c.   practiced greater birth control.
    d.   all of the above

11. The so-called European brain drain was the
    a.   loss of many scientists in the war.
    b.   move of many scientists to the United States.
    c.   lack of interest in science in society.
    d.   control of science by the state.

12. The 1934 British air ministry experiments on air defense led to the development of
    a.   the atomic bomb.
    b.   the double helix.
    c.   jet aircraft.
    d.   radar.

13. The famous 1939 letter to President Roosevelt that predicted the discovery of the atomic bomb was written by
    a.   Albert Einstein.
    b.   Ernest Rutherford.
    c.   General Marshall.
    d.   Winston Churchill.

14. The country that took the lead in Big Science was
    a.   the Soviet Union.
    b.   Germany.
    c.   the United States.
    d.   Britain.

15. Since the Second World War,
    a.   scientists have become more specialized.
    b.   scientists have become subject to greater governmental influence.
    c.   scientists increasingly work together in teams.
    d.   all of the above

16. The political party in Britain that took the lead in establishing a comprehensive national health system was the
    a.   Liberal party.
    b.   Conservative party.
    c.   Workers party.
    d.   Labour party.

17. The 1968 revolt in France that threatened de Gaulle's government was started by
    a.   industrial workers.
    b.   the Communist party.
    c.   students.
    d.   peasants.

18. The student revolt in France in the late 1960s was inspired in part by the
    a. Korean War.
    b. Vietnam War.
    c. Civil War.
    d. Second World War.

19. The welfare-state legislation in Britain since World War II resulted in
    a. greater economic equality.
    b. the disappearance of the aristocracy.
    c. a dramatic rise in the birthrate.
    d. all of the above

20. Since World War Two, the role of motherhood has occupied
    a. more of women's time.
    b. less of women's time.

UNDERSTANDING HISTORY THROUGH READING AND THE ARTS

How has art reflected the ideals and trends in postwar society? The principal artists and the origins of their works are considered in E. Lucie-Smith, *Movements in Art Since 1945** (1986), while the most noteworthy art trends of the 1960s are discussed in *Pop Art** (1985) by L. Lippard et al. The danger of atomic war has fostered the production of a good number of films, including feature films such as *Dr. Strangelove*, *Fail-Safe*, and *Hiroshima, Mon Amour* and documentary films such as *The War Games* and *To Die, To Live*. An analysis of these and other films about nuclear war is found in a book by J. Shaheen, *Nuclear War Films* (1978). A good recent (1982) documentary about the effects of atomic testing in the 1950s is *Nick Mazacco: Biography of an Atomic Vet*.

PROBLEMS FOR FURTHER INVESTIGATION

A number of women of the 1960s began writing about themselves and how they relate to the institutions of marriage, childbearing, and work, and, thereby, contributed greatly to what became the women's movement of our day. Begin your investigation with the Frenchwoman S. De Beauvoir, *The Second Sex** (1953), and then the American G. Greer, *Sex and Destiny** (1985). Those who wish to compare the recent women's movement with earlier movements should turn to K. Rogers, *Feminism in Eighteenth Century England* (1982). On another liberation issue, the emergence of gay

*Available in paperback.

and lesbian minorities into urban politics is the subject of the Academy Award winning documentary film *The Times of Harvey Milk* (1985); it was a PBS television presentation and is available on videotape.

This chapter has suggested that a good number of problems have accompanied the changes in society since 1945. One of the most readable of the futurist books is R. Heilbroner's *An Inquiry into the Human Prospect** (1974). A world future dictated by technology is discussed in J. J. Servan-Schreiber, *The World Challenge* (1981), while the search for ethics in the age of technology is the subject of H. Jonas, *The Imperative of Responsibility** (1984), and R. Hardin et al., *Nuclear Deterrence** (1985), sketches out the positions of strategists and philosophers concerning a number of issues with regard to war and nuclear weapons. The problems and issues surrounding life in a British agricultural village in the 1960s is the subject of R. Blythe, *Akenfield** (1969).

*Available in paperback.

CHAPTER 32

THE RECENT PAST, 1968 TO THE PRESENT

CHAPTER OBJECTIVES

After reading and studying this chapter you should be able to answer the following questions:

Q-1. Why did the world economy shift into reverse gear in the 1970s? What were the social consequences?

Q-2. What were the major political developments in Europe and the United States, and why did the United States enter into a time of troubles?

Q-3. How did these changes interact with Cold War tensions and the evolution of the Soviet bloc?

CHAPTER SYNOPSIS

After about 1968 the self-confidence and the social and economic stability that came to mark the postwar era evaporated. What followed were two decades of upheaval. First, in the early 1970s a combination of factors, including the collapse of the American-dominated world monetary order and a dramatic rise in energy prices, led to a world-wide recession that was to last well into the 1980s. Spurred on by war in the Middle East and revolution in Iran, oil prices skyrocketed, thereby setting into motion the worst world economic decline since the 1930s. Particularly hard hit, western European countries faced massive unemployment and economic stagflation and, as the author points out through the use of a "misery index," the people faced a falling standard of living. All of this was accompanied by increased government spending on benefits for the unemployed and the needy and, correspondingly, by a buildup of huge national debts and inflation. By the late 1970s some, like Thatcher and Reagan, perceived a need to eliminate huge deficits and cut spending, while a whole generation of young people became concerned about their job prospects. The student idealism of the 1960s was over.

One of the few bright developments of this era was the West German initiative, under the Social Democrat Willy Brandt, to bring about reconciliation between Eastern and Western Europe—paying special attention to downplay the idea of German reunification. This policy of détente, as it was called, was furthered with East-West agreements at Helsinki. Meanwhile, the Cold War was reheated as the United States, in an effort to "roll back communism" and after refusing to allow free elections in Vietnam, carried on a long and unsuccessful war in Vietnam—which, by the end, had brought down two American presidents and left America divided and with diminished world prestige. In 1978 the Soviet Union became involved in a similar quagmire in Afghanistan where they used brutal force to preserve their influence, and then, more successfully, put down a rebellion in Poland where a powerful trade union movement had turned into a civil-rights movement. Fearful of the Soviets, the United States under President Reagan reacted with a new nuclear weapons system in western Europe and a proposal for an antinuclear shield called "Star Wars."

In addition to repression in Poland, the Soviet leaders had earlier (1968) engaged themselves in successfully putting down a revolution in Czechoslovakia which sought "socialism with a human face" and carried out at home a program of re-Stalinization that aimed at ending internal opposition and reasserting a unified national spirit. Since 1985 Gorbachav has worked to increase Soviet productivity and to end drunkenness. The author concludes with some cautiously optimistic thoughts about the future of Western civilization—including a look at the prospects of war between the rich nations and the poor nations and that of nuclear proliferation.

STUDY OUTLINE

I. The troubled economy
    A. Money and oil
       1. From 1944 to 1971 the world monetary order was based on the U.S. dollar
          a. The U.S. guarantee that the dollar could be cashed in for gold at $35 an ounce encouraged growth and monetary stability
          b. But U.S. overspending by 1971 caused a run on the dollar
          c. The ensuing abandonment of fixed rates made trade and investment insecure
       2. The era of cheap oil (which had stimulated Western economic growth) came to an end in 1973
          a. Khadafy of Libya activated OPEC price increases
          b. The Yom Kippur War and OPEC oil embargos resulted in vast OPEC price rises

B. Inflation, debt, and unemployment
 1. The world depression of the 1970s was pushed further by the Iranian revolution 1978-1979
 2. The crisis of unemployment and inflation hit western Europe harder than the United States
 3. The crisis gave the Soviet Union leverage over energy-poor eastern Europe
 4. International debt rose as rich and poor states borrowed for oil
 5. Consumers borrowed as a hedge against inflation
C. Some social consequences
 1. Optimism gave way to pessimism
 2. Governments responded with extended benefits for the unemployed and the needy—thereby preserving political stability
 3. Increased government spending without increased taxation led to budget deficits, increased debt, and inflation
 4. Thatcher and Reagan represented a reaction against government spending and deficits
 5. Big Science was cut while many individuals adopted less indulgent lifestyles, and students became obsessed with jobs

II. The Atlantic alliance
A. Germany and the European settlement
 1. In 1970 West Germany's Chancellor Brandt sought reconciliation between eastern Europe and West Germany
 2. Since 1945 West Germany had rebuilt itself and had sought to undermine the East German government
 3. Brandt and the Social Democratic party victory illustrated that democracy was working in West Germany
 4. Brandt recognized the Eastern states, the 1945 land settlement, and the policy of "two German states within one"
 5. This contributed to a reduction to East-West tensions—and began a pattern of West German attempts to defuse Soviet-American tension
B. Political crisis in the United States
 1. American involvement in Vietnam grew out of its fear of communism
 2. The U.S. refused to allow free elections in Vietnam or accept the verdict of such elections
 3. President Johnson vowed not to "lose" Vietnam and therefore carried out massive military buildup and bombing, but without victory
 4. Criticism of the war brought the defeat of Johnson and in 1968 the election of President Nixon
 5. Nixon cut war costs and brought many troops home, but the war continued for another four years

      6. Nixon's illegal activities led to the Watergate crisis and his resignation

      7. Vietnam became unified and the U.S. was left divided and with a decline in prestige

  C. Recent developments

      1. The policy of detente resulted in an East-West agreement at Helsinki guaranteeing frontiers and human rights

      2. Soviet involvement in Afghanistan and elsewhere convinced some that the Soviets were violating the spirit of detente

        a. President Carter applied economic sanctions on the Soviets

        b. Most European governments refused to join the sanctions

        c. President Reagan continued U.S. arms buildup by getting West European governments to accept American cruise missiles on their soil

III. The Soviet bloc

  A. The Soviet Union has steadfastly held to the preservation of Russian communism in eastern Europe—by military means if necessary

  B. The Czechoslovak experiment of 1968

      1. Under the reformer Dubček, the Czech communist party instituted reforms that stressed socialism with freedom and democracy

        a. The reforms were popular but frightened entrenched powers

        b. Other Eastern bloc peoples demanded the same

        c. The Soviets feared Czech nationalism or even pro-Western policy

      2. The Soviets responded in August of 1968 with brutal repression

        a. The Czech leaders backed down; reforms were canceled

        b. Later, the Brazhnev doctrine was enacted, declaring it rightful for the Soviets to intervene in any socialist country

        c. Western Europe stood by without responding because it believed in the sphere of influence principle

  C. The Soviet Union

      1. In the Soviet Union the Czech crisis caused a step backward toward Stalinization

        a. However, the standard of living continued to improve

        b. Russian popular nationalism reinforced re-Stalinization

        c. The Great Russians feared demands for autonomy from East European and non-Russian nationalities

      2. Massive party bureaucracy and centralization hindered economic growth

        a. Gorbachev is tough in international and bloc affairs and is opposed to new American military programs

  D. The Solidarity revolution

      1. Communist Poland has private land ownership and a strong Catholic Church

2. The Polish economy suffered greatly because of poor leadership and because of the world depression of the 1970s
3. The "Polish miracle" was when the economic crisis became a spiritual crisis as well
   a. The former Polish church leader, Pope John Paul II called attention to the rights of all people
   b. Strikes in August 1981 led to revolutionary demands
   c. Lech Walesa led the new democratic trade union movement (Solidarity) in its demands for industrial, political, and economic rights
   d. Solidarity had massive support and a sophisticated organization
   e. It stopped short of challenging directly the communist monopoly of power
4. When Solidarity lost its cohesiveness the Polish army smashed the movement

IV. The future in perspective
   A. The ability to anticipate the future is aided by a knowledge of what has happened in the past
   B. Many predictions for the future are pessimistic and foretell environmental disaster, atomic warfare, or class and race struggles, but the study of history reveals that problems have always existed only to be solved as people and societies evolve

REVIEW QUESTIONS

Q-1. Discuss the causes of the world-wide economic crisis of the 1970s and 1980s. Could anything have been done to prevent it?

Q-2. What were the social consequences of economic stagnation in the 1970s and 1980s?

Q-3. What was the Willy Brandt policy of reconciliation and why was it important?

Q-4. What is meant by the statement that Brandt's election victories marked West Germany's political coming of age?

Q-5. Why did the United States become involved in a war in Vietnam? Why did the Vietcong win?

Q-6. What were the consequences of the Nixon-Watergate crisis?

Q-7. Compare and contrast American presence in Vietnam to Soviet presence in Afghanistan. What are the differences and the similarities?

Q-8. What was the reason for the installation of American nuclear warhead missiles on West European soil?

Q-9. What were the motives of the Czechoslovakian Communist party reform movement of 1968 under Dubček? Why did the experiment fail? Why didn't western Europe give support to Czechoslovakia?

Q-10. What is meant by "re-Stalinization" of the Soviet bloc and the Soviet Union? Give examples.

Q-11. Discuss the Solidarity revolution in Poland in terms of origins, objectives, and outcome. What is meant by the claim that it was a "self-limiting" revolution?

Q-12. Discuss the often presented argument that a global class war between "rich" and "poor" nations is inevitable. If this is a sound argument?

STUDY-REVIEW EXERCISES

Identify the following people and explain their significance.

Willy Brandt

President Johnson

Alexander Dubček

Mikhail Gorachev

Pope John Paul II

Lech Walesa

Define the following key concepts and terms.

Bretton Woods Agreement of 1944

OPEC

"stagflation"

"Two German states within one German nation"

rich nations/poor nations

"Star Wars"

re-Stalinization

the Brezhnev doctrine

détente

Helsinki Conferences of 1973, 1975

the Geneva accords

the Tet Offensive

Vietcong

"socialism with a human face"

Explain what the following events were, who participated in them, and why they were important.

1973 Oil Crisis

Yom Kippur War

Iranian Revolution 1978-79

Solidarity Revolution

Afghanistan War

Vietnam War

Czechoslovakia Experiment

Willy Brandt's electoral victory of 1969

Test your understanding of the chapter by answering the following questions.

1. The world's largest oil producer is _____ .
2. The economic crisis of the 1970s and 1980s *did/did not* result in social and political instability comparable to that of the 1920s.

3. The German chancellor who sought reconciliation between West Germany and

   eastern Europe was _____ .

4. It is apparent that by the 1960s West Germany *had/had not* firmly adopted liberalism and democracy.

MULTIPLE-CHOICE QUESTIONS

1. Between about 1944 and 1971 the international monetary system was based on the
   a. price of silver.
   b. floating rates of exchange.
   c. American dollar.

2. All but one of the following led directly to oil price increases in the 1970s.
   a. The Yom Kippur War
   b. The Vietnam War
   c. OPEC embargos
   d. Khadafy's pressure on oil prices

3. The "misery index" indicates that the people who suffered most from the economic crisis of the 1970s and 1980s lived in
   a. the United States.
   b. Japan.
   c. western Europe.

4. United States involvement in Vietnam had its origins in
   a. fear of French imperialism.
   b. the U.S. attempt to impose free elections on the Vietnamese.
   c. an attempt to stop communism.
   d. U.S. economic interests in Asia.

5. The Czechoslovakia experiment of 1968 sought
   a. socialism with a human face.
   b. the end of communism.
   c. the expulsion of the Soviets.
   d. the adoption of a capitalist economy.

6. The trend in the Soviet Union in the 1970s and 1980s has been
    toward
    a. re-Stalinization.
    b. de-Stalinization.

7. The first initiative to bring about reconciliation between eastern and western
    Europe was undertaken by
    a. Jimmy Carter.
    b. Margaret Thatcher.
    c. Willy Brandt.
    d. none of the above

8. The attempt to undertake a revolution based on the idea of "socialism with a
    human face" took place in
    a. Poland.
    b. the Soviet Union.
    c. Czechoslovakia.
    d. East Germany.

9. Only one of the following did not contribute to the economic crisis that began
    in the early 1970s.
    a. Collapse of the world monetary system
    b. War in the Middle East
    c. Low birth rates in western Europe
    d. Increase in oil prices

10. The American President who vowed not to lose Vietnam was
    a. Lyndon Johnson.
    b. Richard Nixon.
    c. John Kennedy.
    d. Dwight Eisenhower.

11. The American President who applied economic sanctions against the Soviet
    Union was
    a. Richard Nixon.
    b. Lyndon Johnson.
    c. John Kennedy.
    d. none of the above

12. The Brezhnev Doctrine declared that the
    a. Soviets will go ahead with arms build-up.
    b. Chinese were not true Socialists.
    c. Party must reform itself.
    d. Soviets had the right to intervene in any Socialist country.

13. Which of the following is not true with regard to Poland?
    a. Strong Catholic church
    b. Little private ownership of land
    c. Poor economic leadership
    d. Strong independent trade union movement

14. The Czechoslovakian reform movement had the following impact on everyday life in the Soviet Union.
    a. Fall in the standard of living
    b. Decline in nationalist spirit
    c. Decline in bureaucratic influence
    d. Re-Stalinization

15. The leader of the Polish Solidarity movement is
    a. Walesa.
    b. Dubček.
    c. Breshnev.
    d. Gomulka.

16. In 1973 the American dollar
    a. fell in value as against most currencies.
    b. rose in value as against most currencies.
    c. was placed on a fixed rate of exchange as against other currencies.
    d. none of the above

17. The so-called Yom Kippur War began with
    a. the British take-over of the Suez Canal.
    b. the Israeli attack on Egypt.
    c. the Egyptian and Syrian attack on Israel.
    d. all of the above

18. The world's largest oil producer is
    a. Syria.
    b. Iran.
    c. Egypt.
    d. the Soviet Union.

19. With regard to free elections in Vietnam, the position of the United States was
    a. refusal to support elections.
    b. strong support of free elections.

20. The Helsinki agreements of 1975 centered on
    a. the guarantee of human rights and existing political frontiers.
    b. reduction of military spending and arms production.
    c. international ban on nuclear testing.
    d. all of the above

PROBLEMS FOR FURTHER INVESTIGATION

Why were Vietnamese peasants able to withstand the onslaught of American military technology? Did the war contribute to the Watergate scandal? Could the United States have won the war? These questions and many others are considered in H. Higgens, *Vietnam** (1982 edition), in G. McT. Kahin, *Intervention: How America Became Involved in Vietnam* (1986), and in Stanley Karnow, *Vietnam, A History** (1983).

Who were the men who shaped the great postwar alliance between Europe, the United States, and Japan? What were the key events and ideas behind this alliance? Based on interviews, memoirs, and documents, the key figures of the postwar era—Eisenhower, DeGaulle, Kennedy, Schmidt, MacArthur, and others—come alive in R. Barnet, *The Alliance* (1983).

How does one account for the economic woes of Europe and America in the 1970s and 1980s? The causes and significance of Britain's industrial failure is discussed in Keith Smith, *The British Economic Crisis** (1984), and for the United States, begin with L. Thurow, *The Zero Sum Society* (1981).

*Available in paperback.

ANSWERS TO OBJECTIVE QUESTIONS

CHAPTER 12

Provide approximate dates.

1. 1348
2. 1309-1372
3. 1337-1453

4. 1414-1418
5. 1346

6. 1358
7. 1321

Test your understanding.

1. did not
2. bad

3. England, France
4. Lollards

5. economic
6. decrease

Multiple-choice questions.

1. d
2. d
3. a
4. c
5. b

6. a
7. c
8. b
9. b
10. d

11. c
12. c
13. d
14. c
15. b

16. b
17. d
18. c
19. b
20. c

CHAPTER 13

Test your understanding.

1. Niccolo Machiavelli
2. less

3. increased
4. Thomas More

5. declined
6. is not

Multiple-choice questions.

1. a	7. c	13. c	18. b
2. d	8. d	14. b	19. a
3. d	9. a	15. b	20. d
4. b	10. d	16. d	21. a
5. b	11. d	17. b	22. b
6. b	12. d		

CHAPTER 14

Test your understanding.

1. did
2. king
3. political
4. Martin Luther
5. Alexander VI
6. was
7. weaken
8. Protestant

Multiple-choice questions.

1. c	6. b	11. a	16. c
2. d	7. c	12. d	17. b
3. b	8. c	13. d	18. c
4. a	9. a	14. d	19. a
5. b	10. b	15. c	20. c

CHAPTER 15

Test your understanding.

1. Thirty Years' War
2. Cortez
3. Las Cases
4. Edict of Nantes
5. sixteenth
6. Gustavus Adolphus
7. the United Provinces of the Netherlands
8. Amsterdam
9. Elizabeth I
10. skepticism
11. Charles V
12. Concordat of Bologna
13. Portugal

Multiple-choice questions.

1. d	7. a	13. a	18. d
2. b	8. b	14. c	19. d
3. d	9. d	15. b	20. c
4. d	10. c	16. b	21. a
5. d	11. a	17. b	22. d
6. b	12. d		

CHAPTER 16

Test your understanding.

1. stadholder
2. Colbert
3. entered
4. disaster
5. John Churchill
6. Laud

Multiple-choice questions.

1. b
2. d
3. a
4. d
5. d
6. a
7. c
8. b
9. a
10. d
11. c
12. d
13. d
14. b
15. b
16. d
17. d
18. a
19. c
20. c
21. a

CHAPTER 17

Test your understanding.

1. Peter the Great
2. Johann Sebastian Bach
3. increased
4. Suleiman the Magnificent
5. maintained
6. Frederick II (the Great)
7. (1) 4   (2) 1   (3) 3   (4) 2   (5) 5   (6) 6
8. weaker

Multiple-choice questions.

1. d
2. c
3. c
4. a
5. c
6. b
7. d
8. b
9. a
10. d
11. b
12. c
13. b
14. b
15. c
16. c
17. b
18. a
19. d
20. b

CHAPTER 18

Test your understanding.

1. water, earth
2. did not
3. motion
4. universal gravitation
5. philosophy
6. Portugal
7. was not
8. did not
9. skeptic
10. Newton
11. failed

Multiple-choice questions.

1. b
2. a
3. c
4. d
5. d
6. c
7. b
8. d
9. d
10. b
11. a
12. a
13. a
14. b
15. a
16. d
17. b
18. c
19. c
20. d

CHAPTER 19

Fill in the blank line.

1. i	3. e	5. g	7. b
2. c	4. j	6. a	8. f

Multiple-choice questions.

1. b	6. a	11. d	16. d
2. d	7. a	12. b	17. d
3. c	8. a	13. a	18. b
4. d	9. d	14. a	19. a
5. b	10. d	15. a	20. b

CHAPTER 20

Test your understanding.

1. limited	4. potato	7. the common people
2. was not	5. longer	8. Wesley
3. did	6. cowpox	

Multiple-choice questions.

1. b	6. b	11. c	16. c
2. d	7. a	12. d	17. d
3. b	8. d	13. a	18. a
4. c	9. b	14. d	19. d
5. c	10. c	15. b	20. b

CHAPTER 21

Test your understanding.

1. Trafalgar	3. Thomas Paine	5. victory
2. an important	4. a great deal of	6. military ruler

Multiple-choice questions.

1. c	7. a	12. b	17. a
2. d	8. d	13. d	18. b
3. d	9. c	14. a	19. b
4. a	10. d	15. d	20. d
5. d	11. d	16. a	21. d
6. c			

CHAPTER 22

Test your understanding.

1. 1780/textile
2. increased
3. James Watt
4. potatoes
5. Liverpool-Manchester, *Rocket*
6. decrease
7. Crystal Palace
8. increased
9. greater
10. Zollverein
11. decreased
12. factory, decrease

Multiple-choice questions.

1. d	6. b	11. d	16. c
2. b	7. b	12. a	17. d
3. a	8. b	13. b	18. d
4. d	9. b	14. a	19. c
5. c	10. d	15. a	20. a

CHAPTER 23

Test your understanding.

1. defeat
2. Louis Napoleon
3. Eugene Delacroix
4. should not
5. Austrian
6. Johann Herder
7. Louis Blanc
8. competition/victory

Multiple-choice questions.

1. d	6. a	11. a	16. b
2. a	7. d	12. d	17. c
3. b	8. c	13. b	18. d
4. a	9. b	14. d	19. a
5. b	10. a	15. d	20. d

CHAPTER 24

Test your understanding.

1. decreased
2. Bentham
3. antiseptic
4. 1890
5. improved
6. no change
7. labor aristocracy
8. rose
9. music halls
10. love
11. grow stronger
12. more
13. decreased

1. a	7. a	13. a	19. b
2. b	8. d	14. c	20. b
3. a	9. c	15. a	21. d
4. c	10. b	16. d	22. b
5. b	11. a	17. c	23. a
6. d	12. c	18. c	24. b

CHAPTER 25

Test your understanding.

1. approved	4. opposed	6. Protestant, against
2. middle class	5. fell	7. France
3. defeat, freedom		

Multiple-choice questions.

1. b	6. c	11. c	16. d
2. b	7. b	12. b	17. d
3. c	8. c	13. c	18. d
4. d	9. c	14. c	19. b
5. b	10. b	15. c	20. c

CHAPTER 26

Test your understanding.

1. c	3. h	5. d	7. a
2. e	4. b	6. f	8. g

Multiple-choice questions.

1. c	6. b	11. a	16. b
2. d	7. d	12. b	17. c
3. b	8. d	13. c	18. a
4. a	9. b	14. b	19. d
5. b	10. a	15. a	20. a

CHAPTER 27

Number the following.

1. 1   3. 3   5. 5   7. 6
2. 4   4. 2   6. 7   8. 8

Test your understanding.

1. Belgium   7. June 28, 1914   12. Bismarck
2. Vladimir Lenin   8. Alexander Kerensky   13. Black Hand
3. Georges Clemenceau   9. soviets   14. Russia
4. Leon Trotsky   10. T. E. Lawrence   15. Britain
5. Rasputin   11. Brest-Litovsk   16. Duma
6. Schlieffen

Multiple-choice questions.

1. c   7. d   13. c   18. b
2. a   8. c   14. c   19. d
3. c   9. c   15. a   20. d
4. c   10. c   16. a   21. d
5. a   11. d   17. a   22. a
6. b   12. b

CHAPTER 28

Test your understanding.

1. France, Belgium   4. impressionist   6. challenge
2. were not   5. discard   7. J. M. Keynes
3. Germany, Britain, France,
   the United States

Multiple-choice questions.

1. a   6. a   11. c   16. c
2. d   7. c   12. a   17. d
3. c   8. d   13. a   18. d
4. c   9. c   14. d   19. c
5. c   10. a   15. c   20. b

CHAPTER 29

Test your understanding.

1. favored
2. refused
3. victory/disaster
4. right
5. do not
6. Benito Mussolini
7. was
8. Adolf Hitler
9. declined
10. pro-German
11. did not

Multiple-choice questions.

1. d
2. d
3. d
4. a
5. a
6. d
7. c
8. c
9. c
10. c
11. c
12. c
13. d
14. a
15. d
16. d
17. c
18. b
19. d
20. b

CHAPTER 30

Test your understanding.

1. Chiang Kai-shek
2. Marshall Plan
3. Warsaw pact
4. Charles de Gaulle

Multiple-choice questions.

1. c
2. a
3. a
4. b
5. d
6. d
7. b
8. d
9. c
10. b
11. b
12. d
13. b
14. d
15. b
16. c
17. c
18. a
19. b
20. d

CHAPTER 31

Test your understanding.

1. declined
2. fall
3. increased
4. less
5. greater
6. declined
7. an increase
8. less
9. limited
10. greater

Multiple-choice questions.

1. c	6. b	11. b	16. d
2. c	7. c	12. d	17. c
3. d	8. b	13. a	18. b
4. a	9. a	14. c	19. a
5. c	10. d	15. d	20. b

CHAPTER 32

Test your understanding.

1. Soviet Union   3. Willy Brandt   4. had
2. did not

Multiple-choice questions.

1. c	6. a	11. d	16. a
2. b	7. c	12. d	17. c
3. d	8. c	13. b	18. d
4. c	9. c	14. d	19. a
5. a	10. a	15. a	20. a